CAMBRIDGE NATIONAL

LEVEL 1/LEVEL 2

IT

SECOND EDITION

J836

Mo Everett, Richard Howe & Sonia Stuart

Boost

HODDER EDUCATION

AN HACHETTE UK COMPANY

The teaching content of this resource is endorsed by OCR for use with specification Level 1/Level 2 Cambridge National in IT (J836).

All references to assessment, including assessment preparation and practice questions of any format/style are the publisher's interpretation of the specification and are not endorsed by OCR.

This resource was designed for use with the version of the specification available at the time of publication. However, as specifications are updated over time, there may be contradictions between the resource and the specification, therefore please use the information on the latest specification and Sample Assessment Materials at all times when ensuring students are fully prepared for their assessments.

Endorsement indicates that a resource is suitable to support delivery of an OCR specification, but it does not mean that the endorsed resource is the only suitable resource to support delivery, or that it is required or necessary to achieve the qualification.

OCR recommends that teachers consider using a range of teaching and learning resources based on their own professional judgement for their students' needs. OCR has not paid for the production of this resource, nor does OCR receive any royalties from its sale. For more information about the endorsement process, please visit the OCR website.

Orders: please contact Hachette UK Distribution, Hely Hutchinson Centre, Milton Road, Didcot, Oxfordshire, OX11 7HH. Telephone: +44 (0)1235 827827. Email education@hachette.co.uk Lines are open from 9 a.m. to 5 p.m., Monday to Friday. You can also order through our website: www.hoddereducation.co.uk

ISBN: 978 1 3983 5267 4

First published in 2022 by
Hodder Education,
An Hachette UK Company
Carmelite House
50 Victoria Embankment
London EC4Y 0DZ
www.hoddereducation.co.uk

The authorised representative in the EEA is Hachette Ireland, 8 Castlecourt Centre, Dublin 15, D15 XTP3, Ireland (email: info@hbgi.ie)

Impression number 10 9 8 7 6 5 4

Year 2026 2025 2024

Cover photo © LIGHTFIELD STUDIOS - stock.adobe.com
Illustrations by Aptara, Inc.
Typeset in India by Aptara, Inc.
Printed and bound by CPI Group (UK) Ltd, Croydon, CR0 4YYS
A catalogue record for this title is available from the British Library.

Contents

Acknowledgements

The Publishers would like to thank the following for permission to reproduce copyright material.

p. 1 © NatalyaBurova/iStock/Getty Images; **p. 5** © Anatoly Maslennikov/stock.adobe.com; **p. 9** Lost_in_the_Midwest/Shutterstock.com; **p. 10** © T.e.s.l.a. ®/stock.adobe.com; **p. 11** © Have a nice day Photo/Shutterstock.com; **p. 12** © DGTL Graphics sro/stock.adobe.com; **p. 13** © Scanrail/stock.adobe.com; **p. 14** © Wirestock/stock.adobe.com; **p. 16** © Macrovector/stock.adobe.com; **p. 17** © Confidence/stock.adobe.com; **p. 28** *t* © Jpa1999/E+/Getty Images, *m* © Vlad Kochelaevskiy/stock.adobe.com, *b* © Andrew/stock.adobe.com; **p. 29** *t* © Foto-Ruhrgebiet/stock.adobe.com, *m* © Xfilephotos/Shutterstock.com, *b* © Kungverylucky/stock.adobe.com; **p. 36** © Peter Widmann/Alamy Stock Photo; **p. 44** © Andrea Danti/stock.adobe.com; **p. 46** © B Christopher/Alamy Stock Photo; **p. 61** © Scanrail/stock.adobe.com; **p. 62** © Maren Winter/stock.adobe.com; **p. 67** © Ferid Huseynli/Shutterstock.com; **p. 69** © Damon Higgins/The Palm Beach Post/ZUMA Press Inc/Alamy Stock Photo; **p. 72** © Dmitry/stock.adobe.com; **p. 75** © ChrisHepburn/iStock/Getty Images Plus/Getty Images; **p. 77** © Gorodenkoff/iStock/Getty Images Plus/Getty Images; **p. 78** © Ivan Traimak/stock.adobe.com; **p. 83** *l* © TAlex/stock.adobe.com, *r* © Stanisic Vladimir/stock.adobe.com; **p. 84** © Dennizn/stock.adobe.com; **p. 85** © Monopoly919/stock.adobe.com; **p. 87** *l* © Metamorworks/stock.adobe.com, *r* © Dclic-photo.fr/stock.adobe.com; **p. 88** © New photos by Alfonso de Tomas/Alamy Stock Photo; **p. 91** © Pixels Hunter/stock.adobe.com; **p. 145** © Gorodenkoff/stock.adobe.com; **p. 147** © Zapp2photo/stock.adobe.com; **p. 152** *t* © Monopoly919/stock.adobe.com, *b* © Blue Planet Studio/stock.adobe.com; **p. 153** *tl* © Freer/stock.adobe.com, *tr* © Zapp2photo/stock.adobe.com, *b* © Ipopba/stock.adobe.com; **p. 154** © Gorodenkoff/stock.adobe.com; **p. 156** © MONOPOLY919/Shutterstock.com; **p. 157** *t* © Gorodenkoff/stock.adobe.com, *m* © Zapp2photo/stock.adobe.com, *b* © David Becker/Getty Images; **p. 158** © HQUALITY/stock.adobe.com; **p. 162** © R Howe; **p 166** © Nata_zhekova/stock.adobe.com; **p. 168** © Chaosamran_Studio/stock.adobe.com; **p. 171** *t* © Hakinmhan/Shutterstock.com, *b* © PeterPike/stock.adobe.com; **p 172** *l* © Monopoly919/stock.adobe.com, *r* © Zapp2photo/stock.adobe.com.

Every effort has been made to trace all copyright holders, but if any have been inadvertently overlooked, the Publishers will be pleased to make the necessary arrangements at the first opportunity.

The following brands mentioned in this book are trademarks or registered trademarks:

Adobe Aero
Alexa (Amazon)
Amazon
Amazon Web Services
Android
Android Open Source Project
Apache OpenOffice Calc
Apple
Apple HomePod
BBC
Bixby
Bluetooth
BT
Chrome
Cisco
Cortana
DeWalt
Dropbox
Dulux
Dulux Visualiser
eBay
Facebook
Fire OS
Fitbit
Google Assistant
Google Chrome
Google Drive
Google Home
Google Sheets
Gucci
Harry Potter Experience
Hyundai
IKEA
IKEA Place
iPlayer
Kinder
LinkedIn
Linux
Louis Vuitton
Louvre Museum
Lync
Mac OS/iOS
MacDonald's
Microsoft
Microsoft Office Excel
Microsoft OneDrive
Mozilla Firefox
Nest (Google)
PayPal
Pepsi
Pepsi Max
Pokémon GO
Pokémon Gym
Siri
Snapchat
Starbucks
Teams
Transport of London
Twitter
Uber
Ubuntu
Unix
Virgin
Wemo
WhatsApp
Windows
Visa
YouTube

Introduction

This book will help you to develop the knowledge, understanding and practical skills you need to complete your Level 1/Level 2 Cambridge National IT course. As well as preparing you for your final exam and set assignments, the book will introduce you to the IT sector. You will learn how to design, plan, create and review IT products to meet client briefs and target audience demands.

The chapters in this book closely follow all the topics required for each unit in the course specification, which you can find on the OCR website. To help with your learning the book covers the key content in detail and includes a range of real-world examples. There are also lots of activities and learning features; you can find out more about these and how to use them on the next page.

Note for teachers: You can find out more about how we have designed the textbook to support you at: **www.hoddereducation.co.uk/it-teacher-intro**

Qualification structure

The Cambridge National in IT qualification is made up of three different subject units. You will need to complete all of these:

- R050: IT in the digital world
- R060: Data manipulation using spreadsheets
- R070: Using augmented reality to present information

A chapter of this book is dedicated to each unit.

Assessment: Examined unit and final set assignments

- Unit R050 is an examined unit where you will sit a 1½ hour exam paper, which is set and marked by OCR.
- Units R060 and R070 are assessed through a series of tasks for a set assignment that you will be given. The assignments are set by OCR, marked by your tutor and then moderated by OCR.

All the examination questions contain 'command' verbs. These tell you what you have to do to answer the question or complete the task. You should always check the command verb before starting a task or answering a question. For example, if you describe something when an explanation is required, you will not be able to gain full marks; this is because an explanation requires more detail than a description. There are a range of practice questions in this book in Unit R050 to help you get to grips with the command words. A list of command verbs is available on the OCR website.

Once you have learnt all the required parts of the moderated units, you will complete an assignment that will be used to assess your knowledge and skills of the subject. It will be set in a vocational context, which means that it will simulate what it would be like to be given a project by a client or employer in a work situation. You will use the OCR set assignment or a modified version of it for the assessment. This assignment will include a series of tasks that follow the same process and sequence of the topic areas in the R060 and R070 units. The assignment practice features in this book will help you get used to working in the relevant IT contexts.

Note: The practice questions and accompanying marks and mark schemes included in this resource are an opportunity to practise exam skills, but they do not replicate examination papers and are not endorsed by OCR.

How to use this book

This student textbook contains all three units for the redeveloped OCR Level 1/Level 2 Cambridge National in IT (J836).

These are:

- Unit R050 IT in the digital world
- Unit R060 Data manipulation using spreadsheets
- Unit R070 Using augmented reality to present information.

Each unit is then divided into topic areas. All of the teaching content for each topic area is covered in the book.

Key features of the book

The book is organised by the units in the qualification. Each unit is broken down into the topic areas from the specification. Each unit opener will help you understand what is covered in the unit, the list of topic areas covered, and what you will be assessed on, fully matched to the requirements of the specification.

About this unit

An introduction to the topics covered by the unit.

Topic areas

A list of the unit's topic areas, so you know exactly what is going to be covered.

How will I be assessed?

Information on how the unit will be assessed.

Getting started

Short activities to introduce you to the topic.

Key term

Definitions of important terms.

Case study

See how IT concepts can be applied and learn about real-life scenarios.

Activity

A short task to help you understand an idea or assessment criteria.

Test your knowledge

Short questions designed to test your knowledge and understanding.

Research

Research-based activities that draw on the content covered in the book, to reinforce your understanding.

Synoptic link

Links to relevant details in other parts of the book so you can see how topics link together.

Practice questions

Summary questions that allow you to apply the knowledge and skills covered in the unit. This feature appears in the examined Unit R050 and will help you prepare for the exam. The mark schemes are available online at **www.hoddereducation.co.uk/cambridge-nationals-2022/answers**

Note: The practice questions and accompanying marks and mark schemes included in this resource are an opportunity to practise exam skills, but they do not replicate examination papers and are not endorsed by OCR.

Assignment practice

A summary activity that allows you to apply the knowledge and skills covered in the unit. This feature appears in the non-examined units R060 and R070, and will help you prepare for the set assessments.

Unit R050

IT in the digital world

About this unit

We all use IT every day in a range of different ways. When we interact with digital devices, we use a Human Computer Interface (HCI), we create data which is stored and processed, and we create a range of digital communications which are distributed. We interact with smart devices to make our lives easier.

In our interactions with IT, we use different types of devices (hardware), which need software to be able to carry out our tasks. In this unit you will learn about the design tools that can be used to create software solutions or products, and how testing can be used to make sure these work as intended. We interact with devices through an HCI, and you will learn about how these are used in everyday life in a range of different application areas.

Smart devices connect to the Internet of Everything (IoE). You will learn what the IoE is and how it is used in a range of different application areas.

As data is collected, stored and processed when we use IT, it is important that this data is kept secure. You will learn about the different types of threats to data and digital devices and the measures that can be taken to prevent these threats, including the legislation that relates to the use of IT.

Topic areas

In this chapter you will learn about:

1. Design tools (TA1)
2. Human Computer Interface (HCI) in everyday life (TA2)
3. Data and testing (TA3)
4. Cyber-security and legislation (TA4)
5. Digital communications (TA5)
6. Internet of Everything (IoE) (TA6)

How will I be assessed?

Unit R050 is assessed by taking an exam. The mark you are awarded will count towards the final grade you get for this qualification. The exam will be 1½ hours long and will have two sections. Section A will have short-answer questions, which will range from one to two marks per question. Section B will have a context and all the questions in this section will relate to this context. Section B will also include a question where you will need to sketch a solution to a problem and an extended answer question.

You will be assessed on the following performance objectives in the exam:

PO1 – Recall knowledge and show understanding

PO2 – Apply knowledge and understanding

PO3 – Analyse and evaluate knowledge, understanding and performance

Topic area 1 Design tools

Getting started

The first stage in developing any product, resource or system is to design the solution. By designing the solution first it is possible to check that it will meet the requirements, be fit-for-purpose, and enable the end users to use the product, resource or system as intended.

There have been some design failures in the IT world. Research one or two of these failures and investigate the impact they had on the end users.

1.1 Types of design tools

There are different design tools that can be used to design a solution.

Which design tool is used will depend upon the product, resource or system being designed. For example, if the product manipulates data, then a flow chart could be used to show the calculations and decisions, and a wireframe or visualisation diagram could be used to design the Human Computer Interface (HCI).

Synoptic link

The HCI is covered in Topic area 2 of this unit.

There are four design tools you need to learn about. These are:

- flow charts
- mind maps
- visualisation diagrams
- wireframes.

Flow charts

A flow chart can be used to show the steps, decisions and outputs in a process. For example, how the discount on an order can be calculated. You will have learnt about creating this type of design tool in your KS3 study.

A flow chart can also be used to create a simple diagram of all the steps and decisions needed to produce the required output. When using a flow chart as a design tool, each step is set out in the proposed sequence – the order in which the steps and decisions have to be completed.

Each step will lead to the next, displaying the sequence of steps with any decisions which will show the steps to be taken as a result of the decisions. It is important that every flow chart begins with a 'Start' box, with the end of the process being shown by an 'End' box.

Table 1.1 Flow chart symbols

Symbol	Name	Description
	Line	Shows the flow through the process being shown by the flow chart
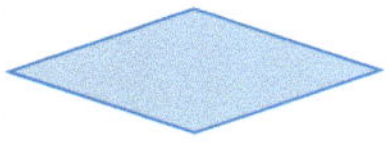	Decision	Shows when a decision has to be made during the process. Two lines must come out of a decision box: Yes/No or True/False
	Start/End	Indicates the start and end of the process being shown by the flow chart
	Step or process	Shows what is done at any specific step, for example: price × quantity = total cost
	Input/Output	Shows an Input or Output. This can be generated by a user or automated, for example a report or invoice

The components of a flow chart are:

- start point
- end point
- decisions
- processes
- input/output
- connecting lines with directional arrows.

These are shown by symbols in a flow chart (see Table 1.1).

Activity

Create a flow chart, using a decision, to show this process:

Ask a user to input three numbers. Add the numbers together. Output the total.

Mind maps

A mind map is based around a central theme (the central node) and has branches to nodes and sub-nodes for the different aspects of the theme. Mind maps are also known as spider diagrams.

The purpose of a mind map is to generate outline ideas or to present ideas to an audience. They can be used to develop and show links between different thoughts, aspects and processes of a project. They are also used to provide an overview, or summary, of a topic or idea.

For all mind maps:

- The main subject, topic or idea is in the centre: this is the central node or central theme.
- The related ideas and information branch from this central node: these are called nodes.

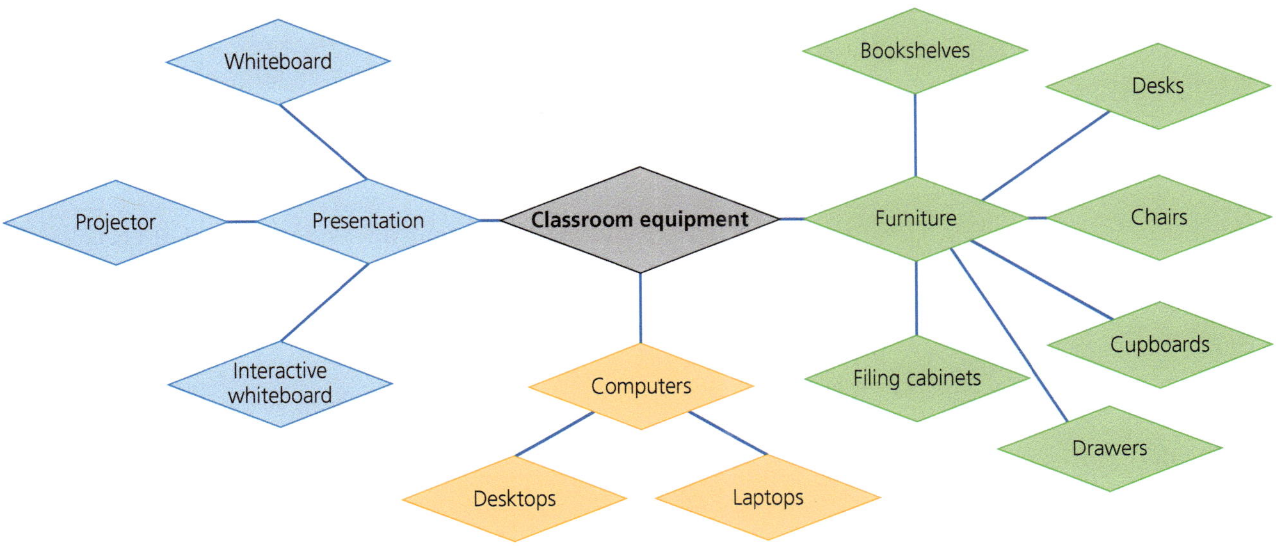

Figure 1.1 A mind map

- Each related idea can have further ideas and information branching from it: these are called sub-nodes.
- The central node, nodes and sub-nodes are connected by lines (or branches).
- The central node, nodes and sub-nodes should each include a word and/or an image.
- Each node can have many branches.

The components of a mind map are:

- nodes
- sub-nodes
- connecting lines (branches)
- key words
- colours
- images.

There are three different types of mind map, each with a different purpose:

- library
- tunnel timeline
- presentation.

Library

Library mind maps sort and organise information to provide a clear understanding of a topic. Figure 1.1 is an example of a library mind map about classroom equipment.

Tunnel timeline

Tunnel timeline mind maps are mainly used for problem solving. The central node is the outcome, or the problem that needs to be solved. The nodes and sub-nodes show the paths that need to be taken to solve the problem.

Activity

Find the basic structure of a tunnel timeline mind map. Use this to create a mind map to show the tasks and subtasks that are involved in decorating a bedroom.

Presentation

Presentation mind maps are used to present ideas to an audience. They should be laid out in a way that the audience can understand.

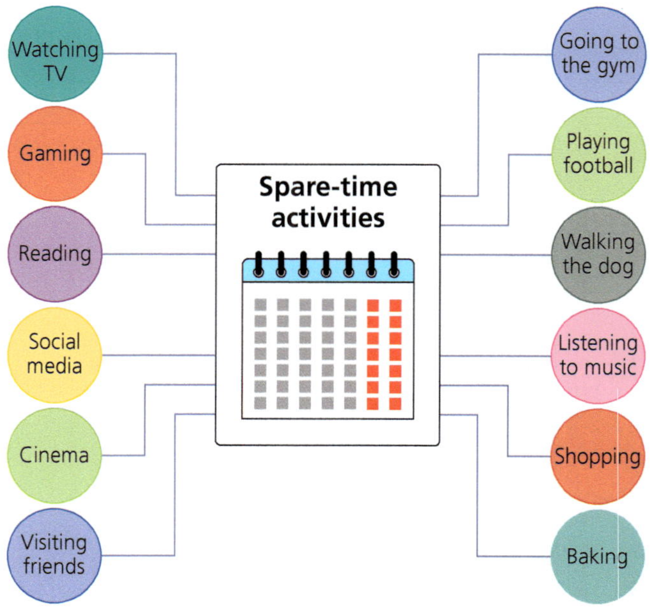

Figure 1.2 A presentation mind map

Visualisation diagrams

Visualisation diagrams are rough drawings or sketches of what a final solution will look like. They can be used to plan the layout of an image in a visual way, and show where text and images will be placed. Visualisation diagrams can be used to check that what is being produced will work and that the objectives of the product can be met.

Visualisation diagrams are usually used when a static product is being created. A static product is one that doesn't move, such as an HCI for a spreadsheet solution or augmented reality (AR) resource. They can also be used to show the format and layout of any outputs, such as a report.

Visualisation diagrams cannot be used for anything that has a timeline.

The components of a visualisation diagram might include:

- multiple images/graphics
- size and position of images/graphics
- position and style of text
- fonts

- labels/annotations, including:
  - size/style of text
  - font
  - size/style of text images/graphics
  - size of other elements
- colours
- themes.

Activity

Draw a visualisation diagram for the front cover of this book.

Wireframes

A wireframe is a plan of what is to be designed – it focuses on what the product will do, rather than what it will look like. Wireframes help people understand the outline or the frame of the design before detailed designing begins. This allows the designer to see if sizes and proportions are correct, and that all the required elements are included. The detail for each element is not included in a wireframe. A wireframe is a layout design tool, meaning changes can be quickly and easily carried out before creation.

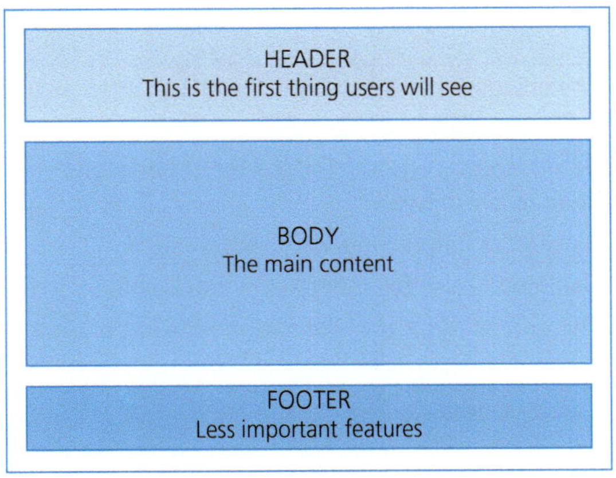

Figure 1.3 A basic wireframe

A well-constructed wireframe will help when creating a solution such as an AR resource or the HCI for a spreadsheet solution. A wireframe could also be created for a website home page. This would show the layout of the home page including the positioning of elements such as buttons.

A wireframe can be low fidelity or high fidelity.

A **low-fidelity wireframe** includes boxes showing the position of basic content and images with no specific details. They use basic shapes, image placeholders and generic 'lorem ipsum' text to show the draft layout of the product. (Lorem ipsum text is dummy text without meaning that shows where text should be placed.) Low-fidelity wireframes:

- are usually created in greyscale rather than colour
- are static, which means the interactive elements are shown in boxes
- do not show the functionality of any interactive elements such as drop-down lists
- are usually a hand-drawn sketch but could be created using software.

A **high-fidelity wireframe** shows the product in more detail. This detail includes fonts, colours, images, text and branding such as logos. If the wireframe has been created using software, then it is possible that the functionality of the user interactions can be shown, for example any drop-down lists. They are usually created using software so the functionality can be shown.

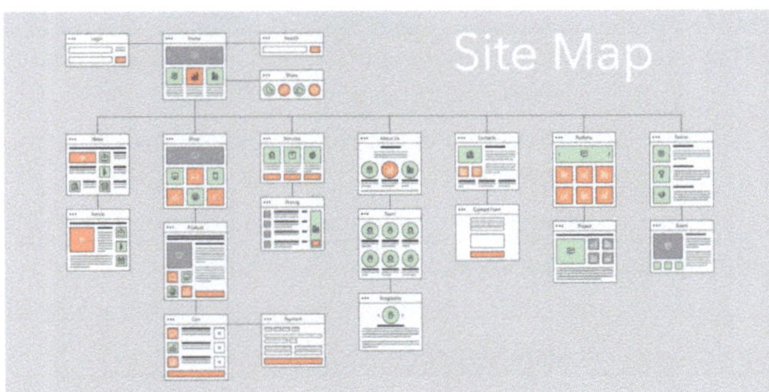

Figure 1.4 A high-fidelity wireframe

Key terms

High-fidelity wireframe A wireframe that shows actual content, fonts, colours, image dimensions and branding.

Low-fidelity wireframe A wireframe that uses basic shapes and image placeholders with limited specific details.

The components of a low-fidelity wireframe are:

- boxes
- box labels
- image placeholders
- layout grids.

A high-fidelity wireframe also includes:

- branding
- colours
- fonts
- text
- user interaction functionality.

Synoptic link

You will need to use design tools when designing your spreadsheet solution and your AR model prototype.

Activity

Create a low-fidelity wireframe for the home page of your school's website.

Test your knowledge

1 What symbol is used to show the start of a flow chart?
2 Identify **two** components of a mind map.
3 What is a tunnel timeline mind map used to show?
4 What sort of products cannot be designed using a visualisation diagram?
5 Identify **two** components of a high-fidelity wireframe which are not used in a low-fidelity wireframe.

Advantages and disadvantages of design tools

Each design tool has advantages and disadvantages (Table 1.2). The choice of design tool will depend upon what is being designed. If a design tool is used that is not appropriate or

Key term

Concurrent processes Processes that can be carried out at the same time.

Table 1.2 Advantages and disadvantages of design tools

Design tool	Advantages	Disadvantages
Flow charts	Can be useful for simple designs with a small number of tasks and decisions. Does not need any specialist knowledge to understand the flow chart. Can show sequence/steps that need to be followed in order.	The processes and decisions are shown sequentially so do not show concurrent processes. Can become complicated if a lot of decisions need to be shown. Cannot be used to create visual designs.
Mind maps	Easy to add ideas at any time. Can help focus on the ideas and links between them. Show dependent ideas.	Can be difficult for others to understand. The correct type of mind map needs to be used.
Visualisation diagrams	Simple to produce. Non-technical so most people can understand them. Ideas can be clearly shown. Can clearly show the layout of documents. Can see if the layout will work before building a prototype.	Can lack detail. A lack of technical details can cause issues, confusion and misinterpretation.
Wireframes	Information and graphical elements can be positioned and moved around. The size of the elements can be changed. The design can be finalised in a low fidelity without the clutter of, for example, font types/colours. High fidelity can be used in the testing process. Changes can be made efficiently.	Interactive features cannot be shown in low fidelity. High fidelity can become over designed.

useful then, in some cases, this is worse than having no design.

Types of software used to create design tools

Software can be used to create a design tool. The type of software selected will depend upon the type of design tool that is being created. The types of software that could be used include:

- DTP (desktop publishers)
- word processors.

Word-processing software can be used to create a flow chart, mind map or low-fidelity wireframe. There are in-built tools and features in word-processing software which allow shapes and lines to be used to create these design tools.

DTP software can be used to create a visualisation diagram where images and text are combined. DTP software can also be used to create a mind map or high-fidelity wireframe. One advantage of using DTP to create a design is that the software allows elements from different files to be combined. This means that images can be imported from, for example, a scanner or a graphics package. Text can be added from a word-processing file or inputted directly. The different elements can be grouped, which means that a group of elements can be moved as one. Elements can also be positioned by using a 'drag and drop' feature which will enable precise positioning to be used.

There is also specific software that can be used to create different design tools. As this software has been specifically created, the features and function it includes can help when creating designs. For example, software created for a visualisation diagram may include features such as automatic lining up of elements, and grids for accurate positioning of elements and templates.

Research

Research the different software applications that are available specifically for creating a mind map and a high-fidelity wireframe. Think about the advantages of using a specific software application to create design tools.

Test your knowledge

6 Identify **one** disadvantage of using the flow chart design tool.
7 Which design tool shows dependent ideas?
8 Which design tools could be created using a DTP package?
9 How can images be imported into a DTP package?
10 What does it mean when components are grouped?

Practice questions

1 One symbol used in a flow chart shows the start and end. Draw and label two other symbols used in a flow chart. [4 marks]
2 Identify **two** advantages of using a mind map to present ideas. [2 marks]
3 Explain how a library mind map will help a client understand the basic ideas for the design of a website home page. [2 marks]
4 Compare the use of low- and high-fidelity wireframes to present a design for a website to a client. [4 marks]
5 Explain how, using an example, a word-processing package could be used to create a visualisation diagram. [3 marks]

Topic area 2 Human Computer Interface in everyday life

Getting started

We all use HCIs every day, for example, every time a smartphone is accessed by a user, an HCI is used.

Think about the digital devices you interact with every day at home and in school. Make a list of these and what you use the digital device and HCI for.

2.1 The purpose, importance and use of HCI in application areas

The purpose of an HCI is to allow communication between the user and a digital system. The communication takes the form of different types of interaction such as type, touch, gesture and voice. The interaction can be captured by the digital system through a keyboard, sensor, camera or microphone.

Synoptic link

You will learn more about the application of an HCI in Unit R060, Topic area 1, section 1.2, and Unit R070, Topic area 2, section 2.1.

An HCI can also be known as a user interface.

A well-designed HCI will:

- be clear in its layout: important information stands out, user interactions are clear
- be consistent in its layout: users know where to find things
- be simple: users can quickly learn how to use the HCI
- be user-controlled: which means the user decides the actions to be taken
- provide feedback: when a user makes an error, the messages should be clear and provide detailed feedback as to how to rectify the error.

There are a range of different application areas where an HCI is used. These include:

- embedded systems
- banking
- entertainment
- fitness
- home appliances
- retail.

Embedded systems

An embedded system is one that is built into a device or system. Washing machines, cars and fridges all contain an embedded system; these are the systems that run the devices. The HCI for these devices shows the user the options that are available for them to change such as the wash cycle temperature, cruise control speed or temperature for the fridge. The range of options available on an embedded system cannot be changed by the user.

Synoptic link

You will need to create an HCI for your spreadsheet solution. This is covered in Unit R060, Topic area 1, section 1.2, HCI, and Unit R060, Topic area 2, section 2.1, User interface.

Banking

Most people have at least one bank account. They may also have a savings account and other types of accounts. Over the last few years there has been a decrease in the number of physical banks and a move to people banking online. It is very important that a high level of security is applied to the banks' websites.

Synoptic links

Security and prevention measures are covered in Topic area 4, section 4.3 of this unit.

HCI design conventions and principles are covered in Unit R060, Topic area 1, section 1.2.

To access online banking, an HCI is presented to the user often on a mobile device or PC. The HCI will provide the user with the ability to access and manage their account. This is done by providing instructions and interaction opportunities for logging in through typing in a username/password, scanning a fingerprint, or recording a phrase using a microphone. Once into the account, options are shown to the user through the HCI regarding the key tasks that they need to do to manage their account.

Entertainment

There is a large range of HCIs available in the entertainment area. These include gaming, e-readers, smart TVs, streaming services and cinema. When a smart TV is switched on, the user is provided with a range of options on the screen to select from. These options are an HCI as each option has a pre-defined action. Some video streaming services require a user to select who is watching; once a person has been selected a further HCI is shown which provides the user's personalised screen, allowing them to customise their experience.

Activity

Investigate other areas of entertainment such as gaming and websites. Look at the HCI and think about how it is used.

Fitness

There has been an increase in the number of fitness devices that are available. These include devices such as wearable fitness trackers, smart bikes and rowing machines. Each device has an embedded HCI which can act both as an output to show users their progress and enable the user to input settings such as the amount of time to exercise or the number of calories to be burned.

It is common for these devices to have a second HCI on a different device such as a smartphone or tablet. This usually takes the form of a downloadable app and allows the user to chart their progress through wireless connectivity between the devices. This is an example of use of the Internet of Everything and smart devices.

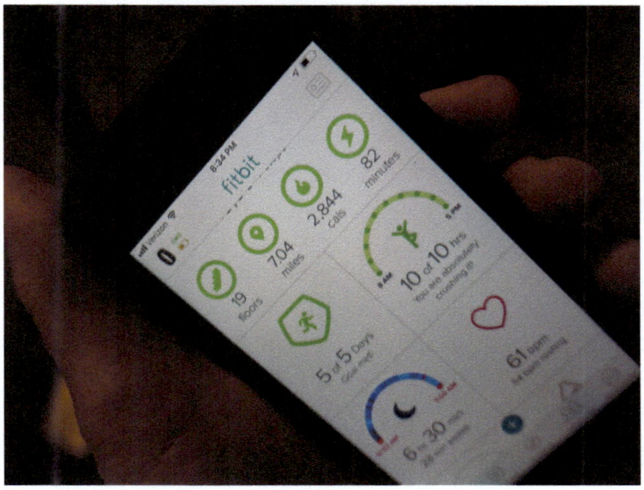

Figure 1.5 A fitness tracker on a smartphone

Figure 1.5 shows the HCI for a fitness tracker on a smartphone. It is possible to see a range of different information such as the number of minutes exercised and for how many days exercise has been taken. This HCI is tailored to a specific user based on the details they first input when they started using the fitness tracker.

Synoptic link

The Internet of Everything (IoE) and smart devices are covered in Topic area 6 of this unit.

Home appliances

Homes today are packed with devices such as cookers, microwaves, heating systems and fridges that are run by small computer systems. As mentioned earlier, these are usually embedded computer systems with their own HCI. However, there is an increasingly wide range of secondary HCIs for these devices that appear as apps on our mobile devices or within smart devices such as the Amazon Show or the Google Nest.

Figure 1.6 An embedded HCI on a washing machine

The secondary HCI on a separate device will enable the user to select options remotely and, if the washing machine is switched on, will send these options to the washing machine which will then start.

Another example is smart lights. These can be controlled through voice commands to a digital assistant that will then carry out the command; this is a voice-activated HCI using a microphone attached to the device. The lights can also be controlled through an HCI on a device where the lights carry out the command using wireless connectivity between the device and the lights.

Advantages and disadvantages of using an HCI

Using an HCI in each of these areas has advantages and disadvantages (Table 1.3).

Activity

In groups of two or three, choose a retail sector, for example fashion, home furnishings, furniture or holidays. Investigate the range of HCIs that are used in your chosen area, and how they enhance the user journey. You should also describe the advantages and disadvantages of using an HCI in your chosen sector. Present your findings to the rest of your class.

Table 1.3 Advantages and disadvantages of using an HCI

Area	Advantages	Disadvantages
Embedded systems	Greater flexibility in use compared to older devices. Ability to set preferences such as specific heating levels.	Limited number of functions/options for the user.
Banking	Increased security. A customer only has access to their own accounts. Can operate bank facilities without the need for bank staff. Flexibility in when and how to use bank.	Cannot access accounts if the HCI fails. Incorrect programming could lead to incorrect accounts being shown.
Entertainment	Offers users a personalised experience. Different users can use the same device.	If connection is lost, then the entertainment device will no longer offer a personalised experience to the user.
Fitness	Personalised settings. Clear set-up of exercise plans. Easy to see and monitor progress.	Device-based HCI can be small to read. Input methods can be very restrictive.
Home appliances	Appliance performance can be tailored to meet the user requirements. Appliance can be user activated or delayed whenever and wherever the user is located.	If connectivity is lost, then the appliance will not work as required.

Test your knowledge

1 Identify **one** way interaction can take place with an HCI.
2 Why is it important that an HCI is clear in its layout?
3 What is an embedded HCI?
4 What is the purpose of a secondary HCI?
5 Identify **one** advantage of using an HCI in the banking application area.

2.2 Hardware considerations

All HCIs are displayed to the user. This can be visually on a display or using audio such as Amazon Alexa's voice. Embedded HCIs are built into a display on the device or system, while others are displayed on a separate digital device.

Display

There are different types and sizes of displays. It is important that these different types and sizes are considered when the HCI is being designed.

Synoptic links

Digital devices are covered in Topic area 5, section 5.3 of this unit.

Devices used with AR are covered in Unit R070, Topic area 1, section 1.3.

The main types of displays include:

- touch screen
- LCD
- LED
- OLED.

Type

Touch screen

There are displays that are touch enabled (touch screens) and displays that are not touch enabled. Touch-enabled displays allow the user to physically touch the screen as part of the interaction. Displays that are not touch enabled will require another interaction method such as a mouse or tracker pad.

Touch-screen devices are becoming more common, ranging in size from smart watches and smartphones to interactive advertising boards and smartboards in the classroom.

For example, touch can be used to select the options available on a car touch screen.

Figure 1.7 A touch screen in a car

Liquid crystal display

Liquid crystal displays (LCDs) are usually found on a range of devices including smartphones, laptops and PCs. LCDs use a separate **backlight** to illuminate the display from behind. This means that sunlight does not affect the view seen. However, the colour representation and contrast are not as good as other display types.

An extra layer is placed on top of the LCD element to provide touch-screen ability. Without this the display would require another device to enable any interaction with an HCI. This

Key terms

Backlight A built-in light source that is needed to produce a readable display.

Liquid crystal display (LCD) A type of display that uses a liquid crystal film sealed between glass plates.

Figure 1.8 The left-hand HCI has the backlight on and the backlight is off on the HCI on the right

type of display can also be navigated using a remote control, for example on a smart TV and smartboards.

Light emitting diode

Light emitting diodes (LEDs) are similar to LCDs, but LED displays generate their own backlight. This means that a backlight does not have to be built into the device. This means that sunlight does not affect the view seen. However, the colour representation and contrast are not as good as other display types. An LED display uses very little power.

Organic light emitting diode

An **organic light emitting diode (OLED) display** produces its own light. This means it uses less power and is thinner than LCD and LED displays. OLEDs are more flexible and can contain the touch response layer in the display itself. Using an OLED means that screens can be folded or rolled.

An active-matrix organic light-emitting diode (AMOLED) is a type of OLED.

Key terms

Light emitting diode (LED) A small device that emits light when an electric current is passed through it; lots of LEDs are used together to make self-illuminating displays.

Organic light emitting diode (OLED) display A type of display that produces its own light; it is flexible and can include a touch response layer.

Size

The display size is the size of the area on the display where, for example, the HCI, pictures and videos are displayed. The size of a screen is usually described by the length of its diagonal, which is the distance between opposite corners.

Research

Investigate the different display sizes available on smartphones.

The size of a display can have an impact on how a user uses an HCI. If the display size is too small, it can mean that the size of the HCI is small or not all of the HCI can be seen. This can mean that the user can find it difficult to use the HCI as they may not be able to touch an icon with their finger.

Embedded HCIs are usually very small. This is because they are embedded into a device and so need to fit with the other components that make the device work. If the embedded HCI is large, then other components may not work as intended or may make the device much larger in physical size.

An HCI for a software application, such as a spreadsheet, will be built into the software itself. This means that the processing power requirements will be reduced but the display area can be quite large on display. The size of the HCI can be reduced by the user with some software such as only showing icons and no text.

Synoptic link

User interaction methods are covered in Topic area 2, section 2.4 of this unit.

Resources

An HCI will also need to use resources, including memory and processing power. When designing an HCI, the size of display, cost of device, method of interaction *and* the processing power and memory requirements should be considered.

Memory

If the HCI has a lot of options then the file size needed to store the HCI will be large, as the HCI is almost a program in its own right. This will take up a lot of memory which could mean there is limited memory for other applications, including an operating system.

Processing power

When a user is communicating with an HCI, processing power will be needed to complete the requested tasks.

The more options, and sub-options, an HCI has, the more processing power is needed. Having an HCI that needs a lot of processing power means there is less processing power available for the device to carry out other tasks, or the response to the options could slow down.

Test your knowledge

6 What does LED stand for?
7 How is backlight generated in an LCD device?
8 How is the size of a screen described?
9 What happens to the processing power needed when more options are included in an HCI?
10 Identify **one** consideration when designing an HCI.

2.3 Software considerations

All HCIs will use software to enable them to provide the display and options to the user.

Figure 1.9 Different digital devices and HCIs

Operating system

Many digital devices have an operating system. The operating system (OS) allows the hardware to communicate with the different applications that the device has. Some cars, fridges and cookers have an operating system that enables them to connect to the internet and other devices – the Internet of Everything (IoE).

Synoptic link

The Internet of Everything (IoE) is covered in Topic area 6 of this unit.

There are several operating systems in use, but the main ones used on digital devices are as follows:

- Windows: mainly PCs, laptops and tablets
- Mac OS/iOS: Apple-based devices including Mac desktops and laptops, iPhones and iPad tablets
- Android: used on mobile devices such as laptops and smartphones
- Chrome: used on Chromebook laptops
- Ubuntu: mainly PCs but can also be used on a server
- Linux: mainly PCs and laptops but can also be used on, for example, cars, smartphones, web servers and networking hardware
- Unix: can be used on devices ranging from supercomputers to mobile devices.

Other devices use operating systems that are based on versions of one of these main ones, for example Amazon's Fire OS is based on the Android Open Source Project.

Operating systems can be graphical user interface (GUI) or command line (CLI) based. A GUI-based operating system uses icons on the HCI to allow users to access the software and features, such as calculators and clocks, included in the operating system. GUI operating systems can also be called **WIMP** interfaces.

Key term

WIMP (Windows, Icons, Menus, Pointer) A type of graphical user interface that uses windows, icons, menus and pointers.

A **GUI** is a very visual interface and is made up of icons – little pictures. When interacting with a GUI the navigation is logical as the user just points at and clicks on/touches an icon to complete a task. A GUI also has menus that provide the user with options that can be selected.

Figure 1.10 The home screen of a device running Windows

Synoptic link

User interaction methods are covered in Topic area 2, section 2.4 of this unit.

A GUI can be used when users don't need to know the technical aspect of opening up software, for example running applications.

They are also used when the interface needs to be easy to use so that users can interact with a device on their own.

A **CLI** uses text to give the device instructions, for example opening software using a keyboard. The user has to input the location of the software they want to access. This is known as defining the file path. An example of this would be typing:

C: \FLS.exe

No icons, or graphics, are used on a CLI which means that not many of a device's resources are used, freeing them up for other tasks. A CLI will also respond very quickly to the user inputting commands.

A CLI is usually designed and used by experienced, technical users who know the required commands. Inputting commands means that users can go directly to a specific location or run a process without having to select lots of different options from menus. This can include technicians who are trying to solve problems with digital devices.

Operating systems, whether GUI or CLI, can also be proprietary or open source. Proprietary means the operating system is owned by a specific company or individual. For example, the Windows operating system is owned by Microsoft. Open source means the software code can be used, and edited, by anyone. There is usually no charge for using open source code.

The operating systems are shown in Table 1.4, and the advantages and disadvantages of GUI and CLI operating systems are shown in Table 1.5.

Table 1.4 Operating systems

Operating system	Proprietary or open source	Interface
Windows	Proprietary	GUI
Mac OS/iOS	Proprietary	GUI
Android	Open source	GUI
Chrome	Open source	GUI & CLI
Ubuntu	Open source	GUI
Linux	Open source	GUI & CLI
Unix	Proprietary and open source	GUI & CLI

When an HCI is being designed it is important to identify the operating system that a device uses. This is because there is some incompatibility between these operating systems. For example, the software and associated HCI that have been developed to run on OS/iOS-based devices (Apple) may not be able to be used on an Android device.

If the HCI can be run on different operating systems, then it may not function as intended with some limited functionality and even limited options for the user. This will have an impact on the user journey while interacting with the HCI.

The difference in functionality may also be evident if the HCI was created for a mobile device but is used on a PC or vice versa. These were

Table 1.5 Advantages and disadvantages of GUI and CLI operating systems

Operating system	Advantages	Disadvantages
GUI	Intuitive and easy to use. Complicated commands do not have to be learnt or remembered. A help feature is usually included. The same data can be shared between different software applications with the results seen as WYSIWYG (What You See Is What You Get).	Very experienced programmers can find these slow to use and select the options needed. The file size is large which means more storage is needed. A large amount of memory and processing power are needed to handle all the graphics and commands.
CLI	An experienced user can quickly interact using the correct commands. Limited memory and processing power are needed. A CLI does not need a GUI to run.	Commands have to be spelt and typed precisely for the operating system to react. There are a large number of commands which need to be learnt and remembered by users.

issues that Microsoft faced when developing a tile system for Windows for use on PCs and mobile devices. There are also differences between some of the software used with the different operating systems. Some software and apps will only work with a specific operating system. This could have an impact on the colours and the clarity of any icons used and how the user can interact with the HCI. This could also impact on the responsiveness and the functionality of the HCI.

Activity

Find a home appliance HCI, for example a heating system app. Look at how it is displayed on a PC or laptop and on a mobile device such as a tablet, and on the device itself. What are the differences between these? Discuss your findings with the rest of your group.

Key term

What You See Is What You Get (WYSIWYG) What is shown on screen is exactly how it will look when printed.

Digital platform

Digital platforms are created using software. Software can also be known as a digital platform. An HCI can be hosted on:

- databases
- mobile apps
- spreadsheets
- websites.

Synoptic link

Databases and spreadsheets are covered in Topic area 5, section 5.2 of this unit.

The purpose of the HCI is to allow the user to operate the digital platform. The main differences in how the HCI will look and work will be due to the OS that it's accessed on, and whether the OS is a GUI or CLI.

The HCI should open as soon as the software is accessed by the user. The HCI will hide the underlying coding of the database or spreadsheet which means there is no danger of a user accessing and changing this.

It is important to consider the performance of the HCI. This means how quickly the user can interact with the HCI to complete their tasks. For example, a GUI will be quicker to interact with than a CLI for most users with limited technical skills.

The user requirements from the HCI also need to be considered. It is important to consider what tasks the user needs to complete using the HCI. It is not possible for an HCI to meet all the user requirements so prioritisation of tasks may need to be considered when designing an HCI.

The HCI needs to be intuitive for the users. This means how well the user can understand and interact with the HCI. The HCI must complete the user-required tasks efficiently. If the user cannot efficiently complete their tasks, then the HCI can be seen as being poorly designed. A well-designed HCI should enable a user who is using it for the first time to predict how it works.

Synoptic link

Design considerations of an HCI are covered in Unit R060, Topic area 1, section 1.2.

An HCI will be used by a range of users, each with a different level of experience. When an HCI is being designed it is important that this experience is considered and that it includes features that are familiar to users, for example the use of red if an error has been made, or icons that are recognisable from real-life situations. Helpful messages should be provided where the user has made an error, including how the error can be corrected.

An HCI on a database and spreadsheet enables the user to carry out tasks using the options presented to them. These could be, for example, printing or editing a data set such as adding or deleting a customer.

The HCI will provide all the functionality required by a client. This functionality and HCI requirements will usually be defined when the database or spreadsheet is being created.

Synoptic link

You will design and create an HCI for your spreadsheet solution in Unit R060, Topic areas 1 and 2.

Test your knowledge

11 What type of devices use Mac OS and iOS?
12 What might happen if an HCI is run on an operating system different to the one it was designed for?
13 Identify **one** digital platform.
14 What does an HCI on a spreadsheet enable a user to do?
15 When should a software-based HCI open?

2.4 User interaction methods

Users can use a range of interaction methods to trigger actions from the HCI.

These interactions can be carried out using a range of different methods including:

- touch and gesture
- keyboard and mouse
- voice.

How the user will interact with the HCI should have been considered during the design phase. This would have involved taking into the account the type of display to be used and the input options available. For example, will it be a touch-enabled device or will a mouse be needed?

Synoptic link

User interaction is covered in Unit R070, Topic area 1, section 1.2.

Touch and gesture

Touch and gestures are used by the user to interact with an HCI on a touch screen. There are many types of gestures that can be used. The most popular ones are shown in Figure 1.11.

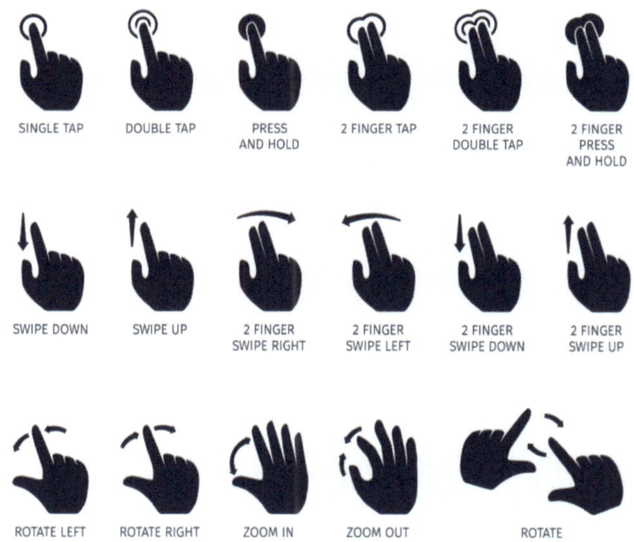

Figure 1.11 Gestures that can be used on an HCI touch screen

By using these as interaction methods, the HCI can be less cluttered as fewer buttons will be needed. Touch and gestures are also easy to use and can make the user journey seamless when interacting with the HCI. Gestures can also be used with an AR product to enable the user to fully interact and become immersed in the AR experience, allowing the user to pan, rotate and select different objects in the AR environment including navigating the layers.

However, gestures may not be accessible for those users who have a physical disability or illness which affects their fingers. While gestures are intuitive and easy to use, any HCI should also have an alternative method of user interaction.

Touch and gestures by using a finger can increase the chances of a user selecting the incorrect action; this is because the surface area of a finger can be large compared to the size of the options.

Keyboard and mouse

A physical keyboard and mouse are the traditional methods of user interaction with an HCI and are used mainly with PCs and laptops. These physical input devices are not usually used when the HCI is presented on a touch-screen device, being replaced by an on-screen keyboard. Many people are familiar with the layout of a standard keyboard which always has the same basic layout. The user can move around the HCI using shortcut keys, such as the Tab key to move onto the next event, or can position and activate the cursor using the mouse and enter the required data using the keyboard.

Figure 1.12 An on-screen keyboard

On-screen keyboards are shown on the screen of a touch-screen device such as a tablet or smartphone. The selection of the keys can be through a tap on the touch screen or by using the mouse and a click. As the action of a tap or a click, the letter or number is shown at the point of data entry.

Using a mouse to select the option required can be precise, meaning the chance of selecting the incorrect option is reduced.

Voice

Voice input allows a user to interact with an HCI by saying commands or key words. Many home assistants such as Amazon Alexa and Google Home are activated and interacted with using voice commands. Voice interaction can also be activated on other digital devices including a PC, tablet or smartphone. Activating voice interaction means that all actions with the HCI can be completed by just speaking. This can be a benefit to those who need assistive technology due to a disability as there is little physical interaction needed to be able to interact with the HCI. Communicating instructions by voice is also a more natural human communication method, which some people find more intuitive. However, if the user has a sore throat or cold which has affected their voice then voice commands may not provide the expected result.

Activity

Research each interaction method and copy and complete the table. Discuss your findings with the rest of your group. Add any extra advantages and disadvantages that your group found that you didn't find to the table.

Interaction method	Advantages	Disadvantages
Gesture and touch		
Keyboard and mouse		
Voice		

Test your knowledge

16 Identify and explain **one** gesture that can be used on a touch screen.
17 Identify **one** task that can be completed using touch and gesture in an AR product.
18 What type of devices usually use a keyboard and mouse?
19 How can keys be selected on an on-screen keyboard?
20 What happens when voice interaction is activated?

Practice questions

1 Explain **one** advantage and **one** disadvantage of using an HCI in the entertainment application area. [4 marks]
2 Describe the interaction method that can be used on a touch screen. [2 marks]
3 Why is it important to consider the memory hardware resource when designing an HCI? [3 marks]
4 Identify **two** different interaction methods that can be used with an HCI. [2 marks]
5 An HCI has been created for a database digital platform. Explain **two** advantages to the user of using a keyboard and mouse to interact with the HCI. [4 marks]

Topic area 3 Data and testing

Getting started

Information and data are all around us. Every day, millions of pieces of data are generated by people, organisations and governments around the world.

One example of data that is held about you is your year group in school. Make a list of all the other data that you think is held about you, including where you think the data is held.

3.1 Information and data

What data is

Data is a big part of our lives. Lots of data is stored by governments and businesses. But anything that is spoken or written down can also be classed as data. If you break down any word, then you will find data.

One definition is that 'Data is raw facts and figures before they have been processed.'

'Raw facts and figures' means they are without meaning; it is not possible to understand what the letters and figures mean.

Key term

Data Raw facts and figures before they have been processed.

Two examples of data are:

NAT23%7

56GHS56

It is not possible to know what these mean. They are just sets of random letters, numbers and symbols.

The main points about data are:

- Data has no meaning.
- Data is raw facts and figures before they have been processed.
- Data can be made up of letters, numbers, symbols, graphics and sound.

What information is

You have already learnt that data on its own is meaningless. Information is created when data is processed.

The formula for converting data to information is:

Information = data + [structure] + [context] + meaning

Sometimes it is not necessary to give data structure and context for it to become information but is it always better to know the full formula.

The structure of data is how it is presented.

One example would be the structure for presenting dates, such as 24/03/2022. The structure for this would be:

- NN/NN/NNNN

  where N shows that it should be a number.

Another example would be the structure for postcodes. The structure for a postcode could be:

- LLNN NLL

  where N is a number and L is a letter.

The context of data is what you need to know and understand to make sense of the data. For example, consider the data of:

- 15, cabbage, rabbits

This data means nothing. But when this data is put into a sentence, or context, the data makes sense:

- 15 cabbage plants were planted but the rabbits ate all of them.

The data now makes sense as a context has been provided. The meaning of data is revealed when it is in the correct structure and put into context.

Table 1.6 How data, structure, context and meaning can be used to get information

Data	Structure	Context	Meaning
01/01/2017	NN/NN/NNNN	A UK date	New Year's Day in 2017
30 40 50 60 70	Integer numbers	Miles per hour	Speed limits on different types of UK roads and motorways
TRNB14	First two letters: type of clothing Second two letters: colour Last two numbers: UK size LLLLNN	A clothing shop stock code	A navy-blue pair of trousers, UK size 14

Activity

Copy and complete the table below to show how data can be turned into information. The first one has been done for you.

	Shoe shop	Sports club	School
Data	MTNSS10		
Structure	LLLLLNN		
Context	A shoe shop stock code		
Meaning	Men's trainers, non-slip soles, size 10		

The relationship between data and information

You have already learnt about how information is:

data + [structure] + [context] + meaning

Data and information are related. This means that there are links between data and information. The main links you need to be aware of are that:

- information is in context, while data has no context
- information is data that has been coded/structured
- data must be processed to become information.

Test your knowledge

1 What can be classed as data?
2 What does 'raw facts and figures' mean?
3 How is information created?
4 What does 'N' mean when defining the structure of data?
5 What is the difference in context between information and data?

3.2 Data use

It could be said that data is all around us as data is used in a range of different contexts. There are different types of data, each of which has a purpose. There are tools that can be used to ensure that the data entered is of the right type and format. But, to be of use, data needs to be processed before it is used.

Use of data types in different contexts

Before data can be processed, the way in which it is to be stored must be considered. There are many different data types that can be used. Which type is chosen will depend upon the data that needs to be stored and how it is to be processed. The data types that could be used include:

- **alphanumeric**
- Boolean
- date
- numeric (currency, decimal, integer, percentages, real)
- text.

You should have learnt about some of the different data types in your KS3 study.

Synoptic link

You will need to use different data types in your spreadsheet solution. Data types are covered in Unit R060, Topic area 2, section 2.1.

Key term

Alphanumeric A combination of letters and numbers.

Activity

Copy and complete this table to show how each data type could be used in the areas shown.

	School	Online retailer	Sports club
Alphanumeric			
Boolean			
Integer			
Date			

Test your knowledge

6 What are the three choices in the Boolean data type?
7 Which data type would be used to store money?
8 What is represented by the integer data type?
9 How could the percentage data type be used?
10 Describe the real data type.

The difference between validation and verification

Validation and verification are two tools that can be used to check that the data entered into a digital system is entered correctly. Data that has been incorrectly entered is of little use. Validation and verification can be used to reduce the number of errors in data entry.

Validation:

- checks that the data being entered into a digital system is sensible and reasonable
- does not check that the data is correct
- checks the data against pre-set rules
- is usually carried out by the digital system at the point at which the data is being entered
- is usually set as part of the creation of a solution.

Table 1.7 Different data types and how they could be used

Data type		Characteristics	Example of data	How it could be used
Alphanumeric		Any combination of letters, symbols, spaces or numbers	AjcY6&9£4	To store postcodes or stock codes as these contain numbers and letters
Boolean		There are only two choices, such as True or False. It can sometimes be shown as a drop-down list, radio buttons or a tick list where only two options are shown.	Yes or No, True or False, 1 or 0	To answer a closed question such as 'Are you over 16?' or to select a delivery option
Date		There are different formats of date that can be used. Which one is chosen will depend upon how the date is to be stored and processed.	09/03/2022 9/3/22	To show a date, such as 09 March 2022
Numeric	Currency	Shows data in the format of money. It can be used to show currency signs (such as £ or $) and have decimal places to show the full currency details.	£29.99	To store prices
	Decimal	A number format that shows an exact number using a decimal point and numbers after the decimal point	12.75 100.50	To show the result of a calculation expressed as a decimal
	Integer	Whole numbers	2012 4	To store number of items in stock, number of lengths swum in a pool, number of tickets sold in one day to a live concert, television channel number, years
	Percentage	A number format that includes a percentage sign (%) and can include decimal places	25%	To show a percentage of a discount, such as 25% off the price
	Real	Any number, with or without decimal places	12.30	To store height/weight
Text		Any character	DB7&~?→hT5	To store names of items or people Phone numbers are usually stored as text as this means they can have spaces and start with a 0.

It is important that the validation tool used is appropriate to the data type being entered, and also how it will be processed and what it will be used for.

Verification is a check to see whether the data being entered into a digital system is identical to the source from which it came. Verification can be carried out manually or by the digital system.

Data validation tools

A range of validation tools can be used to check that the data being entered is sensible and reasonable. The aim of validation tools in a solution is to alert the user if there are any errors in the data that has been entered. The errors could be highlighted by, for example, an error message or a red box around the data entry field.

The data validation tools are shown in Table 1.8.

Table 1.8 Data validation tools

Validation tool	The purpose	Example
Data type check	Checks that the data entered is of the required type.	A name must be in text form. A quantity must be a number.
Input mask Format check	An input mask can be set to make sure the input data is in a specific format. The input mask defines which type of character can be in each position. When the data is being entered a format check will be carried out to make sure the input mask has been followed.	A UK postcode usually follows the format of LLNN NLL – this would be set as the input mask. The format check validation tool would check that the data entered followed this format.
Length check	Sets the length of the data entry.	A password has to be 8 characters in length.
Limited choice	Includes drop-down lists, radio buttons and tick lists. Provides users with a limited choice to select for data entry.	Providing a drop-down list of months in a year for a user to select from. Giving a user the choice of having a present gift wrapped.
Lookup	Looks up acceptable values in a list. This is not a search but a comparison against a set of values in the list.	Checks that a postcode or a car manufacturer is valid by looking up the data in a list.
Presence check	Checks that data has been entered into a specific field. This makes sure data has been entered in the field.	When data is a key field, such as a delivery postcode, as this cannot be left blank.
Range check	Sets an upper and lower boundary for data entry. The entered data must be between these values.	In a secondary school a student can be in Years 7 to 11. The lower boundary is 7 and the upper boundary is 11. Any number not in the range 7–11 will produce an error alert.

Synoptic link

You will need to use different data validation tools in your spreadsheet solution. Data validation is covered in Unit R060, Topic area 1, section 1.2 and Topic area 2, section 2.1.

Data verification tools

Verification is performed to make sure that the data entered exactly matches the original source. But, as with validation, verification does not check the data is correct.

There are two different verification methods. These are:

- double entry
- manual checking.

Double entry is entering the data twice. The data is then checked by comparing the two sets of data to make sure they are the same. If any difference is found, then the user is alerted by an error message. The comparison can be done manually by a person or through a check by the digital system.

Manual double entry can be done by the same person or different people. The main problem with double entry verification is that if the same error is made each time the data is entered, then the method will not find a difference so the data will pass the verification check.

Figure 1.13 Confirming a password

Double entry verification can be carried out by a digital system. One common use is that of setting, or resetting, a password. When carrying out this task, the password needs to be entered twice. The second entry is checked against the first entry to make sure they are the same.

A manual checking verification method is basically proofreading. This involves visually comparing the source data with the data entered into the digital system. This verification method involves a person being able to follow two sets of data and identify any differences. This is not a very reliable method as it is difficult to keep track of where you are on the source document and on the screen.

If verification checks are carried out manually then this is time consuming and can be expensive in terms of workload.

Test your knowledge

11 What is the purpose of verification?
12 Which validation tool would check a postcode is in the correct format?
13 Identify **one** type of the limited choice validation tool.
14 What sort of error does the presence validation tool check for?
15 How does the double entry verification tool check for errors?

3.3 Data collection methods

All data needs to be collected. How it is collected will depend upon:

- the type of data to be collected
- where the data and information are to be collected
- how the collected data and information will be stored
- if the data is collected using a primary or secondary collection method.

Data and information can be collected using primary and secondary collection methods.

- A primary collection method is where the data and information collected is fresh data collected for a specific purpose.
- A secondary collection method uses data and information that has already been collected. A good example of secondary research is using a book to find out statistics that have already been collected and, possibly, processed.

The main difference between primary and secondary collection methods is the source of the data and information. There are other differences between primary and secondary collection methods. These are shown in Table 1.9.

Table 1.9 Differences between primary and secondary collection methods

	Primary	Secondary
Meaning	Research that collects first-hand or fresh data for a specific purpose	Research that uses data and information that has already been collected
Based on	Raw data and information	Analysed and processed data and information
Carried out by	The researcher	Someone else
Data	Specific to the purpose	May not fully meet the specific needs
Process	Very involved	Quick and easy
Cost	High	Low
Time	Long	Short

There is a range of primary and secondary methods that can be used to collect data.

Primary collection methods

Email

Data and information can be gathered using email. An email can be sent that includes an interactive form to be completed or a link to an online questionnaire or survey. If the email contains an interactive form, then the email has to be replied to. The form can then be completed and returned to the sender. It is possible for information gathered in this form to be imported into a spreadsheet or database.

The interactive form must be in the same structure as the spreadsheet or database and include the same fields. This allows the information to be inputted automatically into the software with little risk of human error. If the email contains a link to an online form, then the process is the same as that mentioned in the section below on questionnaires and surveys.

Interview

An interview is a conversation between two people in which questions are asked. For this reason, interviews are usually completed one to one, face to face. The questions to be asked need to be planned in advance, based on how the data and information collected will be processed. The **interviewer** asks questions of the **interviewee**.

The type of questions asked will depend upon the data and information that is to be collected and how it will be stored and processed. An interview will not usually contain rank or rating questions but may contain some closed questions. Most of the questions will be open and qualitative.

The data and information gathered during the interview will need to be manually input into the software being used to store and process it.

Online questionnaire and survey

A questionnaire/survey contains a set of questions that are designed to collect data and information from the people completing the questionnaire or survey. A range of types of questions can be asked, including:

- **closed question**
- **open question**
- **rank order**
- **rating**.

Online questionnaires and surveys are technology-based. The questionnaire/survey can be provided by email, on a website or in the cloud. As each person completes and submits their answers, the data and information can be automatically input into the software used for the analysis. This method means there is less chance of errors in the data and information being stored and processed.

Questionnaires and surveys must be created knowing how the data and information will be stored and processed. They are an excellent way to collect statistical data and information. Rating and rank order questions can be very useful if statistical information is required, as all the answers will be numerical. **Qualitative** and **quantitative** data and information can be collected using a questionnaire or survey.

Key terms

Closed question A question where there is only a set number of answers to be chosen. For example, the question 'Can you ride a bicycle?' can be answered either 'Yes' or 'No'.

Interviewee The person answering the questions.

Interviewer The person asking the questions.

Open question Allows the person completing a questionnaire to give a detailed answer in their own words.

Qualitative data Data that is descriptive and cannot be measured.

Quantitative data Data that is measurable and is usually in numerical form.

Rank order Requires the person completing a survey or questionnaire to compare a list of the same type of items. The items are then ranked, for example from 1 to 10 where 1 is most important and 10 is least important.

Rating Requires the person completing a survey or questionnaire to compare different items. The items are then ranked, for example from 1 to 10, where 1 is most important and 10 is least important.

Activity

Create a questionnaire or survey to ask your classmates about their screen time, including what they access, when and for how long. You should use a range of different question types.

Find a free online survey tool and create an online questionnaire/survey from your questions.

Secondary collection methods

Books and magazines

Books and magazines can be used to collect data and information. However, the data and information these include can be out of date. This is because of the time it takes for these to be published. For example, it can take about 18 months for a book to be published. This means the data and information contained in it will be at least 18 months out of date.

However, if historical data and information needs to be collected, then books and magazines can be a useful source. This is because the data and information provided by books and magazines has been checked so they can be seen as valid and reliable sources.

Government statistics and websites

A wide range of statistics that have already been collected can be found on websites. These statistics can be analysed to provide further data and information.

Websites can be a good source of data and information. What is important is that the website chosen to collect the required data and information demonstrates **validity** and **reliability**. Statistics can be found on many websites, but the validity of these should also be confirmed before they are used. It is always best to find statistics on websites that can be trusted, for example the websites of the different government departments.

It is sensible to collect data and information from well-known organisations such as the BBC. One website that stores valid and reliable statistics is **www.streetcheck.co.uk**. This website enables people to search for statistics based on a postcode. The categories of statistics that can be found include the population, types of housing and broadband speeds.

Key terms

Reliability Data and information from a reliable source can be trusted to be correct or true.

Validity The quality of being correct or true; valid data and information is also, generally, reliable.

One of the largest collections of statistics can be found from the census. The census takes place in the UK every 10 years and is completed by every household. The census is carried out by the Office for National Statistics (ONS), which also processes all the data. There are many different datasets on the ONS website, such as the value of e-commerce sales. This dataset shows the increase in sales through e-commerce related to different areas, such as retail and hotels.

Other government departments such as the NHS also provide statistics on a range of different areas. For example, the NHS website contains statistics about the average waiting times for treatments.

By looking at collected statistics it is possible to spot trends or patterns. For example, the website **www.metoffice.gov.uk** provides statistics on weather, including hours of sunshine and amount of rain, for the United Kingdom. By looking at these statistics, some of which have been processed into graphs, it is possible to see trends. The website has also developed, in conjunction with the BBC, a climate change visualisation tool.

Activity

Access the Met Office website and look at the climate statistics for your local region.

Try to analyse the statistics. Are they a good representation of the weather in your region?

The advantages of using websites to collect data and information include the speed aspect. It is much quicker to input a search and have results returned often within five seconds, compared to visiting a library to look for material. Websites tend to be more up-to-date than books and magazines as they can be quick to update.

Each collection method has advantages and disadvantages; these are shown in Table 1.10. Which collection method is chosen will depend upon:

- where the data and information will be collected
- what data and information is to be collected
- how it is to be stored and processed.

Table 1.10 Advantages and disadvantages of different collection methods

Collection method	Advantages	Disadvantages
Email	The same email can be sent to many people at the same time. The results from the emails can be automatically input into software for analysis/manipulation. Little risk of human error occurring when the data collected is input into the software.	Emails may be diverted into spam/junk folders by the email provider. If the fields or data types are not exactly the same as the fields being used for analysis/manipulation then the data collected may be worthless.
Interviews	Questions can be modified based on the answers given to previous questions. A rapport can develop between the interviewer and the interviewee that may result in questions being answered honestly. Additional questions can be asked to clarify any answers already given.	Can be time consuming and costly to carry out. Poor interviewing can lead to misleading or insufficient data and information being gathered. Not suitable for gathering data and information from large numbers of people.
Online questionnaires and surveys	Large numbers of people can be asked to fill in the same questionnaire/survey. Comparisons are easy to formulate (for example, 75% of people liked the new company logo). Cheaper than interviews for large numbers of people.	People need the technology and a stable connection to be able to complete it. A badly designed question may not get the data required in the right format.
Books and magazines	Can be reused for a range of data collection. Likely to be reliable and valid as data and information will have been checked before being published. Can be used to collect historical data.	Can become out of date very quickly. Data could be over 18 months old on publication. May have to use a range to collect the required data and information. Can be biased to the viewpoint of the author(s) or contributors.
Government statistics	A trusted source. Readily available statistics which are reliable and valid. Cover a range of topics. Statistics can show trends and patterns that can help with decision making. Can be updated regularly.	Some statistics may not be available. Can be difficult to collect the exact data needed in large datasets. Some processing may have already been carried out meaning the data may not meet the required purpose. Statistics need to be collected knowing how they are going to be analysed/processed and stored. Statistics can just show data from a sample of people.
Websites	The data has already been collected and possibly processed. Data collection is quicker than having to collect the data first-hand.	May not have been collected for the same purpose so may not provide clear and full data. Can be biased to the viewpoint of the contributors. The data may not be exactly what is required. It is not always possible to tell if the website is real/genuine.

Test your knowledge

16 Identify **two** primary collection methods.
17 What is an interview?
18 What is a closed question?
19 What is qualitative data?
20 Identify **one** advantage of using a questionnaire to collect data.

3.4 Storage of collected data

When data has been collected, it needs to be stored ready for processing. The data can be stored in a logical or physical location.

Logical location

The logical location is the cloud. The cloud has a very large storage capacity and is made up of servers that store and locate data and information. The cloud refers to software, services and storage areas that run on the internet rather than being stored and accessed on a physical location storage device.

Cloud

Cloud services and storage are accessed through a web browser, such as Mozilla Firefox or Google Chrome. An increasing number of cloud service providers also offer access through an app. Cloud services include Dropbox, Microsoft OneDrive and Google Drive. Many people store files – including documents, pictures and videos – in the cloud. By doing this, the files can be accessed from anywhere as long as an internet connection is available.

Using the cloud to store and view large files – such as documents, photo collections and videos – means that the user requires less physical memory on their devices, such as their laptop, tablet or smartphone. Storing data on the cloud means that space can be saved on a physical location device.

The cloud servers process and store the files, so users do not need to buy high-specification devices to access and work on the files. Many businesses use the cloud to enable collaborative working on files. This means that many employees can now work remotely and do not have to travel into an office.

Automatic backups of data can be scheduled where the backup is stored in the cloud. This means that if there is a problem with a physical location device, the data will still be available in the cloud.

The biggest problem with using the cloud to access and work on data and files is that it requires an internet connection. Without an internet connection, or with a slow/unstable connection, the files, software and apps stored in the cloud can be inaccessible. The files, software and apps are also inaccessible if the cloud servers stop working or 'go down'.

The other problem with storing files in the cloud is that of security. As the data and information 'lives' in the cloud, there is always a risk of it getting into the wrong hands if the storage space in the cloud is hacked. There are prevention measures that can be put in place, but it is wise to carefully consider what data and information is stored in the cloud.

Physical location

Physical locations for storing data are actual devices; they can be touched. They can be internal or external. Internal means they are built into a digital device. External means they can be portable and used with different digital devices if they have the right connection.

Using a physical location to store data means that data can be accessed without needing to access the cloud. If there is no broadband connection available, data can still be moved, and shared, between digital devices. It is possible to encrypt the data stored on a physical location. It is also possible to use security measures such as a PIN or password to access data stored on a physical location.

Physical location devices can be dropped or lost. It is also possible that components of the device may stop working, meaning that the data stored on them could become inaccessible.

If the physical location is external, then it may need power for it to work. This means that if there is a power cut, then the device may stop working. This can also apply to the internal physical locations as all digital devices need power to work. Some digital devices do have a battery but when the battery has run out, the digital device and the data stored on the internal physical location will become inaccessible.

Each physical location storage device has different characteristics, advantages and disadvantages. These are shown in Table 1.11.

Table 1.11 Characteristics, advantages and disadvantages of storage devices

Device	Characteristics	Advantages	Disadvantages
Internal storage devices			
Primary hard drive 	A primary hard drive uses solid-state or magnetic disks, or both, for storing software and data in files. This is the main storage in a digital device and is integral to the device. The software, including the operating system, is stored on this drive when the digital device is bought. The primary hard drive can store huge amounts of data.	Data files can be read, edited, re-written or deleted on many occasions. Internal to the digital device so cannot be lost unless the device is lost.	The disks can be susceptible to dirt and dust. The disks can be damaged if suddenly moved. When the disks fail all the stored data may be lost.
Network drive 	A storage location that is part of a network. There can be one, or more, network drives on a network. These are not physically on a digital device.	Different user profiles can be set up to limit access to data and software. Data can be backed up to a network drive from any digital device on the network.	They can fail, which means that data can be lost if not backed up to a different location.
External storage devices			
Portable solid-state drive (SSD) 	A solid-state drive uses flash memory to store software and data in files.	As there are no moving parts, they are reliable and durable. The reading and writing of data times can be fast.	More vulnerable to abrupt power loss and electro-magnetic fields. If one of the components becomes damaged, the stored data may become inaccessible.

Device	Characteristics	Advantages	Disadvantages
Portable USB flash drive 	There are no moving parts. Can be used in a range of digital devices where a USB port is available to connect to.	Low power consumption. Portable, small and lightweight. Range of capacities available. Fast speeds, with no moving parts.	Constant plugging into a device can degrade the physical USB port or the USB connector. The speed of access to the data is dependent on the USB connection. Limited number of read/write cycles possible.
Network-attached storage (NAS) device 	Connects to a network using the router. Extra storage disks can be added when extra space is needed.	Multiple users can access the drive at the same time. Files can be shared among users and devices. Remote access is possible. Can be a cheaper option than a network drive.	File transfer speed can be slow. Requires some network knowledge to install and configure. Uses bandwidth so can run slow if there are network/broadband problems.
Portable wireless drive 	A hard drive placed inside a protective case. Uses SSD technology. No wires or connections are needed to access the data. Can be used directly with a digital device via USB or plugged into a router via an Ethernet cable.	Can be located in one place with data still accessible. Can be accessed remotely. Multiple users can have access at the same time. Has own battery/power source.	Can be discoverable by other devices if security protection methods are not used.

Research

Research the features, advantages and disadvantages of a portable external hard drive disc (HDD).

Test your knowledge

21 What is the cloud?
22 How can cloud services be accessed?
23 Identify **one** disadvantage of using physical location devices to store data.
24 Identify **one** internal storage device.
25 Describe **one** advantage of using a portable USB flash drive to store data.

3.5 Application of testing to a range of contexts

Importance and purpose of testing

Testing is the process of checking that a solution, the final product, meets the needs of the end users and is fit for purpose. Testing is also needed to make sure that the solution contains no errors that could impact on the functioning of the solution when it is being used.

If full and complete testing is not carried out, then the final solution could have errors which will limit the functionality. A solution which does not work as intended is as bad as not having a solution at all.

During testing it is important that every part and aspect of the solution is tested to make sure it works as intended.

There are advantages and disadvantages of testing. These are shown in Table 1.12.

Table 1.12 Advantages and disadvantages of testing

Advantages	Disadvantages
The final solution will be fit for purpose and be of high quality.	Creating a full and complete test plan can be time consuming.
Testing will have covered all functions and features so all errors should have been identified and rectified.	The planned tests must cover all functions and features of the solution.
Technical testing means that the solution will have been tested on a range of digital devices and operating systems.	If the test plan is not full and complete then errors may not be identified if the tests are not specifically detailed.
User testing will ensure the user journey is error free and intuitive to use.	Full and complete testing can take a long time.
Carrying out testing can ensure the reliability and robustness of the solution.	If testing does not identify errors at the testing stage, then the completion of the solution may be delayed as errors may be identified later in the creation process.
	If the solution is complex then many people may need to test it, meaning a large number of resources in terms of time, people and money may be needed.

Test data

There are three different types of test data that can be used during the testing process. These are:

- extreme
- invalid (erroneous)
- valid.

During the testing process, data needs to be entered and processed by a solution. Testing should use all possible acceptable (valid) data as well as data that should cause errors. By using the different types of data, the solution can be checked that it performs as expected.

A well-designed solution should produce error messages when data has been used during testing that is not acceptable. Table 1.13 shows the different types of test data and how they can be used during the testing of a solution.

Table 1.13 Different types of test data

Type of test data	Description	How it can be used during testing
Extreme	A data value that is on the boundary between valid and invalid data. This type of data will not cause an error.	A range validation tool has been set as having acceptable values between 18 and 64. The test data for this is set as 18 or 64. These values would be accepted as they are on the boundary of the acceptable range.
Invalid (erroneous)	A data value that will cause an error. This will be unacceptable but could also be incomplete or not meet the validation.	A password has been set as having 8 characters including 1 capital letter and 1 number. The test data for this is set as Bnhdtypu. This would cause an error as no number has been included.
Valid	A data value that is acceptable, sensible and reasonable. This type of data will not cause an error.	A postcode has been set in the format LLNN NLL. The test data is set as CV99 9ZZ This would be accepted as it matches the input mask and format check.

Synoptic links

Validation tools were covered in Topic area 3, section 3.2 of this unit.

You will need to test your spreadsheet solution. Testing is covered in Unit R060, Topic area 3, section 3.1.

You will need to test your AR prototype. Testing is covered in Unit R070, Topic area 4, section 4.1.

Activity

Locate a booking form on a website, for example for a hotel, festival or holiday. Copy and complete this table to show the three different types of test data (extreme, invalid (erroneous), valid) with examples that could be used to test each field. You will need to add more rows to the table.

Field	Type of test data	Example of test data

Types of testing

When the solution is ready to be tested, there are two different types of testing that can be carried out. These are:

- technical
- user.

Both of these types of testing has advantages and disadvantages. Some of these are shown in Table 1.14.

Research

Find **two** more advantages and **two** more disadvantages for each type of testing.

It does not matter which type of testing is carried out, a test plan must be created. The test plan should be in enough detail that someone else can carry out the planned tests.

An example test plan is shown in Table 1.15.

Technical testing

Technical testing is checking the functionality of the solution. This also includes checking that the solution works on a range of digital devices, different operating systems and, if connectivity is needed, that it works on a range of connectivity methods.

Table 1.14 Advantages and disadvantages of different types of testing

Type of testing	Advantages	Disadvantages
Technical	The solution will be fit-for-purpose and error free. The solution will have been tested on a range of digital devices. All functionalities will work as intended.	It can be time consuming to carry out full and complete technical tests. If all functionality is not tested the product will have errors on release. It may not be possible to test on a range of digital devices and operating systems. It can be expensive in terms of time and money.
User	Real users will interact with the product, following a complete user journey. An increased confidence in the product from users. A range of user demographics (population type) can be used to test the product. The development team can observe where users get stuck or muddled.	If the incorrect demographic users are selected, their user journey may not be indicative of the actual or target demographic group. It can be expensive in terms of time and money. Only a small group of users can test the product.

Table 1.15 An example test plan

Date	Test number	Test purpose	Type of test data	Test data	Expected result	Actual result	Remedial action needed	Retest number

Technical tests can cover:

- links on a web page or mobile app to take the user to the intended internal or external page
- testing an HCI to make sure the buttons and macros work as intended
- calculations used in a spreadsheet solution
- how a solution loads on opening on a range of digital devices and operating systems
- user interaction in an AR product
- how an AR product loads on a range of digital devices
- output including the contents and layout
- data validation on a form.

Activity

Find a website which includes a range of features. Copy and complete this table to show each feature, its purpose and the type of technical tests that could have been carried out. You will need to add more rows to the table.

Feature	Purpose	Technical tests

Synoptic links

HCI was covered throughout Topic area 2 of this unit.

Operating systems were covered in Topic area 2, section 2.3 of this unit.

User interaction methods were covered in Topic area 2, section 2.4 of this unit.

Digital devices are covered in Topic area 5, section 5.3 of this unit.

Connectivity methods are covered in Topic area 5, section 5.4 of this unit.

Demographics are covered in Topic area 5, section 5.5 of this unit.

User testing

User testing is carried out by a range of users who are likely to use the solution. User testing can be carried out when the solution is still in the creation stage. This is known as beta testing.

User testing can also be carried out when the solution is ready for release. This type of testing focuses on how the users interact with the solution in the real world. The users will carry out specific tests and record the results. This will ensure that, when the solution has been released, the user journey is free from error and the user can interact with the solution as intended.

When users are testing a solution, they can either use specific tests on a test plan individually or they may be observed carrying out the tests.

User tests can cover:

- data entry including validation
- functionality of an HCI
- output format
- different user interaction methods
- ease of use
- whether it is intuitive with informative error messages.

Activity

Using the same website as in the previous activity, add a column to the table titled 'User tests'. In this column, write details about the user tests that could have been carried out on each of the features.

Test your knowledge

26 Identify **one** advantage of testing.
27 Which type of test data is on the boundary of a range?
28 Identify **one** technical test that can be carried out.
29 What is user testing?
30 Identify **one** user test that can be carried out.

Practice questions

1 An online retailer provides customers with an order total. Identify and explain the data type that should be used for the order total. [3 marks]

2 Explain, using an example, how the validation tool length check can be used when a customer is selecting a username on a website. [3 marks]

3 Describe **one** advantage and **one** disadvantage of a charity using an online survey. [4 marks]

4 Discuss the advantages and disadvantages to a team who are working remotely of collecting, storing and using data in the cloud. [9 marks]

5 Identify **two** examples of technical tests. [2 marks]

Topic area 4 Cyber-security and legislation

Getting started

Data is a valuable asset to people and organisations. It must be kept secure against threats and to comply with legislation. Breaches in security can occur, however. In May 2014, eBay reported that a hacking attack, lasting 229 days, had exposed account detail for all its users, reported to be 145 million people. The account details included names, addresses, dates of birth and encrypted passwords.

Investigate other high-profile hacking attacks and think about the impact of these for the organisations and the people whose data they held.

4.1 Threats

There are many different threats to data and information.

Cyber-security attackers can attack a digital system, which can lead to data and information being stolen, leaked or made unusable. The impact of this can be huge for an organisation or an individual. As more organisations and people use the cloud to store data and information and use the internet for financial transactions and shopping, the security level of this data has to be high to ensure that the information and data cannot fall into the wrong hands.

Some of the most common cyber-security threats to data security and digital systems are a denial of service, hacking, malware and social engineering.

Key term

Cyber-security The practice of defending digital devices, including computers, servers, mobile devices, electronic systems, networks and data, from malicious attacks.

Denial of service

A denial of service (DoS) is an attempt to make a digital system, for example a network or website, unavailable to its users by flooding it with network traffic. A DoS is usually focused on preventing an internet site or service from functioning efficiently, or at all, either temporarily or indefinitely. The attacks usually target sites or services hosted on high-profile web servers such as banks, payment websites (such as PayPal) and mobile phone companies.

A DoS is carried out by usually only one attacker. A DoS attack is often simple to identify and stop as the attacker is easy to identify and block.

Hacking

Hacking means finding out weaknesses in an established system and exploiting them. A computer hacker is a person who finds out weaknesses in a computer system to gain unauthorised access. A hacker may be motivated by a multitude of reasons, such as profit, protest or challenge.

There are three main types of hacking that can take place: black hat, grey hat and white hat.

Black hat

Black hat hacking is where the hacker hacks into a computer system with malicious intent. This intent can include stealing, exploiting the data stolen or seen, and selling on the data. Black hat hackers carry out illegal hacking activities and can be prosecuted under UK IT legislation.

Grey hat

Grey hat hacking is where the hacker hacks into computer systems for fun or to troll, but does not have malicious intent towards the computer system. If a grey hat hacker finds a weakness, then they may offer to fix the vulnerability – but for a fee! Grey hat hackers can also manipulate the rankings of websites when a search is done on a search engine.

White hat

White hat hacking is where the hacker is given permission to hack into systems to identify any loopholes or vulnerabilities. As this type of hacking is done with the permission of the computer system owner, it does not break any of the legislation that relates to hacking. White hat hackers are motivated to keep the system as safe as possible from malicious hacking attempts.

Malware

Malware (malicious software) is installed on a computer system and collects information about users without their knowledge. There are many types of malware, but the main types are adware, botnet, ransomware, spyware, Trojan horse, virus and worm (see Table 1.16).

It is simple to protect against many forms of malware by installing, running and keeping updated security software. It is also not wise to open any suspicious files or click on any links in emails.

Table 1.16 Types of malware

Type of malware	Why it is used	How it works	How to mitigate
Adware	Adware generates revenue for its author.	Adware is also known as advertising-supported software. This is any software package that automatically shows adverts, such as pop-ups. It may also be in the user interface of a software package or on an installation screen. Adware, by itself, is harmless, however some adware may include spyware such as key loggers.	Install, run and keep updated a security software package. Do not open any files from an unknown source. Do not click any links in emails.
Botnet	A botnet, and the person who created it, attempts to take control of digital systems.	A botnet is an interconnected network of several digital systems infected by bot malware. Bot malware is a type of malware that allows a cyber-security attacker to take control of an infected digital system without the user's knowledge.	Install, run and keep updated a security software package. Do not open any files from an unknown source. Do not click any links in emails.

Type of malware	Why it is used	How it works	How to mitigate
Ransomware	Ransomware holds a computer system captive and demands a ransom, usually money, to release it.	Ransomware can restrict user access to the computer system by encrypting files or locking down the digital system. A message is usually displayed to force the user to pay so that the restrictions can be lifted and the user can have access to the data or digital system. It is spread like a worm and can be started by downloading an infected file or by a vulnerability in the digital system.	Do not open any files from an unknown source. Do not click any links in emails. Install, run and keep updated a security software package.
Spyware	Spyware can collect data from an infected digital system, including personal information like websites visited, user logins and financial information.	Spyware is usually hidden from a user and can be difficult to detect. It is often secretly installed on a user's personal digital system without their knowledge. Some spyware such as key loggers, however, may be installed intentionally to monitor users. Spyware can also install additional software or redirect web browsers to different websites. Some spyware can change system settings, which could lead to slow internet connection speeds or changes in web browser settings.	Do not open any files from an unknown source. Do not click any links in emails. Install, run and keep updated a security software package.
Trojan horse	A Trojan horse is a standalone malicious program designed to give full control of an infected digital system to another digital system.	Trojans often appear to be something that is wanted or needed by the user of a digital system. They can be hidden in valid programs and software. Trojan horses can make copies of themselves, steal information, or harm the host digital system(s).	Do not open any files from an unknown source. Do not click any links in emails. Install and run a security software package, and keep it updated.
Virus	A virus attempts to make a computer system unreliable.	A virus is a computer program that replicates itself and spreads from one digital system to others. Viruses can increase their chances of spreading to other digital systems by infecting files on a network file system or a file system that is accessed by other digital systems.	Do not open any files from an unknown source. Do not click any links in emails. Install, run and keep updated a security software package.
Worm	A worm is a standalone computer program that replicates itself so it can spread to other computers.	A worm can use a network to spread. Unlike a virus, it does not need to attach itself to an existing program. Worms almost always cause some harm to a network, even if only by consuming bandwidth.	Do not open any files from an unknown source. Do not click any links in emails. Install, run and keep updated a security software package.

Social engineering

Social engineering is the art of manipulating people so that confidential information can be found out. It can take many forms. The most common ones are described in Table 1.17.

Table 1.17 Types of social engineering

Type of social engineering	Why it is used	How it works
Baiting	Baiting tries to get victims to give cybercriminals the information they need.	Baiting is very similar to phishing. The cybercriminals make a promise of goods to get the information they need. An example would be to promise free downloads of films or music in return for log-in details.
Phishing	Phishing tries to get users to input their credit or debit card numbers, or security details or log-in details into a fake website.	Phishing uses a fake website that looks identical to a real one. The most common targets for phishing are bank, building society and insurance websites. For example, the attackers send out emails or text messages that pretend to be from a bank. A link is contained in the email, which the user is asked to click on. This link takes the user to a fake website.
Pretexting	Pretexting is when a cybercriminal lies to get data or information.	Pretexting usually involves a scam where the criminal pretends to need the information to confirm the identity of the person they are talking to.
Quid pro quo	Quid pro quo tries to disable anti-virus software so that software updates, usually malware, can be installed to gain access to a digital system.	Quid pro quo is very similar to baiting, except the promise is that of a service rather than goods. A common method is a telephone call claiming to be from an IT service provider. These people offer assistance in fixing IT problems.
Scareware	Scareware tries to scare people into downloading and buying useless software.	Scareware is malware, usually pop-ups, that attempts to convince a user that there is a problem with their digital system, such as a virus or hacking attack.
Shoulder surfing	Shoulder surfing aims to steal data and information.	Shoulder surfing is when a person's private and confidential information is seen. For example, an attacker may stand very close to someone using a cash machine in order to see their PIN. This is very effective in crowded places when a person uses a smartphone or mobile device and log-in details can be seen.

Figure 1.14 Social engineering

Activity

Identify a method that could be used to mitigate against each type of social engineering shown in Table 1.17.

Test your knowledge

1. What does DoS stand for?
2. What is a black hat hacker?
3. Why is a Trojan horse used?
4. How does phishing attempt to get financial details from a user?
5. Identify **two** types of social engineering.

4.2 The impacts of a cyber-security attack on individuals and/or organisations

If a cyber-security attack takes place and is successful, this can have an impact on individuals and organisations. Sometimes, a successful attack on an organisation can have an impact on both the organisation and its customers. A cyber-security attack can result in a range of impacts.

Data destruction

Data destruction is when data is destroyed by a cyber-security attacker and no longer exists.

If there is a backup, then it is possible to restore the data that has been destroyed. If an organisation carries out a daily backup, then this means that at least only one day's data and information will have been lost or corrupted.

There is always a time delay before the most recent backup can be used to reinstate data. This delay can have an impact on how the organisation is able to interact with its customers and suppliers. With many transactions happening online (for example, e-commerce), customer orders may be lost. The loss of this data can have consequences for customers as their **personal data** and the goods they ordered may be lost.

Data manipulation

Data manipulation is when data is edited, usually to meet the needs of cyber-security attackers.

For example, the attackers could change the data in a news feed on social media platforms. This could result in false news being published on these sites. This type of cyber-security attack is usually found quite quickly.

Data modification

Data modification also changes data to meet the needs of the attacker, for example changing the amount of money in a bank account. The attacker can then withdraw the increased amount of money, causing the bank to lose money. In some cases, the crime may not be found for a long time. Data modification is very similar to data manipulation, but the attackers usually have different aims.

> **Key term**
>
> **Personal data** Any information relating to an identified or identifiable living individual.

Data theft – in transit and at rest

Data theft is when cyber-security attackers steal computer-based data from a person or organisation, with the intent of compromising privacy or obtaining confidential data. Data that can be stolen includes passwords, personal details and financial data. Data theft can also be committed by stealing portable storage devices or mobile digital devices.

Data theft can occur when the data is at rest or in transit. Data at rest means that the data is not moving from device to device or network to network. Data at rest is when the data is stored on, for example, a hard drive, laptop, flash drive, or archived/stored by an organisation.

Data can also be intercepted and stolen when it is in transit. Data in transit means the data is being sent, or moving, from one location to another, for example across the internet or through a private network.

> **Synoptic link**
>
> You will learn about the measures that can be used to protect data and digital systems in Topic area 4, section 4.3 of this unit.

Denial of service to authorised users

A denial of service (DoS) attack can have an impact on the authorised users of the website that is being attacked. This can lead to authorised users being unable to access the website while it is under attack or after the attack has finished. For example, if a banking website was the victim of a DoS attack then customers who use that bank website would be unable to access their accounts, pay bills, transfer money or complete other online banking activities.

In December 2015, the BBC was the victim of a DoS attack, with iPlayer being taken offline, preventing online viewing of BBC news and other programming. In February 2020, Amazon Web Services (AWS) was the target of a DoS attack which lasted 3 days, with 2.3 terabytes of useless traffic flooding the servers each second.

Identity theft

Identity theft is when personal details are stolen, and identity fraud is when those details are used to commit fraud, for example taking out a loan in someone else's name. If cyber-security attackers get hold of someone's name, address and date of birth then this is enough for them to create a copy of that person. If a person's identity is stolen then this could result in, for example, big debts being run up in their name or passports being issued and possibly used for criminal activity. In 2001, Abraham Abdallah stole the identities of several famous and wealthy people, including Steven Spielberg, in an attempt to steal millions of dollars.

Impacts

Many cyber-security attacks result in data and information being stolen or corrupted so it can no longer be used. If there is a backup then it is possible to restore the data and information, but most organisations back up only once a day. This means that at least one day's data and information will have been lost or corrupted.

The organisation may have backups, but the time taken to reinstall the data can have an impact on its operations. An organisation relies on data to carry out its day-to-day functions, both internally and in the interaction between it and its suppliers and/or customers. The time delay in restoring lost or corrupted data will mean that the organisation cannot carry out its day-to-day business. While the organisation is recovering from the cyber-security attack it may not be able to operate, as the internal data required to be shared between departments and external data, such as links with suppliers and customers, may have been lost or corrupted. This will have a negative impact for the organisation and can cause disruption to its function.

Synoptic link

You will learn about firewalls and secure backups in the section on logical prevention measures below.

If an organisation has been the target of a cyber-security attack and data has been destroyed, manipulated, modified or stolen, then its reputation will be negatively affected. It is very likely that the organisation will no longer be seen as trustworthy and customer confidence will be reduced. This could mean customers moving their custom elsewhere which could result in the organisation stopping trading.

It is also possible that the individual customers may suffer identity theft leading to a personal financial impact. If the data includes sensitive data such as a customer's name, address and date of birth, then criminals could use that information to, for example, get credit cards or loans. The person whose data is used might have no idea they have been the victim of identity theft until credit card statements or other letters arrive at their address. It is then very difficult to prove that the card or loan was taken out by someone else.

If personal data has been the target of the cyber-security attack, then the organisation may also have to pay compensation. Legislation requires organisations to pay compensation to the people whose data has been destroyed, stolen or corrupted. This compensation can be very high, sometimes running into thousands of pounds. If the cyber-security attack has affected more than one person's data then this sum of money will increase. The cost of this compensation may result in the organisation having to be shut down if it does not have enough money to pay the compensation or to carry on trading.

Synoptic link

You will learn more about IT legislation in Topic area 4, section 4.4 of this unit.

Test your knowledge

6 What is meant by data destruction?
7 What is the difference between data at rest and data in transit?
8 What does a DoS attack aim to do?
9 Identify **one** type of data that could lead to identity theft being committed.
10 Identify **one** impact on an organisation of a cyber-attack.

4.3 Prevention measures

Data and information are very valuable assets, not only to the organisations that collect, store, process and use them, but also to each individual person.

Data and information are used for a variety of purposes including customer shopping records, financial data and health data. It is important that all data and information is kept secure with prevention measures put in place to protect it from threats.

Physical prevention measures

Physical prevention measures are usually hardware based. The aim is to stop unauthorised access to digital devices and the data and information stored on them.

Biometric devices

Some devices include biometric prevention measures. These use a physical characteristic of the user, such as a fingerprint, eye scan or voice.

It is common for laptops, smartphones and tablets to need a biometric measure to be positive before the device can be accessed. The owner of the device will have stored their characteristic as part of the security settings on the device. For example, when a fingerprint is used to access the device, this is checked against the stored fingerprint. If there is a match, then access is granted. This means that only people whose characteristic is stored and recognised can access the device. If anyone else tries to gain access, the characteristic will not be recognised, and access will be denied.

Large organisations can use biometric prevention measures to, for example, protect server rooms. When someone tries to access the server room, they must scan their fingerprint, for example. This is then checked against the database of authorised personnel fingerprints and, if there is a match, access will be granted.

There are some disadvantages to using biometric prevention measures. For example, a person's voice can change if they have a cold. This can cause problems if the device they are trying to access does not recognise the voice pattern. If someone injured their finger, for example with a burn or cut, the pattern of their fingerprint would change and may result in access being denied. Similarly, if someone has been swimming, their fingers become wet and wrinkly. This would also change the pattern of the fingerprint.

Keypads and radio-frequency identification

Keypads and **radio-frequency identification (RFID)** access badges can be used to protect areas in a building where digital devices are stored or kept. This can include server rooms.

Keypads are a type of lock. The correct code must be inputted before the lock opens. The code can be given only to people who need to access the room; this limits the number of people able to enter. The main disadvantage of keypads is that the access code may not be changed regularly. This means that the number of people who have the code may increase, which reduces security.

Access badges use RFID. When the access badge is near or tapped against a lock, the lock opens as long as the badge owner has the authority to access it. If the badge owner does not have the authority, then the lock stays closed. This means that an audit log can be kept of who accessed a room or area. The main advantage to using RFID is that different access can be given to different people. For example, only IT support staff will have access to the network and/or server rooms.

Key term

Radio-frequency identification (RFID) Access badges or tags that use radio frequency to transfer data from the tags to a digital system, for example to allow access to a room.

Activity

Investigate the physical security measures used in your school. Think about the effectiveness of the measures. Could anything be improved?

Test your knowledge

11 What is the aim of physical protection?
12 Identify **one** characteristic that could be used in a biometric device.
13 How do keypads allow access into a room?
14 What does RFID stand for?
15 How does RFID transfer data?

Logical prevention measures

Logical prevention measures use software-based techniques for authenticating a user. There are many logical protection measures that can be implemented and used. The choice of measures will depend upon the data and information being protected.

Access rights and permissions

Digital systems, software, files and folders containing data and information have **access rights** and **permissions**. Authentication, usernames and passwords, can be used to set access rights and permissions for each person. This means that only those users who have the correct log-in credentials can have access.

The access rights can inform what a user can do with a file and folder. These are called permissions. A user can have permission to read, write, edit or delete data and information.

An organisation can use access rights and permissions to control which files employees are allowed to look at by setting different access

Key terms

Access rights Control over who has access to a digital system, folder, files, data and/or information.

Permissions A set of attributes that determine what a user can do with files and folders, for example read, write, edit or delete.

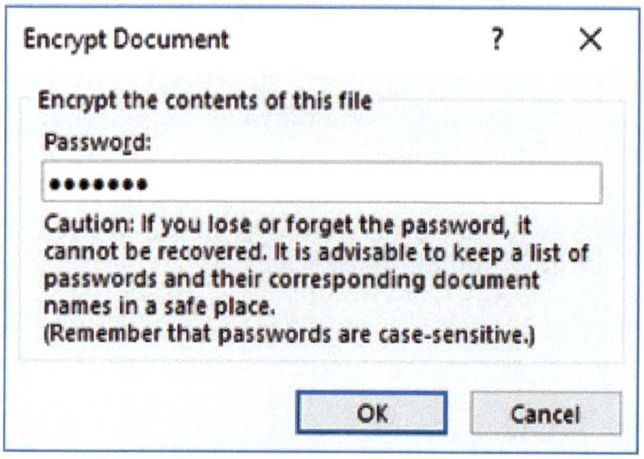

Figure 1.15 Protecting a document with a password

permissions to the folders or files. Managers can have access to folders or files that other office staff do not. A personnel manager would be able to look into the files and folders that contain staff personal details, but a warehouse manager would not have the access rights and permissions to do this.

Files and folders can be protected by setting the access rights to read-only so that the files cannot be altered. Individual documents can have passwords set on them so that only authorised staff can open the file to read and/or edit the contents. As well as protecting the whole document with a password, restrictions can be set on just parts of the document. This is useful in spreadsheets, where formulae must not be changed when an office worker is entering data. The data they are working on can be changed but the formula calculations must remain the same.

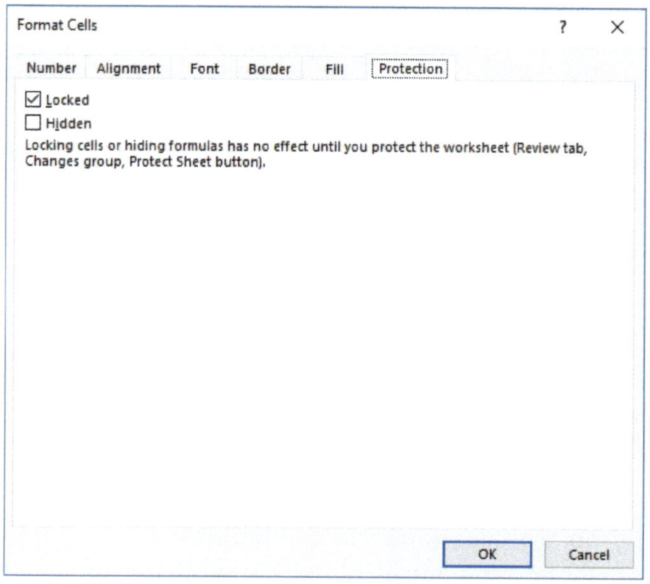

Figure 1.16 Protecting a cell in a spreadsheet

Anti-virus/malware software

Anti-virus and anti-malware programs are security software which are designed to prevent, detect and remove viruses and other malware, including adware, Trojans and worms. It is essential that any digital system connected to the internet has some form of security protection. If security software is not installed, then it is possible that within minutes of connection to the internet it will be infected. There are approximately 60,000 new malware or viruses created each day.

Security software performs several tasks including:

- scanning files or directories for any viruses, malware or known malicious patterns
- automatic real-time scanning
- performing a manual scan of a digital device
- removing any malicious code detected – sometimes you will be notified of an infection and asked if you want to clean the file; other programs will automatically do this behind the scenes
- blocking unsafe websites or alerting a user about infected emails.

When security software finds a malicious program on a digital system, the user is usually offered two options:

1. Quarantine the malicious program so the software cannot infect the digital system; this option gives the vendor the opportunity to analyse the program so that they can offer an update to users.
2. Delete the malicious program; this option clears the digital system of the infection.

Anti-virus and anti-malware scans can also be carried out by the software. These can be scheduled to run automatically at a selected time and day or can be done by the user at any time. These scans will search for any viruses or malware that may be on the digital system and that have not been detected by the anti-virus package.

It is important that the software is kept up to date. When the package is bought and installed, it will be the most up-to-date version. New viruses and malware are being created and distributed all the time, however, so the software vendor releases updates to reduce the risk from these new threats.

Automatic updates

Some software updates automatically. This process is usually completed in real time. This means that when the computer system is connected to the internet the anti-virus software will automatically be checking all the time for new updates. If an update is found, then the software will automatically download and install the update. This happens because threats covered by the software are being released all the time. This means that the user does not have to remember to manually check for updates and so the digital system is always protected from any threats.

If an organisation uses automatic updates of the software then the user does not have to remember to manually check for updates and can be sure that their digital system is as up to date as possible. This also means that any vulnerabilities identified by the vendor are solved before an attack can take place.

Manual updates

Manually updating security software can be dangerous to the digital system and the data and information held on it. People can forget to carry out manual updates and this can leave the digital system vulnerable to threats.

A manual update for the software could be completed on an ad-hoc basis or can be set to check at a specified time by a user.

There are some problems with manual updating:

- It can take time to download the patch.
- There may be a time delay between the patch being released by the software vendor and the time when the manual update takes place.

- The digital system must be switched on and connected to the internet for the update to be downloaded. If the manual update has been scheduled for a time when the digital system is switched off, then the user will never get updates or download patches. This can leave the digital system open to attacks and threats and could result in data being lost or stolen.

Some users, however, may prefer to update their software manually because they want to look at the updates to decide whether or not to download them. Some users may consider the updates to be intrusive or not appropriate.

Activity

Choose any two providers of anti-virus and anti-malware software – look on the internet to see the different providers available.

Copy and complete this table to show the features which are available (two features have been given for you). You may need to add more rows to the table.

	Provider 1	Provider 2
Internet links scanner		
Live support		

Two-factor authentication

Some digital systems use two-factor authentication (2FA). The most common authentication protection is that of using a token.

When a user tries to access a secure website, the username and password are entered. When these are submitted and checked, the system creates a token code, usually made up of numbers, which is sent to the email address (or by text message to the mobile phone number) linked to the username and password. To access the secure area, the user must input the token code. 2FA is used on, for example, financial websites and an organisation's secure cloud sharing area.

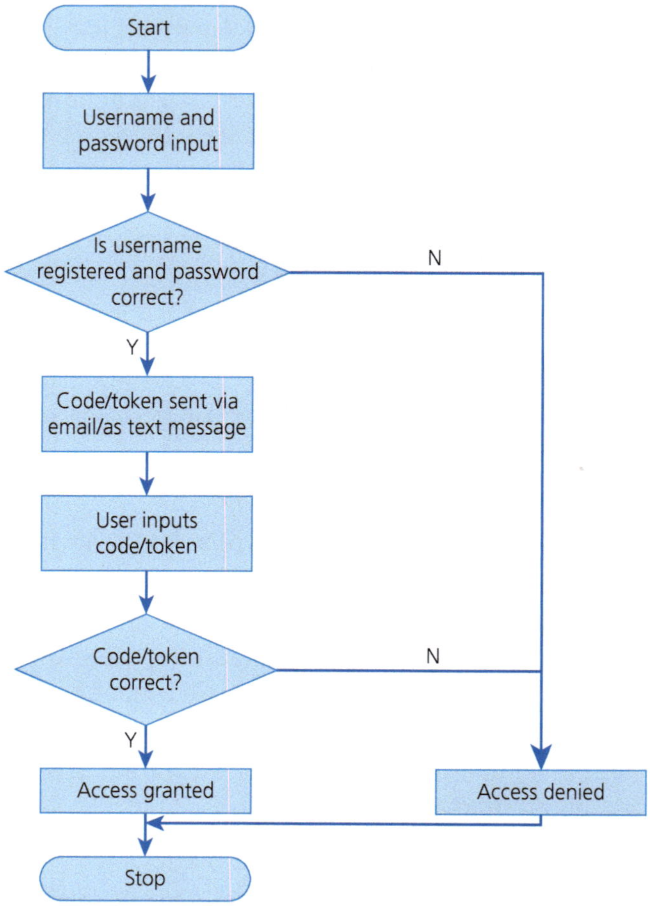

Figure 1.17 Two-step authentication

Encryption

As has already been discussed, the most valuable assets to an organisation or individuals are data and information.

Encryption can help to prevent the data being accessed and used by hackers and other attackers. Data can be scrambled by using **encryption software** when it is stored or transmitted between digital devices over networks.

Key term

Encryption software Software that is used to encrypt a file or data.

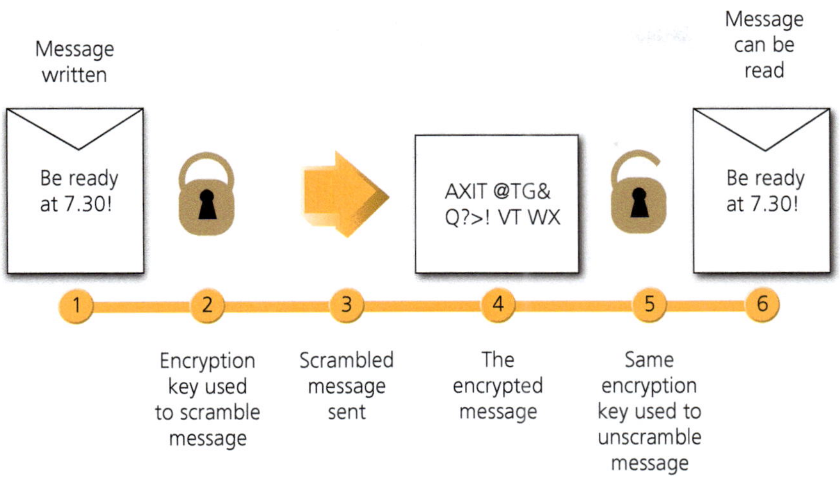

Figure 1.18 Using an encryption key to encrypt and decrypt a message

Encryption software uses an **encryption code (or encryption key)** to scramble (encrypt) the contents of data files. The proper code is needed to unscramble the file (decrypt it) so it can be read and used. If the encrypted file is accessed by anyone without the correct code to unscramble it, the data is meaningless.

Data can be encrypted at rest and/or in transit. It is common practice, especially where the data is sensitive, for example financial or personal data, to encrypt the **data at rest**. This can help mitigate the loss of the data in an attack.

It is also good practice to encrypt the **data in transit**. By doing this the encryption can mitigate against the loss of the data while it is being transmitted by, for example, email or uploading to a cloud storage area.

Asymmetric and symmetric encryption

There are two main types of encryption: asymmetric and symmetric.

Key terms

Data at rest Data stored on a digital device or storage media.

Data in transit Data being sent to two or more authorised users.

Encryption code (or encryption key) A set of characters, a phrase or numbers that are used when encrypting or decrypting data or a file.

Asymmetric encryption is also known as public key encryption. This is when the encryption key is available to anyone to use and encrypt data but only the person who receives the data receives the decryption key.

Figure 1.18 shows the process of symmetric encryption. This is when the encryption and decryption keys are the same.

Encryption can also be used on websites. When customers buy goods online, book cinema tickets online or enter personal details into any website, the data should be encrypted before being transmitted. This will keep the details from being read or used by others even if they are intercepted. Everyone should check that a website they are using to enter personal detail uses encryption.

A secure website using encryption will use https instead of http in the URL and will show a small padlock. Different web browsers will show the use of https in different ways.

Figure 1.19 shows a web address beginning with https and also shows the padlock to confirm that the website uses encryption.

Figure 1.19 A website using encryption

Firewalls

A firewall is a security device that mitigates against threats by examining **data packets**. A firewall can be either hardware or software or both, but hardware and software firewalls work in the same way.

The purpose of a firewall is to establish a barrier between a digital device and/or a network and incoming traffic from external sources, such as the internet. Firewalls monitor the traffic that flows into a digital device and/or a network through an internet connection. The firewall blocks malicious traffic like viruses and hackers based on security rules.

Figure 1.20 A firewall acts as a barrier against threats to a system's security

Firewalls can either be software or hardware, though to maximise the efficiency it is best to have both.

- A software firewall is a program installed on each digital device that monitors traffic through port numbers and applications.
- A physical firewall is a piece of hardware installed between the network and the gateway.

Firewalls monitor and analyse incoming traffic based on pre-established security rules. Traffic that does not meet the rules, for example from unsecured or suspicious sources, is blocked.

Firewalls monitor the traffic at the entry point – called ports. Ports are where the information is exchanged with the external devices or websites.

There are two main types of firewalls:

- Packet-filtering firewalls mitigate against threats by analysing the data packets and blocking any packets that do not meet the pre-defined security rules.
- Inspection firewalls mitigate against threats by marking the key features of any outgoing requests for information and checking for the same key features of the data coming into the system and deciding if the incoming traffic is relevant.

Secure backups

A secure backup of data is a copy of data or files that are currently in use. Backups are made regularly and stored away from the computer system, preferably in another building in a secure place.

How often a backup is made will depend upon what the data and files contain. A retailer will make backup copies of its data and files every day, usually at a set time, after most of the day's work has been done. Banks and other financial institutions carry out **real-time backups** because their data is so important.

Backups created by organisations are kept safely so that they are protected from theft or fire. The data on the backups is often encrypted so that even if the backups are lost or stolen, no one will be able to understand the data without the encryption key.

Creating backups is so important that most large organisations are prepared to spend large sums of money to ensure they have adequate backups that can be used to recover any lost data. The expense of using their own tape drives or additional hard disks can be too much for some organisations, so many use the cloud as an online backup, as

Key terms

Data packets Small units of data which are sent and received when accessing the internet or any other type of network.

Real-time backup When a backup is made automatically each time the data changes.

shown in Figure 1.21. This means the backups are stored on servers managed by external companies, which charge for the service but take responsibility for providing the systems and for security of the stored data. The cost of these services can be much lower than paying for in-house IT technicians to manage and run backup systems or for buying and maintaining dedicated backup servers.

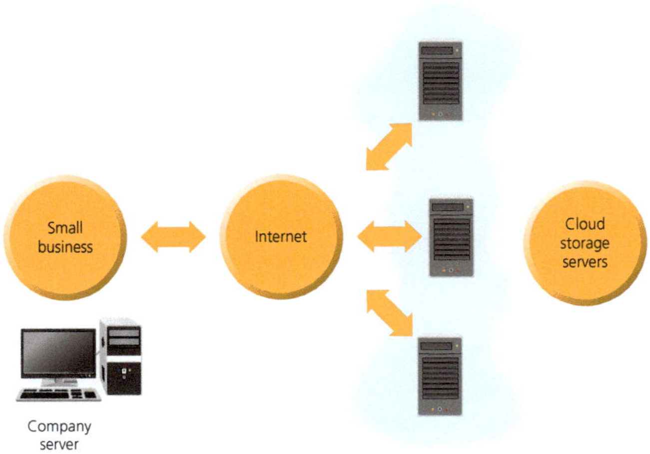

Figure 1.21 How cloud storage is used by a business for backup

Usernames and passwords

Usernames and passwords are a two-part logical prevention measure. The username acts as authorisation while the password acts as authentication. Without both parts being correct, access will be denied to the digital system that is used to store data and information.

The username is a unique identifier for a user and identifies who the user is to the digital system. The username can be allocated to a group, for example in your school to a group of teachers and a group of students. Each group will have access rights and software allocated to them.

The password is the method of restricting access. Without the correct password being linked to the correct username, access is denied. The password lets the system know that the user is who the username says they are. It is also good practice for external storage devices to be password protected.

Passwords are only effective if they are strong and not easily guessed.

Activity

Rules can be set about choosing a password. Create a digital communication for new students at your school, to show the rules that should be followed when creating a password.

Test your knowledge

16 What permissions can be given to a user?
17 What does 2FA stand for?
18 Identify the two different types of encryption.
19 What does a firewall do at a port?
20 What does a password act as?

Secure destruction of data

This should be carried out when data is no longer required or when it should be securely destroyed for legal reasons. This is to make sure that no data falls into the wrong hands. Even if data is deleted using the operating system software, it can still be located and used from the physical device, for example a laptop's hard drive.

There are many ways in which data can be securely destroyed. Which way is used will depend upon what data is to be destroyed and the storage device.

Data sanitation

Data sanitation is the process of deliberately, permanently and irreversibly removing or destroying the data stored on a storage device to make the data unrecoverable. A storage device that has been sanitised has no usable data left on it and the data will never be able to be recovered. Depending on the method of data sanitation used, it may or may not be possible to reuse the storage device again.

Data sanitation can be achieved by data erasure, magnetic wiping and physical destruction.

Data erasure

Data erasure uses software to overwrite the data on a storage device. All the data on the storage device is removed, usually by overwriting it with 1s and 0s. All **sectors** of the storage device are overwritten. Other methods of data erasure include reformatting the storage device, but this method can leave data recoverable so is not secure.

If data erasure is used to securely destroy the data, then it is highly likely that the storage device can be used again.

Magnetic wipe

A magnetic wipe is when the magnetic field part of a storage device is removed. This makes all the data stored on the storage device unreadable. Using this method can also make the storage device unusable. This is because the wipe also removes all the basic commands stored on the storage device – these are the commands that make the storage device operate.

Physical destruction

The most secure, but probably the most expensive, way to securely delete data is through the physical destruction of the storage device. The physical destruction of a storage device may mean that it is so thoroughly destroyed that the data cannot be recovered. One example of physical destruction is the use of a hard drive shredder that shreds hard drives, a bit like a paper shredder. Another method is to use a drill or hammer through the hard drive.

In 2017, a hard drive containing unpublished and unfinished novels by Terry Pratchett was destroyed after his death. The method of destruction was extreme: the hard drive was run over by a steamroller!

Key term

Sector An area on a storage device that stores data.

Figure 1.22 A destroyed hard drive

It is also important that any paper-based forms that contain personal or confidential data are securely destroyed. Paper-based forms can be securely destroyed by using a paper shredder to shred them so no information can be read, or by burning them.

Test your knowledge

21 What is one reason why data would need to be securely destroyed?
22 What is a sector?
23 Can a storage device be reused when it has been magnetically wiped?
24 Identify one physical destruction method.
25 How can paper-based forms be securely destroyed?

4.4 Legislation related to the use of IT systems

Important: The details of each Act in this topic were correct when this book was published. During your study for this course, you must make sure that you know about and understand the most up-to-date versions of each of the Acts, including any changes or additional pieces of legislation that are relevant to IT.

Computer Misuse Act

The Computer Misuse Act (CMA) was brought into UK legislation in 1990 and has seen many amendments over the years. This Act aims to protect data and information that is held on computer systems. The CMA relates to illegal access to files and data stored on digital systems. It was introduced to cope with the increase in hacking, malware and viruses.

There are five main parts to this Act.

1 Unauthorised access to computer material

This means that any access to materials that you do not have permission to view is against this law, as is using a computer to access data or programs stored on another computer. This is often what people refer to as 'hacking'. Hacking is only illegal if you do not have permission to access the data or use the computer to access the data.

Synoptic link

You learnt about hackers in Topic area 4, section 4.1 of this unit.

2 Unauthorised access with intent to commit or facilitate the commission of further offences

Accessing computer material and then intending to use the information to commit further offences is against this law. This means that if you access information, even if you have permission to do so, with the intention of using it to commit fraud or blackmail, you are breaking this law.

3 Unauthorised acts with intent to impair, or with recklessness as to impairing, operation of a computer

This means that any unauthorised alteration made to computer materials is against this law. If files or data are changed when you do not have permission, this is breaking this law. For instance, if you access someone else's digital system files and change the contents, then you are breaking this law. Also, unauthorised altering of files to make the digital system malfunction, to alter how it works or to alter other data also breaks this law – so sending a virus is a crime under this law.

4 Making, supplying or obtaining any articles for use in a malicious act using a computer

This means that anyone who creates a malicious program is breaking the CMA, for example if you downloaded a program to take remote control of a friend's digital system without their knowledge but you didn't get a chance to use it before you were caught. This offence covers the creation, use or possession of 'malware' but also any legitimate software that you were going to use to commit an offence.

5 Unauthorised acts causing, or creating risk of, serious damage

This part of the CMA is focused on the most serious cyber-security attacks, for example those on essential systems controlling power supply, communications, food or fuel distribution. These could have a significant impact, resulting in loss of life, serious illness or injury, severe social disruption or serious damage to the economy, the environment or national security.

Penalties for breaking this law can be a prison term of several years or a fine, or both. But to be found guilty of breaking the CMA, intent must be proved. If a digital system is not well protected, data could be accidentally accessed, for example a document may be accidentally edited.

For anyone to be found guilty, it has to be shown that they intentionally accessed and changed data.

Copyright, Designs and Patents Act

The Copyright, Designs and Patents Act (CD&PA) was brought into UK legislation in November 1988 and, like other legislation related to the use of IT and digital systems, has seen many amendments over the years.

The CD&PA establishes copyright and that this copyright lasts:

- 70 years after the work was created or published
- 70 years after the death of the author
- 50 years for computer-generated work.

The CD&PA protects the creative work of individuals or businesses. The creator of an original piece of work automatically owns the 'copyright'. The CD&PA aims to protect **intellectual property (IP)** rights.

Among the works that the CD&PA covers are:

- images
- software
- writing
- music.

The creator can decide what others do with their work. For example, they can decide to sell or allow it to be used with a credit. The creator may also decide to invoke a Creative Commons licence. This type of licence is public copyright which allows the free distribution of a copyrighted work. The creator gives people the right to share, use and build on their work. Open-source software is an example of a Creative Commons licence.

Research

There are six Creative Commons licence options. Investigate these six options and how they can be used.

The CD&PA protects against:

- illegal download of video and audio files
- software piracy, either by illegal download or illegal distribution
- theft of intellectual property, for example text/written work, including on websites
- use of software without the relevant licence
- using/downloading images without permission of the copyright holder.

The CD&PA protects the creator of the work by making it a crime for anyone to download, copy and share their work without first paying for it, or in some cases asking for permission to use it first.

There are three main ways in which the CD&PA is broken:

1 Using software without the correct software licence

If software has been bought by an organisation with a licence to install it on three digital devices but the organisation installs it on four devices, then the CD&PA has been broken. Some applications or programs will only run if a special piece of hardware is plugged into the computer or if a unique code is entered for that specific device.

2 Downloading files from the internet

If text, images and other files are downloaded and used, then permission from the copyright holder must be obtained. The name of the copyright holder should also be acknowledged. Sometimes a fee may have to be paid to use the work.

3 Copying music, DVDs, CDs and software

Any copying or sharing of digital files that you have not created yourself is a breach of the CD&PA. This includes copying and sharing MP3 and MP4 files made from streaming services or from music CDs and DVDs. Copying and sharing films copied from DVDs or from streaming services are also breaches of the CD&PA. It is also illegal under the CD&PA to make and share copies of software.

Key term

Intellectual property (IP) Creative work which can be treated as an asset or physical property. IP covers four main areas – copyright, trademarks, design rights and patents.

Test your knowledge

26 What is meant by unauthorised access?
27 How many parts does the Computer Misuse Act have?
28 How long does copyright last for on computer-generated works?
29 What is intellectual property?
30 Identify **one** way the CD&PA can be broken.

Data Protection Act

The current Data Protection Act (DPA) became law in 2018 and attempts to control how personal data and information are used by organisations and the UK Government. The Act also seeks to give people (the **data subjects**) control of their personal data and to support organisations with their lawful processing of personal data.

The Act sets out rules on how the data should be stored and processed. If people think their data is being misused, then the DPA can be used to complain and to claim compensation.

Storing data on digital systems makes it easier for that data to be accessed and used by the organisation, but it can also make the data more available to those who would misuse it. The DPA tries to protect individuals by giving them rights to access any data about themselves stored by others and to try and make sure that the data is processed appropriately. Most people would prefer that their personal data is kept private and cannot be accessed or used by anyone.

The DPA gives everyone the right to know what data is stored about them on a digital system and the right to see it. If someone feels that they are not being allowed to see their personal data or feels that the data is not being processed properly, they can contact the **Information Commissioner's** Office and ask for help. The Information Commissioner's Office will investigate the matter and, if necessary, can take action against the organisation.

There are six principles of the DPA:

1 Used fairly, lawfully and transparently

This means that you should be told about data which is being collected about you and should be asked for your permission to collect it.

You should also be made aware of the reason why the data is to be collected and for what it will be used.

2 Used for specified, explicit purposes

The **data controller** has to state why they want to collect and store information when they apply for permission to be able to do so. If they use the data they have collected for other purposes, they are breaking the DPA.

3 Used in a way that is adequate, relevant and limited to only what is necessary

This means that the data that is stored should be just enough for the task to be carried out, only relevant to the task, and not include other data. For example, a bank would need to hold a customer's name and address, but not any details of their qualifications.

4 Accurate and, where necessary, kept up to date

This means the person storing the data has a duty to ensure that any data they hold is accurate and free from errors. This is the principle that most people worry about because inaccurate data stored, for example by their bank, can cause many difficulties. Most people who ask to see the data held about them are concerned that an organisation holds data that is not accurate and want to get it corrected.

Key terms

Data controller The person who needs to apply for permission to collect and store data. The data controller is often the person in charge of the business, but sometimes a different person who works in the business may have this responsibility. This person decides what data needs to be collected and what it will be used for and how.

Data subject The person the data is being held about.

Information Commissioner The person who enforces the Data Protection Act. This is the person who organisations need to apply to in order to gain permission to collect and store personal data.

5 Kept for no longer than is necessary

Data should be destroyed or deleted when it is no longer needed. This should be carried out to ensure that others cannot read or access it.

6 Handled in a way that ensures appropriate security, including protection against unlawful or unauthorised processing, access, loss, destruction or damage

Data should be protected by some form of security. Effective data protection relies on IT systems being protected from malicious intent. The DPA requires organisations that handle personal data to evaluate the risks of processing such data and implement appropriate measures to mitigate those risks. These measures can include cyber-security controls.

The DPA also covers user consent. Consent must be given before, for example, an organisation or charity sends a marketing message. The consent must be knowingly and freely given and must be clear and specific.

The consent needs to be given for the organisation and the type of marketing communication to be used, such as a phone call, automated call, email or text. The consent should be a positive action, for example ticking a box, clicking an icon or sending an email.

The person must fully understand that they are providing consent. It is not acceptable to only provide information about marketing as part of terms and conditions or a privacy policy as these can be hard to find, difficult to understand or rarely read.

The clearest way to obtain consent is to ask the person to tick a box confirming they are happy to receive marketing calls, texts or emails. This is called **opt-in**.

It is important that clear records of what has been consented to are kept, including when and how the consent was given. This means that compliance can be proved in case of a complaint.

Consent can be withdrawn at any time, so it must be easy for someone to do this. This is called **opt-out**. For example, a link at the bottom of a marketing email enables the receiver to unsubscribe, as shown in Figure 1.23.

Some organisations provide opt-in boxes that are automatically pre-ticked. However, pre-ticked boxes do not give valid consent.

Key terms

Opt-in When a person has to take a specific positive step, for example ticking a box, sending an email or clicking a button or icon, to say they consent to receiving marketing.

Opt-out When a person must take a positive step to refuse or unsubscribe from marketing.

Test your knowledge

31 Who can people complain to about the DPA?

32 Define 'data subject'.

33 Identify **two** principles of the DPA 2018.

34 How can people opt in?

Figure 1.23 An unsubscribe link

Freedom of Information Act

The Freedom of Information (FoI) Act was brought into legislation in November 2000. The Act deals with access to official information and people being able to find out any information on any topic from any public authority. This is known as 'a right of access'. The FoI Act is overseen by the **Information Commissioner's Office (ICO)** and applies to all **public authorities**.

The Act allows anyone to make a request for information. The process begins with a request made by letter, email or message to the authority that the information is required from. The name and address of the person wanting the information is needed so the information can be returned. The request should also detail the information required.

There is usually no charge for the information, although a small charge may be made if information has to be scanned or copied if it is not in electronic form. The information may include printed documents, computer files, letters, emails, photographs, and sound or video recordings

The authority has 20 working days to comply with the request.

The main benefit of the FoI Act is that information that was not accessible to anyone outside the authority is now available. This increases accountability as it is no longer possible for decisions to be made and then 'hidden'.

Any information can be requested, but this does not mean that it will be received. The FoI has a list of information that does not have to be returned. These are called exceptions.

The request should be very clear and specific in what information is needed. The authority has to confirm or deny the existence of the information requested. If the request is too vague then either the request will be denied, or the information may not be found. Requests for information will not be replied to if the information is:

- already in the public domain
- contained in court records.

A request must be made under the correct Act. The FoI enables access to information about public authorities. If information is required about yourself, then a request needs to be made under the DPA.

Synoptic link

The DPA was covered previously in this topic area.

Health and Safety at Work Act

The Health and Safety at Work Act provides guidance to employers and employees about health and safety at work. The part of the Act that applies to people working with digital systems is the Health and Safety (DSE) Regulations. DSE stands for '**display screen equipment**'. The Act also defines actions that an employer should take to protect employees who work with digital systems in their job.

Almost everyone – not just all employees and employers – has a duty under the Health and Safety at Work Act to work and behave safely.

Key terms

Display screen equipment (DSE) Devices or equipment with a display screen, such as laptops, touch screens, smartphones and other similar devices.

Information Commissioner's Office (ICO) The organisation that oversees the Freedom of Information Act; it reports to the UK parliament.

Public authorities These include government departments, the National Health Service (NHS), state schools and the police force.

The Act makes it illegal to act recklessly or intentionally to act in such a way as to endanger yourself or others. Employees must take reasonable care for their own and others' safety and must cooperate with their employers in doing so.

The Health and Safety (DSE) Regulations apply to people using digital systems for their work but not necessarily to those using them at home, unless the employee works at home. The DSE regulations apply to any form of display screen. This means that employees working with, for example, PCs, laptops, tablets and smartphones are all covered by these regulations. The DSE regulations cover employees who work with DSE for an hour, or more, during their working hours.

The Health and Safety (DSE) Regulations state that employers (organisations) must do five main tasks to ensure the safety of their employees.

1 Analyse workstations and assess and reduce risks

Employers, and employees working from home, should complete a DSE workstation assessment. A DSE assessment should also be completed when:

- a new workstation is set up
- a new employee starts work
- a change is made to an existing workstation or the way it is used
- employees complain of pain or discomfort.

Employers need to check that the digital system equipment and the area around it is safe. If any risks are found during the assessment of the workstation and surrounding area then action needs to be taken to make it safe.

2 Ensure that workstations meet the minimum requirements

Employers need to make sure that adjustable chairs and suitable lighting are provided for employees. Tilt and swivel monitors should also be provided, and the workstation should have sufficient space for the keyboard, monitor and any paperwork needed by the employee.

3 Plan work so that there are breaks or changes of activity

Employees should not be expected to work at a digital system all day. Regular breaks should be provided or a change in the activity that the employees are carrying out. The regulations do not say how long or how frequent the breaks should be.

4 Arrange and pay for eye tests and glasses (if special ones are needed)

Working with DSE does not cause permanent damage to eyes. But if DSE is used for a long time without a break it can lead to:

- tired eyes
- discomfort
- temporary short-sightedness
- headaches.

Employees, who are covered by the DSE, can ask that eye tests are arranged and paid for. The eye tests can be repeated as advised by the optician – the organisation will have to keep paying for these but will only have to pay for the glasses if special ones are required.

5 Provide health and safety training and information

Employers must provide training to make sure that employees can use their computer equipment and workstations correctly (see Figure 1.24). This could include training on how employees can use the equipment to minimise risks to their health. The employers should also provide information to their employees about health and safety when using screen equipment and the steps that have been taken to minimise the risks.

Where employees are using DSE, the employer has a responsibility to:

- provide adjustable chairs and suitable lighting
- provide tilt and swivel monitors
- ensure that a workstation has sufficient space for the keyboard, monitor and any paperwork.

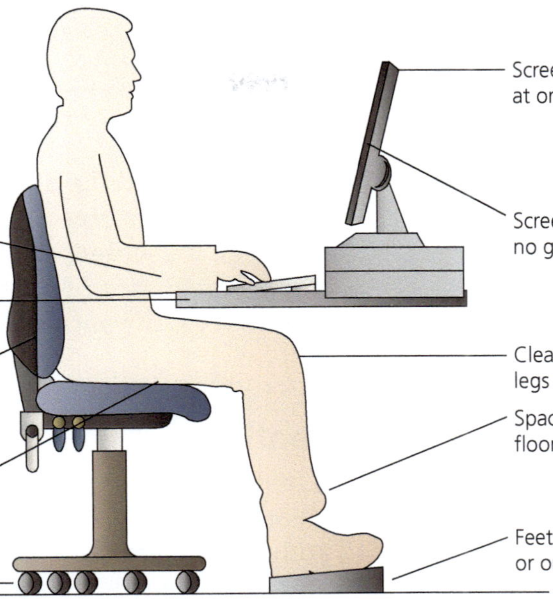

Figure 1.24 Correct and safe arrangement of a workstation

When working with DSE it is the responsibility of the employee to:

- check their screen is well positioned and properly adjusted
- make sure lighting conditions are suitable
- take regular breaks from screen work.

Activity

Investigate the Health and Safety policy, which applies to digital systems users, at your centre. Write down the main points of the policy and summarise how the policy affects the users.

Test your knowledge

35 Who oversees the Freedom of Information (FoI) Act?

36 Identify **one** type of information that does not have to be provided under an FoI request.

37 Identify **two** tasks that an employer must complete to ensure the safety of their employees.

38 What health issues could occur when working with DSE?

39 Identify **two** responsibilities of an employee when using DSE.

Practice questions

1 Discuss the different types of hacking. [9 marks]

2 Identify and describe **two** different types of social engineering. [6 marks]

3 Explain how encryption can be used to mitigate against security risks. [3 marks]

4 Explain, using an example, the importance of the Health and Safety at Work Act when working with display screen equipment (DSE). [4 marks]

5 Describe **one** way in which the Copyright, Designs and Patents Act (CD&PA) should be considered when selecting images for a website. [3 marks]

Topic area 5 Digital communications

Getting started

Information and data is presented to us every day. Most of this is presented using different types of digital communications such as an infographics, social media posts and presentations.

Make a list of all the digital communications, the information and data that has been presented, and how you accessed them, in the last 48 hours. Discuss your findings with the rest of your group.

5.1 Types of digital communications

Communication between people is important. People interact every day using a range of methods. Digital communication involves sending and receiving information electronically.

There are many types of digital communications. They include: audio, collaboration tools, leaflets, infographics, newsletters, presentations, reports, social media, video, websites and Voice over Internet Protocol (VoIP). Each has a purpose.

Synoptic link

Websites and Voice over Internet Protocol (VoIP) are covered in Topic area 5, section 5.4 of this unit.

Audio

Audio includes talking in a conversation or at a meeting (either in person or using cloud-based collaboration tools). It can also be sounds – such as music and special effects that can be included on a web page, an AR experience, or in a presentation.

Collaboration tools

Collaboration tools can be used to help people work together in groups and share files and documents. They include video conferencing and cloud-based storage areas.

Synoptic link

The cloud is covered in Topic area 5, section 5.4 of this unit.

Leaflets

A leaflet provides a message or information clearly and concisely. They can be electronic and sent via email, or printed and distributed on paper. Many businesses and organisations use leaflets to advertise their products and services, for example new stores, special offers and events. Leaflets can also be used to advertise a community event, such as a car boot sale; the leaflet can provide key information such as location, time and costs.

Infographics

An infographic is a collection of images, charts, graphs, statistics and text that provides an easy-to-understand overview of a topic. The infographic communicates the information clearly and quickly to the target audience.

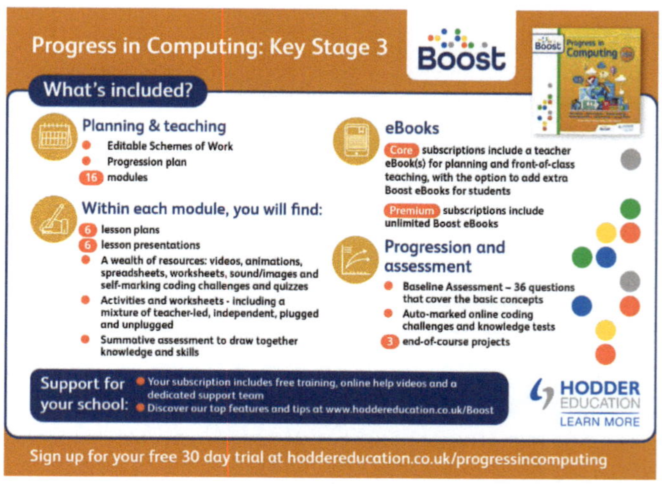

Figure 1.25 Infographics can be displayed in many ways

Newsletters

A newsletter can be in printed or electronic format. A newsletter provides the audience with news from an organisation or business, such as a sports club or school. A newsletter can include elements such as images, graphics, text and charts/graphs. These elements may have been created in a range of software and integrated into the newsletter using different layouts.

Activity

Look at two or three different newsletters created by your school. What elements are consistent, and what elements change?

Presentations

Presentations can be used to inform an audience about an idea or concept or to provide information. Presentations can include elements such as sound, text, graphics, hyperlinks and weblinks. A presentation can be used either with a speaker or automated running on a loop. The automated setting can include a display screen in, for example, a railway station, airport or festival.

Reports

A report usually focuses on one topic area in a formal format. Reports are usually written to communicate information to a specific audience. Many businesses and organisations use reports to provide an update on their performance.

Social media

Social media allows individuals to keep in touch with friends and family. It can also be used by businesses and organisations to keep in touch with their customers to, for example, promote new products or raise brand awareness. Social media can be used for a range of activities including finding out about a brand, keeping up-to-date with news events, and sharing photos and videos.

Research

Investigate how social media is used to provide details of news stories.

Video

A video is a collection of moving images and/or graphics and usually includes audio. The purpose of a video is to convey a message or entertain. Using a video to convey information can be more informative than providing the same information in text format, for example showing practical demonstrations of how to carry out a task.

Advantages and disadvantages of digital communication

Each type of digital communication has advantages and disadvantages which need to be considered when deciding which type is suitable for specific contexts. These are shown in Table 1.18.

Synoptic links

The purpose, advantages and disadvantages of VoIP and websites are covered in Topic area 5, section 5.4 of this unit.

Demographics is covered in Topic area 5, section 5.5 of this unit.

Test your knowledge

1. What is the purpose of collaboration tools?
2. What is an infographic?
3. Identify two elements that could be included in a presentation.
4. Identify one advantage of using a report to communicate information.
5. Identify one disadvantage of social media.

Table 1.18 The advantages and disadvantages of digital communication

Type of digital communication	Advantages	Disadvantages
Audio	It is a fast communication method. It can reach one or more people at once. It provides an instant message.	The audio message may be incorrectly interpreted. It can only be heard within a short distance. It can distract people from the intended message. It cannot be understood by a hearing-impaired person.
Collaboration tools	People can work from any location where there is an internet connection. Documents and resources can be shared in real time.	If there is no connection, then collaboration cannot take place. Personal contact can be reduced, leading to a feeling of isolation.
Leaflet	A template can be set up and reused to maintain consistency of layout. A house style can be used to provide recognition and consistency. It focuses on one topic so can provide a high level of detail. It can be targeted at one, or more, demographic group.	It can be easily ignored or recycled without being read. Information in the leaflet may be out of date.
Infographic	It provides a quick overview of a topic. It can explain a complex topic in a simple way. It can increase interest about a topic.	It can become too complex if too many elements are used. It can simplify a complex topic too much.
Newsletter	A template can be set up and reused to maintain consistency of layout. A house style can be used to provide recognition and consistency. It can be sent via email as an attachment.	Not every newsletter will be read so important information could be missed. It takes time to create a newsletter. The information may be out of date when it is read.
Presentation	Slides can include a range of different components (elements), for example text, images, graphs. A house style or template can be used. Links to other resources or files, for example a hyperlink to a web page, can be included. The contents can be presented by a speaker or automatically with no human involvement. Audience handouts can be created from the presentation.	Too much text on a slide can make the information difficult to read. Effects such as animations or transitions between slides can become distracting. Presentations may become unprofessional if too many features and effects are used.
Report	Information about a topic can be collated and presented as a report. Headings and subheadings can be used to enhance the structure of the report. A range of elements, for example a table of contents and graphs/charts, can be included.	If too much information is included then the user may not read the report thoroughly. If the information does not 'flow' then the user may become confused. The report must be checked for spelling and grammar errors – these can detract from the message of the report.
Social media	Posts can be uploaded which can be seen by many people. Posts can be shared to increase awareness. Up-to-date information can be provided. It increases awareness of a business or organisation. Links can be provided to other resources.	Negative posts can be seen by many people and shared. Posts can be made anonymously as profiles can be set up in a false name. It needs to be kept up to date and monitored which can take time.
Video	It can grab attention and get instant feedback from audience. It can be uploaded to social media, AR experiences and websites.	It can take a long time to create. Too many effects can detract from the message being communicated.

5.2 Software

All types of digital communications have to be created using software.

Desktop publishing (DTP)

Desktop publishing (DTP) is used to create documents including newsletters and leaflets. These documents could be produced in word-processing software, but DTP provides features and characteristics including pre-defined templates, frames, and drag and drop which makes it more suitable. These make DTP better for creating complex layouts. DTP uses **WYSIWYG**, which means the document looks the same on a screen as it does when printed on paper or posted to the internet.

Synoptic link

DTP was covered in Topic area 1 of this unit.

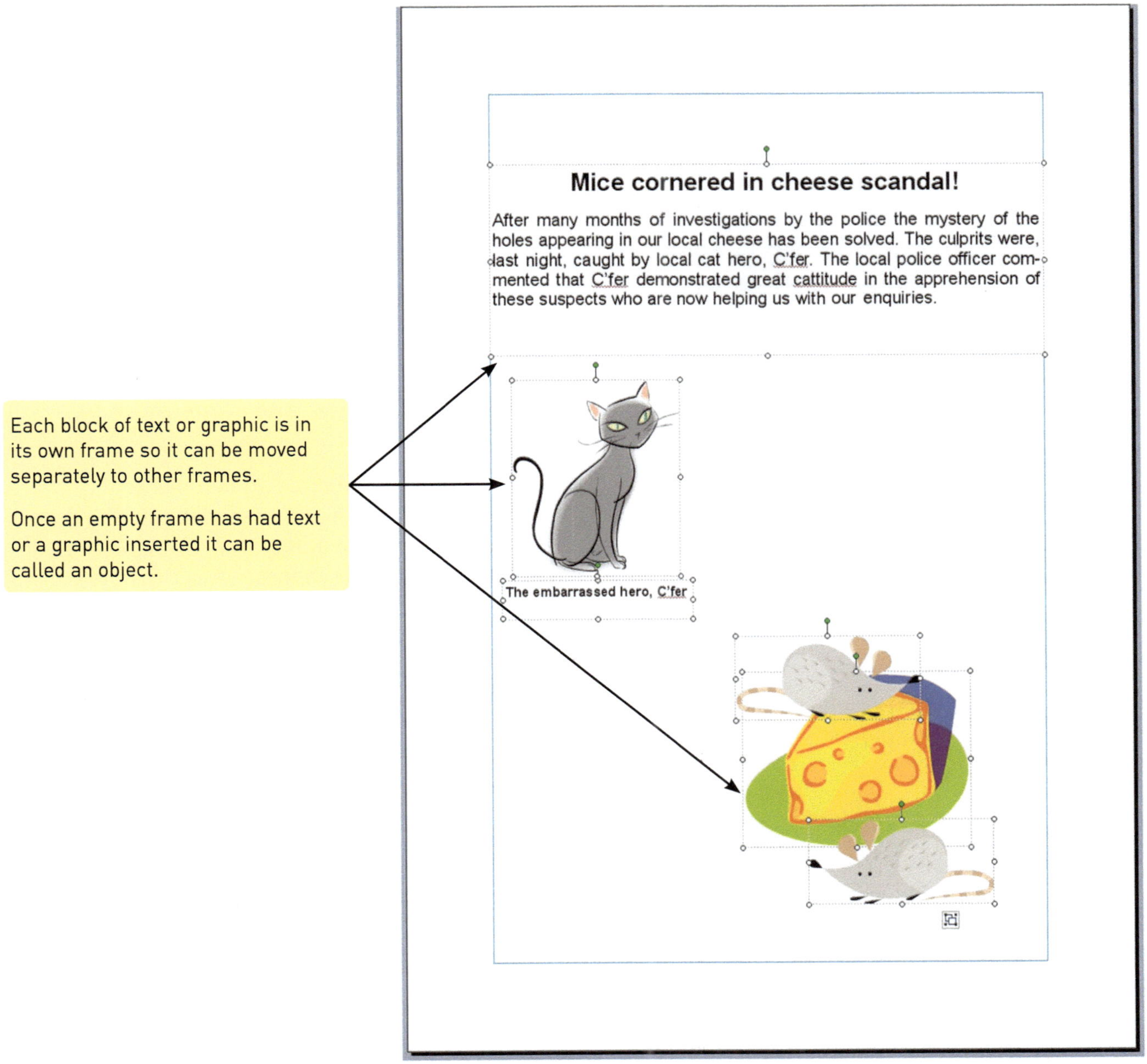

Figure 1.26 Using frames in a DTP package

Templates are pre-defined layouts that can be used to base the layout of a document on. A template enables a professional-looking document to be created with limited creative skills. However, because templates are included in DTP packages many other people may have used the same template.

Frames are boxes that contain elements of the final document such as text or graphics. Frames can be moved around a page and resized without losing the content in the frame.

DTP software also includes layout tools which assist the user in placing and aligning elements accurately. These include rulers, adjustable guidelines, layers, object snapping and grouping.

Activity

Access the DTP software used in your school. Investigate the features and create a user guide which explains each of these.

Standard office applications

There are a wide range of standard office applications. The most commonly used are:

- word processing
- spreadsheet
- database
- presentation
- collaboration tools.

You will have learnt how to use word processing, presentation and spreadsheet software in your KS3 study.

Word processing

Word-processing software is used to create, edit, save and print documents such as reports. Text can be input by typing on the keyboard or imported from an existing text file. Text can also be input by using a microphone or touch screen. Word processing includes tools which enable the user to copy, move, delete and format text (for example, font, bold, italics, underline). Tables can also be inserted into a word-processing document.

Word-processing software enables elements – such as images and photographs – from different applications to be embedded into a document. This is called an integrated document.

Most word-processing applications have a spelling and grammar feature which allows the user to set their language. The software will then check for spelling and grammar errors based on this language.

Word-processing software can be used with a database or spreadsheet to carry out a mail merge.

Spreadsheet

Spreadsheet applications are mainly used for calculations and modelling. The formatting tools in word-processing applications are also available in spreadsheet applications. For example, the contents of a cell can be made bold, italicised and underlined, and the font type and size can be changed. The colour of cells can be changed, and borders can be added.

Formulae and functions can be used to manipulate the data in a spreadsheet. The data can be presented to a user in a graph or chart to provide a visual representation of the data.

Synoptic link

You can find more information about features, including formulae and functions, of spreadsheet applications in Unit R060.

Database

Database applications can store almost any type of data in a structured and organised manner. They allow a user to enter, store, edit, process and retrieve data. They can be used to, for example, store customer details, stock details or cars for sale.

Databases are stored in files made up of **records**. A record is a collection of **fields** where each field holds one item of data about an object. Records and fields can be stored and displayed in **tables**. A database can be just one table of records (a flat-file database) or it may hold many tables of records that are connected together by relationships (a relational database). There should be a key field in every record. A key field holds data that is unique so that each record can be identified from all other records.

Relational databases separate data into tables, which allows the data to be accessed and arranged in many different ways without having to change the tables of data. A relational database can have two or more tables of data linked together in different ways. The links are called relationships and are made between fields in the tables. The key field holding the unique data is a record called the primary key and is usually, but not always, used to link the table to another table. A table receiving the link will have the same field in its records, but here it is called a foreign key. A foreign key must be of the same data type as the primary key.

Activity

Your centre may have a database about students in the school. Identify the fields that could be used for each student record. What other data may be stored in the database and how could the data be linked? Discuss your findings with the rest of your group.

Tables can be created manually and the data typed in, or the data can be imported from spreadsheets or other files. The relationships between database tables are then created.

Relationships can be one of three types:

1. One-to-one: Where both tables have only one record.
2. One-to-many: Where the table with the primary key has only one record that relates to many records in the other.
3. Many-to-many: Where each record in one table can relate to many records in the other. A third table is often needed in cases of many-to-many relationships.

Activity

Investigate how a database could be used by an online retailer. Create a document detailing the results of your investigation. You should include different elements in your document.

Database applications can also be used with word-processing applications to carry out a mail merge. A mail-merge function allows you to produce numerous customer letters using one template document and a table with customer names and addresses in the database.

Presentation

Presentation applications are used to create slideshows to present data and information to an audience, such as a room of delegates. A slideshow is made up of a number of slides. Each slide can include, for example, text, images, hyperlinks, sound, video and animation.

Each slide can move to the next through automatic or manual transition. Automatic transition is when a slide is set a specified time to be shown before it moves on. Manual transition is when an action – for example, the presenter pressing a button – is taken to move the slide to the next one.

A presentation can be used to provide brief information and data which is then expanded on

Key terms

Field An individual data item within a record. Each field has a unique name and contains a single data type.

Record A collection of data about a single item, such as a single student or customer. Each record must be unique.

Table Contains data about 'things', such as students, customers or orders. Each table has a unique name and contains data held in records.

by the presenter or can be used to provide full and complete details about a topic.

The features of presentation applications include:

- Slide master – this is applied to set the appearance and maintain consistency of the slides.
- Animations – these are visual effects that can be added to elements on each slide. They control the way the elements become visible.
- Transitions – these are the different ways that one slide can change to the next.
- Speaker notes – these appear on the presenter's screen and can be used as a reminder about what to say about the contents of each slide. The audience cannot see these notes.

Activity

Create a presentation to provide details about your school to new Year 7 students.

Collaboration tools

Collaboration tools are used to make teamwork more productive and effective, using the cloud. The tools provide a range of features including video calling, document sharing and screen sharing. Meetings can be set up with people invited to join. An invitation is sent to everyone which is then used to join the meeting. During the meeting, screens can be shared – for example, to show documents. A chat facility can be used to post comments and questions as well as discussions.

The meeting can be recorded to provide an audit trail and a record of the meeting. This is like the minutes of a face-to-face meeting. People involved in the meeting can mute their microphone, turn off their camera and raise their hand if they want to speak.

Other collaboration tools facilitate document sharing via a document store on the cloud. Files can be stored in the cloud and be accessed by other people at the same time; this allows real-time editing and collaboration. People can have upload, download and editing rights for these files. Access rights, such as a username and password, may be required to access the files, which helps keep them secure.

Uses of software

Each software can be used to create and use different types of digital communications. These are shown in Table 1.19.

Table 1.19 Software and applications used in different types of digital communications

Software/ application	Can be used for
DTP	Infographics Leaflets Newsletters
Word processing	Infographics Leaflets Letters including mail merge Newsletters Reports
Spreadsheet	Creating elements to be used in other digital communications Data manipulation Graphs and charts
Database	Creating elements to be used in other digital communications Data manipulation Mail merge
Presentation	Slideshows
Collaboration tool	Recording meetings Sharing screens Sharing documents

Test your knowledge

6 Identify **one** feature of DTP.
7 Identify **two** documents word-processing software can be used to create.
8 What does a graph provide in spreadsheet software?
9 What is a record in a database?
10 Where do speaker notes in a presentation appear?

5.3 Digital devices

Digital communication needs digital devices so that the communication can be seen, heard or accessed.

There are many different digital devices available. The ones you need to know about are:

- smartphones, tablets and laptops (mobile devices)
- smart TVs
- PCs
- smartboards.

Synoptic link

You will learn about the devices that can be used with augmented reality (AR) in Unit R070, Topic area 1, section 1.3.

Smartphones, tablets and laptops

Smartphones, tablets and laptops can be classed as mobile devices. A mobile device is a device that can be easily moved and is portable. It can usually be used on the go.

Here are some examples of the characteristics of mobile devices.

- They have a battery that powers them for several hours.
- They have an on-screen or physical keyboard which is used to enter data and/or information.
- They have cellular or Wi-Fi access to the internet.
- They usually have a touch screen.
- They are of a size and weight that allows them to be carried.
- Many have a virtual assistant (such as Alexa, Siri, Cortana, Google Assistant, Bixby).
- They can download, and store, data and information including websites, apps, photographs, books and music.

Smart TVs

Smart TVs are televisions that connect to the internet. The television includes software that allows the user to access a wide range of apps. These apps include streaming services, catch-up TV and web browsing. The televisions can also be used to play games, check social media and control other smart devices, such as a virtual assistant. Some of these types of television have voice capability, so the user can control the television's power, adjust its volume, and change channels using their voice and pre-set commands.

Figure 1.27 A smart TV home screen

A smart TV uses a home network to provide access to the apps on the television. It can be connected using the built-in Wi-Fi or using a cable.

Research

Investigate the different apps that can be accessed through a smart TV.

PCs

Many people use PCs to carry out a variety of tasks. These tasks include using standard office applications to create and edit digital communications and using the internet.

Desktop PCs are usually not mobile – this means they cannot be easily moved.

Activity

Investigate the different types of PCs and laptops. Create a guide showing what they can be used for and the different characteristics of each including hardware and software.

Smartboards

There are currently two different types of smartboards:

- projected
- television style.

Projected smartboards

The projected type of smartboard allows images from a computer screen to be displayed onto the smartboard using a digital projector. The user can interact with the display by using a stylus pen or a finger directly on the screen.

Figure 1.28 An interactive whiteboard

Television-style smartboards

The television-style smartboard uses the same technology as a smart TV. The smartboard is connected to the internet so files stored in the cloud can be accessed and edited. This means that there is no connection via a projector to a source digital device.

This type of smartboard provides access to applications which can include software. These smartboards enable users to interact with the display using a stylus pen and eraser. Each user has access details which means that the apps displayed can be specific to each user.

Test your knowledge

11 Identify **two** characteristics of a smartphone.
12 What is a smart TV?
13 How can a smart TV be connected to a home network?
14 Identify **one** difference between a PC and a laptop.
15 How does a user interact with the display on a smartboard?

5.4 Distribution channels

Types of distribution channel

When a digital communication has been created, it needs to be distributed to the target audience. There are different ways the digital communication can be distributed – these are called **distribution channels**.

Cloud

Cloud-based distribution methods are totally reliant on access to the internet. Documents can be stored in the cloud and can then be accessed by other people. Access rights may be required to access the information, which helps keep the information secure. The size of the files containing the information to be distributed must be considered. If the files are too large then they may take time to download or become corrupted during downloading.

Synoptic link

Access rights were covered in Topic area 4, section 4.3 of this unit.

Email

Email is the abbreviation for electronic mail. Email provides a way in which a user can

Key term

Distribution channels The methods (channels) that can be used to share data and information by individuals, organisations or businesses.

communicate with others. Email can be sent from a range of devices, such as computers, laptops, tablets or smartphones, as long as there is a connection to the internet. Attachments can be sent, which can enable files – such as documents, videos and images – to be distributed between users.

Messaging

Messaging services are another distribution channel that could be used. Messaging services include email, social media and internal messaging channels.

Social media is a very popular distribution channel with businesses. Social media is the term given to a dedicated website that allows members to interact with others. A business may have a page on social media that allows posts to be made, videos to be uploaded and members to react by posting comments, liking/disliking posts or sharing links about the business. A business can use its social media page to keep customers and other interested people up to date.

Many organisations and businesses have an internal messaging service. This is likely to be on the home page of the business intranet and can be used to keep staff informed, for example about any events or important information.

Mobile apps

Mobile apps are applications (apps) that are designed to be run on a mobile device such as a tablet or smartphone. Apps are available for many different purposes. They include fitness trackers, transport and travel apps and social media. Apps, unlike websites, focus on one thing. For example, Transport for London (TfL) has several apps, each focused on a different part of the London transport network. One app checks the **real-time data (RTD)** of the bus network; another app shows a tube map and allows travellers to plan their journey.

Key term

Real-time data (RTD) Data that is delivered immediately after it has been collected.

There are apps that relate to people's lifestyles and appliances that they own. NHS England has created apps to help people track various aspects of their health, for example to help with healthy eating by working out how many calories are in a meal. Other apps include being able to control the central heating at home while you are out and about. An app called Wemo enables users turn the lights on automatically when they arrive home, or randomly turn the lights on and off in different rooms when they are away.

Research

Investigate the apps available for fitness and health. Look at the main purpose of each app, how it could be used by people, and the benefits of its use. Discuss your findings with the rest of your group.

Multimedia

Multimedia is the term given to a collection of elements. These elements include text, sound, video and graphics.

Multimedia as a distribution channel can be used to provide information in an informative yet entertaining way. It can be very powerful and have a huge impact, but only if the elements are carefully combined. Some multimedia can include user interaction, meaning that a user can interact with the multimedia to provide a personalised experience. For example, links to other sections of a site can be included so users can go to the sections they are interested in. Other user interactions can include being able to stop, pause, go back or forward.

Multimedia can be uploaded directly to sharing sites such as YouTube or can be embedded into a website or social media page. A website or social media page can also have links to the sharing site to directly access the multimedia.

Multimedia can be used as a distribution channel via a web conference. A web conference is when people who are remote from each other interact through speech via the internet. A webcam can be used so that the people taking part in the conference can see each other. During the conference, different documents can be seen and shared by all the people taking part in the conference. A web conference could be used as a distribution channel when people who are remote from each other need to access the information. A stable internet connection is needed, as are a webcam, speakers and microphone.

Voice over Internet Protocol

Voice over Internet Protocol (VoIP) is a system that enables voice calls to be made over the internet. A device or hardware is needed to convert the analogue signal made by the voice to digital to enable the voice to be transmitted.

This distribution channel is useful when information has to be 'talked through'. Files can be sent to the person accepting the call via email. VoIP can also be used with video calling using a webcam. There are programs that can be downloaded, usually for free, that allow calls to be made to anyone else who has the program installed. Some providers require a subscription to use the service, while others charge on a call-by-call basis. Examples of providers include Teams and Lync.

Websites

Websites are a popular way of distributing information, especially to lots of people at the same time. However, websites need to be kept up-to-date and monitored, which can take time.

There are different types of websites that can be used to distribute digital communications.

Blogs and vlogs

One type of website is a blog. A blog is a regularly updated website or web page that is usually run by one person, the blogger, or by a very small group of people. A blog can be used by an organisation or business to provide details about its services and products to its customers. The content of the blog is generally written in an informal style. A blog can be used to distribute information by the blogger writing about something. As with other internet-based distribution channels, information can be uploaded to a blog so the readers can either download it or read about it on the blog.

> **Key term**
>
> **Voice over Internet Protocol (VoIP)** A system that enables voice calls to be made over the internet.

Vlogs are like blogs in that one person usually runs them, but this person may be posting on behalf of a business or organisation. The main difference between a blog and a vlog is that a blog is usually mainly text-based, while a vlog distributes the information through video. The videos can be downloaded to watch or watched online. As with blogs, it is sometimes possible to download a text file that provides more information.

If the blogs and vlogs are run by one person, there is a possibility that only one viewpoint is distributed. This can mean that the information contained in these does not provide a balanced viewpoint.

Intranet/internet

An intranet is a private network that is accessible only to those people who have log-in, or access, details. An intranet can provide information to authorised users that is not available to those without access details. As a distribution channel, an intranet can be used if the information is to be kept to a small number of authorised people. An intranet could provide the platform for an internal messaging service. An intranet can also enable an internal website to be created and used by a business. The web pages on the internal website can be used to distribute information, provide links to information or an internal blog, and allow files to be downloaded.

Figure 1.29 An intranet home page

A website hosted on the internet is one that can be accessed by anyone who is connected to the internet. Most organisations and businesses have a website and can distribute information through this website. A website can enable information to be posted directly or allow the information to be downloaded in the form of a file. A link to a blog or vlog can be given on a website that, when clicked, will take the user to the blog or vlog.

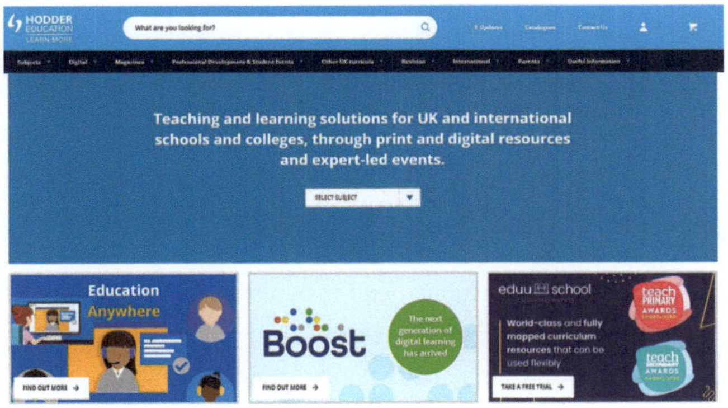

Figure 1.30 The internet website home page of the publisher Hodder Education

Advantages and disadvantages

Each distribution channel has advantages and disadvantages. These are shown in Table 1.20.

Test your knowledge

16 What does RTD stand for?

17 What is a mobile app?

18 What does VoIP stand for?

19 What is the difference between an intranet website and an internet website?

20 Identify **one** disadvantage of using the multimedia distribution channel.

Distribution channel connectivity

Each distribution channel needs connectivity so that the communication can reach the target audience. There are different connectivity methods.

4G/5G

5G began to be rolled out in the UK in 2018 as the new generation of wireless technology. The 5G mobile telecom network follows from the rollout of 3G and 4G. The introduction of the 3G network led to the introduction of the smartphone, while 4G provided a faster mobile browsing experience.

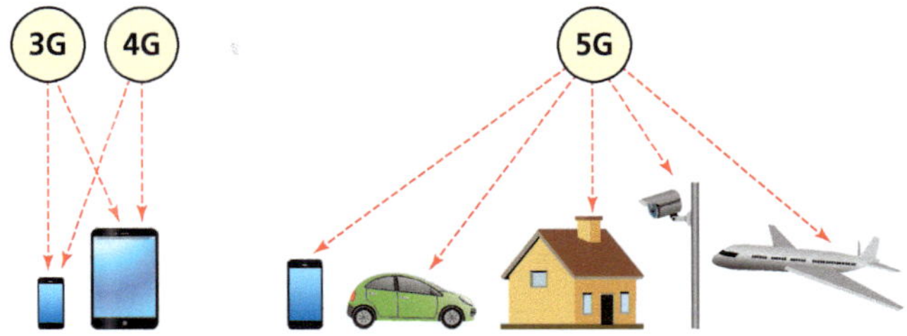

Figure 1.31 5G will be able to support many more devices at once than 3G and 4G

5G is designed to provide faster download speeds, and greater capacity. 5G also enables billions of devices to be connected to each other through the internet, including in the areas of AR and the Internet of Everything (IoE). As 5G gets better it will be possible to have many devices connected to the same network at the same time without dips in connection or interruption.

Synoptic links

The Internet of Everything (IoE) is covered in Topic area 6 of this unit.

AR is covered in Unit R070.

Bluetooth

Bluetooth is a wireless technology that allows the exchange of data between different devices.

Bluetooth uses wavelength, rather than cables and wires, to transfer information but can only be used over a short distance for the devices to stay connected.

Bluetooth can be used to transfer files, including music and photos, from one digital device to another. Other uses of Bluetooth include connecting:

- a smartphone to a vehicle such as a car or van
- keyboards, mice and printers to a digital device
- smart watches and activity trackers to other digital devices including smartphones and tablets.

Table 1.20 Advantages and disadvantages of different distribution channels

Channel	Advantages	Disadvantages
Cloud	Files are stored off-site so can be used as a backup. Access rights can be given so documents can be shared. Security can be implemented. More cloud storage space can be bought when needed so large files containing a number of elements can be uploaded. Access can be restricted to those who need it. Accessible anywhere and anytime if an internet connection is available.	Must have internet access to be able to download stored files. If the internet connection is slow or unstable the communication can take a long time to download. Communications can become corrupted during download. The cloud provider has access to the data and information stored on its cloud storage area.
Email	Communications can be sent to a large number of people at once. Communications can be sent as attachments. The communication can be targeted to specific groups of people. Can be used as a marketing tool to gather feedback. Can be accessed on a range of digital devices. Emails can provide an audit trail.	Emails may go into the junk/spam folder so may not be seen. Some email providers have an attachments file size limit so large attachments may not be delivered. Security settings need to be considered. Accounts can be hacked, leading to identity theft. Attachments could contain a virus.
Messaging	Posts and messages can be sent to alert users about the communication. Links can be provided for more detailed communications. All users in a group will see the message. Users can react to the communication in real time. A wide range of people can be sent or can access the communication. The communication can be targeted to specific groups of people. Can be used as a marketing tool to gather feedback. Files and images, and so on, can be sent/uploaded.	Messaging needs to be kept up to date. The messaging service needs to be monitored to make sure any posts meet the rules. Trolls and negative posts can be posted. Security settings need to be considered. Accounts can be hacked, leading to identity theft.
Mobile apps	Can be used to provide communication 'on the go'. One specific topic area, leading to focused communication. Features can be included in the data/information to increase user interaction. Money can be raised if people have to pay for the app. Apps can be linked to social media.	Need connection to access the apps. Apps need to be constantly monitored and updated. Regular maintenance needs to be carried out. The app needs to be included on app stores or promoted so that people know about it because search engines do not search for apps.
Multimedia	Can include a range of elements such as text, graphics and sound. Information can be seen visually rather than read. The data/information can be shown or made available to one or many people. Links to the multimedia can be embedded on websites or social media. Demonstrations can be included, for example to show how a product works. As the multimedia is easy to change, it is flexible and can be used for many purposes.	The message given through multimedia can be lost if too many elements are used. If the quality of the multimedia is low, then the message may not be seen as reliable. Too much information can be given. If the users do not have the correct hardware/software then some elements may not work as intended. If distributed via the cloud or email they can take a long time to download and access.

Channel	Advantages	Disadvantages
VoIP	Can be easier to have a discussion where questions can be asked. Features such as call forwarding, three-way calls, call waiting and voicemail can be used. Files can be sent at the same time as the call is being made.	Needs a stable connection. May have lag or distortion if the connection degrades. Each end of the call must have the right hardware and software to speak to one another. No calls can be made during a power cut. Using the digital device to complete other tasks during the call can reduce the call quality.
Websites	Websites are used by many people. Communications can be uploaded and kept for access. Communications can be archived to provide an audit trail.	Some indication of where the communication is located needs to be provided. Must have a connection to access the website.

Figure 1.32 The Bluetooth symbol

Mobile Wi-Fi hotspots

A mobile Wi-Fi hotspot is a hotspot that's mobile and can be set up anywhere. A hotspot is a location where the internet can be accessed. A regular Wi-Fi hotspot is a physical location, such as in a coffee shop or hotel.

Many smartphones have a mobile hotspot feature which is available through the phone network provider. Some cars now include a mobile Wi-Fi hotspot feature. A mobile hotspot can be created by, for example, using your smartphone's data connection to connect your laptop to the internet. This is called tethering.

Wi-Fi

Wi-Fi is the wireless technology that allows a digital device to access the internet through a wireless connection. It uses radio signals to send and receive data between devices and the wireless access point (WAP). The main requirement for Wi-Fi is a device, the WAP, that receives and transmits a wireless signal. The WAP is usually a router but can sometimes be a smartphone or computer.

A router receives and transmits the broadband internet connection from an **internet service provider (ISP)**. This connection is then sent to devices within range of the router and the wireless signal. Many digital devices can connect to the WAP including smartphones, desktop and laptop computers, tablets and smart TVs. The connected devices receive the internet connection via Wi-Fi from the router.

Many homes now contain routers to provide broadband access to the internet. These routers are sometimes referred to as a 'hub' by the ISP. These hubs are in fact hybrid devices that contain modems, hubs, wired routers and wireless routers all in one device. This saves the homes having to have several devices all needing power sockets. The hybrid device (the hub) only needs one power supply to carry out several roles to allow us to connect to the internet.

Key term

Internet service provider (ISP) A company that provides access to the internet to both personal and business customers.

The hub part of the hybrid then distributes the internet connectivity around a home. This can be through Wi-Fi or using a wired connection.

Wired

The wired connectivity method uses cables and wires to provide the connection. The cables and wires connect the router and hub or a hybrid device and the digital devices using it. This forms a network. The cables used are usually Ethernet.

Advantages and disadvantages

Each distribution channel connectivity has advantages and disadvantages. Some of these are shown in Table 1.21.

Table 1.21 Advantages and disadvantages of distribution channel connectivity methods

Connectivity method	Advantages	Disadvantages
4G/5G	Increased bandwidth for all users which means faster transfer speed.	Possible less coverage as more transmitter masts will be needed to provide the increased bandwidth. Environmental impact on the countryside because of increased number of masts. Limited coverage in rural and hard-to-reach areas. New devices may have to be bought to access 5G.
Bluetooth	No cables are needed so paired devices can be moved. Most devices, for example cars and smartphones, have Bluetooth capability. Requires limited technical knowledge to set up and use.	Slow compared to, for example, Wi-Fi and wired connections. The range between the paired devices is relatively low, about 10 m. The security level is low, and the connection can be hacked. Objects can disrupt the signal.
Mobile Wi-Fi hotspots	Provides internet access wherever it is needed. Will allow multiple devices to connect to the same hotspot.	Speed can be lower than other connectivity methods. Some mobile data charges may be applied by the ISP.
Wi-Fi	Increased mobility as devices can be moved and still be connected to the WAP. Can be simple to set up as most devices have a 'discover me' feature. No cables or wires are needed.	The WAP (router) needs to be password protected or unauthorised people could access the Wi-Fi. Wi-Fi signals can have a limited range and extra equipment may be needed to extend the signal range. The more devices that are connected to the WAP, the slower the data transfer. Objects can block signals, for example thick walls, so boosters may be needed.
Wired	Greater bandwidth so increased transfer of data speeds. Lack of interference from, for example, walls and closed doors meaning the signal is stable. There is a higher distance connectivity range without the signal degrading. The digital devices are not discoverable so unauthorised people/hackers cannot use the wired connection so this increases security.	Devices cannot be moved as a wired connection may not be available. The wires and cables could become unplugged from devices meaning the connection is lost.

> **Test your knowledge**
>
> **21** What was 5G designed to provide?
> **22** What is Bluetooth?
> **23** What is a mobile hotspot?
> **24** What does WAP stand for?
> **25** Identify one disadvantage of the wired connectivity method.

5.5 Audience demographics

Digital communications need to be presented to an audience; this is called the target audience. The target audience should be considered when the type of digital communication and its distribution channel are being selected.

There are different factors that should be considered when selecting the type of digital communication and the distribution channel. These factors are called demographics and include:

- accessibility
- age
- gender
- location.

It can sometimes be very difficult to separate these demographics when selecting the type of digital communication and distribution channel, but it is important they are considered.

Accessibility

The accessibility of the information needs to be considered. The information in the digital communication must be accessible to the target audience. This may result in the information being presented in a number of ways. A report, infographic or presentation could be created to be presented at a face-to-face meeting. If the information is then to be shared via the cloud, every person who needs to access the information must have access to the internet. If the information is a large file, then a stable internet connection is needed.

Accessibility also means providing access for people with disabilities. A visually impaired person may find it difficult to read information that is presented in a text format, such as a leaflet, newsletter or report. Solutions include providing the information in a large print or Braille format.

Most websites offer accessibility options where text can be made larger or read out by a screen reader. A person with a hearing impairment may not be able to hear music and sound effects in a presentation or video product. It may be possible, with the aid of a signer, to interpret any spoken words to sign language.

Figure 1.33 Interpreting spoken words to sign language to increase accessibility

Age

Age is very important when selecting a type of digital communication and distribution channel to present information. Age groups could be classified as ranges, such as: 6–12, 13–18, 19–39, 40+ years. The communication type selected must be appropriate for the age group the information is targeted at. For example, if the message of the information relates to the launch of a new primary after-school club, then the audience may be children aged between 5 and 11 years old. It would not be appropriate to use a report to tell the children about the after-school club as a report would be mainly text-based. A presentation or infographic may be a more appropriate method for presenting this information.

Gender

The gender of the target audience should be considered. For example, some colours are associated more with men or women, or may be considered gender neutral, so the colours used in a presentation in a meeting may need to be considered. Different audiences might respond to certain colours in different ways. You should also consider other identities such as transgender and non-binary, and whether to use gender-neutral language, such as they/their instead of he/his or she/her.

Research

Research the use of different colours. Consider how different colours could be used to present information to different genders.

Location

Where the information is being presented – the location – may also have an impact on how the information is to be presented. A report could be created to be distributed internally, for example to staff members, while a presentation could be created to be shown to people external to the business. The report and presentation could show the same information but in different formats.

Another way of looking at location may be to categorise it into local, national and international. Location is also related to the increased use of mobile devices. If the information is being presented over the internet, then the location of the devices used to access it can be very important. Parts of the UK have limited access to 4G or 5G services and have intermittent 3G access. This means that if the presentation method has a lot of content and will take a long time to download, people in those areas may not be able to access it on their mobile devices.

Synoptic links

You will need to consider the target audience when designing your AR prototype in Unit R070, Topic area 2, section 2.1.

4G and 5G were covered in Topic area 5, section 5.4 of this unit.

Test your knowledge

26 What is meant by demographics?
27 How can a digital communication be presented to a user with a visual disability?
28 Identify **one** accessibility option that can be found on a website.
29 Identify **one** method of presenting information to primary school students.
30 Identify **one** category of location.

Practice questions

1 Explain **one** advantage of using an infographic to inform people about a new service at a doctor's surgery. [2 marks]
2 A leaflet can be created using DTP or word-processing software. Discuss the advantages and disadvantages of each type of software to complete this task. [9 marks]
3 Explain the difference between automatic and manual transition in a presentation. [2 marks]
4 Explain **two** disadvantages of using email to communicate with friends. [4 marks]
5 Describe **one** advantage of using the Bluetooth connectivity method. [2 marks]

Topic area 6 Internet of Everything (IoE)

Important: There are constant developments in smart devices, and how the Internet of Everything (IoE) can be used in different application areas.

During your study for this course, you must make sure that you keep up to date with emerging technologies, including smart devices, and how the IoE is used in different application areas.

Getting started

The IoE is a collection of smart devices which can connect to each other and exchange data using the internet. The IoE is full of data and information. Having access to this and being able to make decisions is one positive aspect of the IoE.

What positive decision would you take to make the world a better place? What data and information would you need to be able to make this decision? Discuss your decision and required data with the rest of your group.

6.1 Use of IoE

What is the IoE?

The IoE is a collection of devices connected to each other that exchange data using the internet or other specific data network. These devices are often called smart devices because they can connect to the internet and send/receive data. Most people have access to at least one smart device such as a smartphone, smart speaker, smart lights or smart heating.

Most smart devices communicate with each other using wired and wireless connections. A smart watch will send data wirelessly using Bluetooth to a smartphone, which can then use Wi-Fi or 4G to send the data to the cloud. This data can then be accessed on a digital device which has a wired or wireless connection by logging into an account.

The IoE is made up of a range of smart devices, for example smartphones, smart wearable devices, smart lights, smart doorbells, that are connected or interrelated. The devices collect and transfer data over a wireless network without human intervention.

When these smart devices are combined with automated systems, it is then possible to gather data and information, analyse it and create an action. This can be to learn from a process or to help someone carry out a particular task. Think of the IoE as being about networks, devices and data. Devices that are on closed private internet connections are able to communicate with other devices on other private internet connections because the IoE brings these networks together. The IoE creates a connected world.

Many confuse the internet with the World Wide Web (WWW/W3) – the web.

The internet can be defined as:

> *a network of networks which are the connected devices (the hardware) that the web needs to transfer data and for a user to select and interact with web pages.*

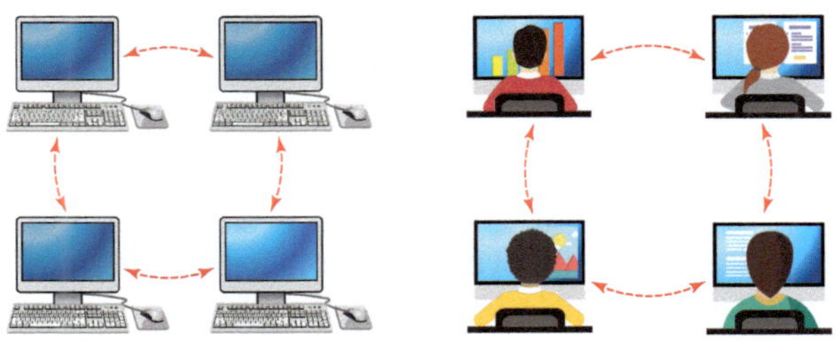

Figure 1.34 The internet connects computers and the WWW connects people

The World Wide Web (WWW/W3) can be defined as:

> *an information space in which the items of interest, referred to as resources, are identified by global identifiers called Uniform Resource Identifiers (URI) – the websites and web pages, the software, that are seen when you are online.*

This means that the way the devices automatically connect and communicate is carried out on the internet, but the web is used when people need to interact with the devices on a website.

The IoE is a system of interrelated, internet-connected devices that collect and transfer data over a wireless network without human intervention. It is built on a connection between humans (people), processes, data and devices. These are called the pillars.

The four pillars of the IoE

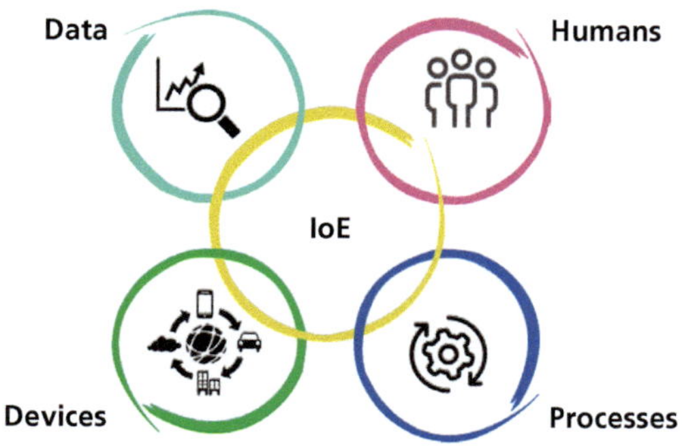

Figure 1.35 The four pillars of the IoE

Humans

The way people connect to the internet has changed dramatically over the last two to three decades. People now use wearable technologies and smart devices which have transformed the way we obtain and share information. There are self-monitoring devices such as the 'Fitbit', which allows people to track exercise, monitor the function of vital organs such as the heart, and even the quality of their sleep. It connects people in the most relevant and valuable ways.

Processes

The IoE has revolutionised the way organisations work and how they manage their business. Think of an e-commerce company such as Amazon and how people's shopping habits have changed to buying online, bringing the convenience of shopping from home with fast delivery times. (Of course, this also has a negative impact on the high street stores.) The process there is the delivery of the correct information to the correct person/machine at the correct time.

Data

This is about maximising data into more useful information for decision making. The world is flooded with data and one of the main functions of the IoE is to gather huge amounts of data to improve operations and functionality. Data could be hours of footage from a surveillance camera, how much exercise you have done in a day, what TV programmes you watch. These are examples of individual data but imagine the vast amounts of data that can be collected, processed and analysed from organisations on a global scale. All you have to do is consider social media platforms such as Facebook, Twitter, WhatsApp and LinkedIn.

Synoptic link

Data is covered in Topic area 3 of this unit.

Devices

These are the physical devices and objects connected to the internet and each other for intelligent decision making. The devices include desktop computers, laptops, smartphones, tablets and servers. But devices also include devices that are not traditionally connected, such as manufacturing equipment and cars. Cisco – one of the world's largest technology corporations – has estimated that 99 per cent of physical objects will one day be connected.

There are many devices that we can interact with on a daily basis that are connected to the internet. Smartphones can be used for online banking, paying for goods or just checking the weather. Another example is that lighting and heating in homes can be controlled through the IoE when people are away from their homes.

The interactivity between the four pillars

Each of the four pillars interacts with the others. Each pillar can interact with one or more other pillars. For example, you have already learnt that heating can be controlled by a smartphone when the user is away from home. This control involves interaction between all the pillars: processes, devices, data and humans.

- The **human** interacts with the **device** (smartphone) to set the required heating temperature (**data**).
- **Data** is sent from the smartphone to the heating controller (**device**).
- The heating controller (**device**) interacts with the **data** by **processing** the **data**.

IoE digital interactivity

Device to device

Device to device (D2D), also known as machine to machine (M2M), connections occur when data is transferred from one device or 'thing' to another over a network. Devices include sensors, robots, computers and mobile devices. An example of D2D is a home assistant such as Amazon Alexa or Google Nest automatically switching on smart lighting light bulbs based on user-set times before the user arrives home. Another example would be a laptop communicating with a printer using a Bluetooth or wireless connection. This communication is because they are directly connected.

Human to device

Human to device (H2D) interaction usually happens using an HCI. This could be carried out using a visual HCI or with a voice command to a digital assistant such as Amazon Alexa. The human will speak to the digital assistant using command words that the device 'understands'. Another example is interacting with a heating or lighting control HCI to provide user-set values. For example, setting the bathroom heating to come on at 6.30 a.m. and off at 8.30 a.m. on a weekday.

The HCI used on these devices will usually be an embedded system with a secondary HCI on a different device.

Synoptic link

HCI is covered on Topic area 2 of this unit.

Activity

Create a detailed bulleted list showing the IoE pillar interaction between:

- an autonomous (driverless) car and traffic lights
- a smart doorbell and a smartphone.

How devices can be tailored to meet the needs of the user

There is a huge range of devices that can be connected to the IoE. What is important to remember is that as technology changes so too does the number of devices that can be connected to the IoE. The devices that can connect to the IoE include:

- lights
- fitness trackers
- heating controls
- smart TVs
- smart electric plugs
- autonomous (driverless) cars
- printers that automatically order ink when supplies are low
- smart energy meters.

Research

Research the different devices that can be connected to the IoE in:

- the home
- transport
- manufacturing
- health.

Devices can be tailored to meet the needs of a user. This is usually done through an HCI. For example, some towns have installed smart street lighting to reduce energy costs and light pollution. These can be tailored to switch on at dusk and switch off at sunrise. The street lights also make the streets safer for people. The street lights can also be equipped with a sensor that automatically detects the amount of daylight and can switch on when the reading gets below a user input value. These lights will form part of the **smart city** concept.

Another example is tailoring a digital assistant to recognise different voices. By recognising different voices, the options provided can be different. For example, a child's voice saying a command word will only activate those options that the parent has activated. This could mean any automatic shopping ordering and payments being disabled. The digital assistant can also respond by saying the child's name.

The same principle can be applied to cars. By the driver speaking to, or touching a button on, the car's HCI, the driver's seat and steering wheel can move to that driver-preferred position.

Activity

Select a device related to entertainment or a smart home appliance. Investigate how the device can be tailored to meet the needs of the users. Create a digital communication, using text and images, to explain your findings. Present your findings to the rest of your group.

Advantages and disadvantages of the IoE

There are advantages and disadvantages to the use of the IoE. Some of these are shown in Table 1.22.

Key term

Smart city An urban area that uses the IoE and digital devices to collect data to allow well-informed decisions to be made and to improve the quality of life of the people who live and work there.

Table 1.22 Advantages and disadvantages of using the IoE

Advantages	Disadvantages
Increase in technology-based jobs.	Reduction in some job roles carrying out tasks that are repetitive and can be automated.
Increase in automation and control in homes and cities via smartphones. This control can increase personal protection so increasing security of people, homes and buildings.	People can become reliant on the IoE which could lead to a decrease in control of people's personal and working lives.
Increase in information and data available.	Security – how strongly is the data being transmitted being encrypted? If hackers got hold of information this could cause problems for users such as identity theft.
Time can be saved as devices could complete tasks.	If there is no power, the IoE will 'fall over' and no interaction between the four pillars can take place.
Monitoring of, for example, food in a fridge and automatic reordering to have the food delivered.	Compatibility between devices as there is, currently, no agreed standard.
It can assist in the smarter control of homes and cities via mobile phones. It enhances security and offers personal protection.	Safety – if a hacker were to change some of the automated tasks, then safety could reduce. For example, changing traffic light sequences.
Information is easily accessible anywhere there is a signal, with the information being regularly updated in real time.	Any failure, hacking attacks, viruses or bugs in the software or hardware will cause problems for users as this could cause the IoE to fail.

Synoptic links

Hacking and identity theft are covered in Topic area 4 of this unit.

Real-time data is covered in Topic area 5, section 5.4 of this unit.

Test your knowledge

1 What is the IoE?
2 Identify **two** pillars of the IoE.
3 What does H2D stand for?
4 Describe **one** advantage and **one** disadvantage of the IoE related to jobs for people.
5 Identify **one** smart device that can be found in a home.

6.2 Application areas in everyday life

The IoE has impacted on many parts of our everyday lives. We now take for granted the presence of smart devices in our lives and, usually, do not give them a second thought. In every part of our lives, smart devices are being used to ensure that useful data and information is collected, and to make lives safer and save time.

Energy management

The threat of climate change is becoming more evident. One of the goals of governments around the world is to have a net carbon zero target. This can be achieved by people and businesses using less energy and switching to energy that is generated in a climate-friendly way. One way this target can be worked towards is by people understanding how and when they use energy.

A smart meter and a portable in-home device can help people understand how and when they use energy so that decisions can be made as to how the use of energy can be reduced.

Smart meters monitor energy consumption 24/7 and send the energy consumption data to the energy provider automatically on a secure network. This differs from traditional energy meters where a manual reading has to be taken and sent to the energy company approximately four times a year.

Smart meters are an example of a D2D IoE system using a bespoke wireless network that is separate to the internet. The meters communicate with the digital devices at the energy supplier.

Figure 1.36 A smart meter portable device HCI

The smart meters include a portable digital device which can be located in the house. This device includes a screen-based visual HCI. The HCI shows the actual energy being used at any given moment, how much energy has been used that day/week and, in some case, the cost of the energy used. Some HCI displays also provide energy usage light indicators. These show the energy use as low (green), medium (amber), or high (red).

Smart meters can also help when analysing the cost of charging an electric car (EV). A comparison can be made with the cost of fuel, petrol or diesel, and the cost of the electricity.

By using smart meters, the energy suppliers can predict how much energy will be needed at any time based on people's use. The suppliers can also use the data gathered from the meter readings to monitor the amount of energy that can be used from alternative energy sources such as wind and solar power as well as from traditional methods.

Using the IoE in energy management means that carbon footprints can be reduced, and a smart energy system can be created and used. Suppliers are able to match supply and demand to integrate more renewable energy sources into the supply system. By doing this, less CO_2 will be put into the atmosphere which means less air pollution.

Energy management can also be achieved by using smart lights and heating controls.

The advantages and disadvantages of using the IoE in energy management are shown in Table 1.23.

Table 1.23 Advantages and disadvantages of using the IoE in energy management

Advantages	Disadvantages
Accurate consumption readings leading to more efficient supply of energy.	If there is a power cut, devices will not work so readings can be delayed.
Renewable sources energy can be used to supply energy based on analysed data about energy consumption.	If the network to provide smart meter readings is not available, for example in remote or rural areas, smart meters will not work as intended.
Less air pollution and CO_2 in the air leading to better health.	Installing smart devices to monitor energy can be complicated and require a restructured distribution system.
Data is provided automatically so analysis can be carried out on accurate readings.	Smart devices may not work correctly if a customer changes energy supplier.
Faulty supply equipment can be identified and fixed with little, if any, break in supply of energy.	Security of data.

The main security issue with the use of the IoE in energy management is that of the security of the constantly transmitted data – data in transit. This real-time data includes sensitive customer and supplier data. If this data was the target of a cyber-security attack, there would be impacts on the suppliers and customers. Suppliers have to ensure the data is safe while it is being transmitted in real time, which may include an increase in prevention measures which could lead to an increase in costs.

The security of the network used to send the real-time data will also need to be increased. It may be possible for hackers to modify or manipulate the data as it is being sent, meaning the customer could receive higher energy bills than expected. The supply network could be disrupted with a virus infecting the system, having been deliberately introduced to the data network. Another threat could be a denial of service (DoS).

Synoptic links

Cyber-security threats and DoS are covered in Topic area 4, section 4.1 of this unit.

The impacts of a cyber-security attack are covered in Topic area 4, section 4.2 of this unit.

Prevention measures are covered in Topic area 4, section 4.3 of this unit.

Health

Health devices connected to the IoE can help people keep track of their health on a personal level. The IoE allows medical staff to stay in touch with patients through the monitoring of real-time data. Vital medical data can be sent from a land or air ambulance to the hospital while the patient is being transferred. This means that the doctors and nurses already have a detailed picture of the patient's condition before they arrive.

Smart devices allow constant health monitoring in our everyday lives. Smart devices include fitness bands, smart watches and mobile health trackers. These monitor a range of different health readings including heart rate, blood pressure and glucose levels. Medical staff can access these data readings and monitor the patient for any abnormal readings. The monitoring of the readings can be beneficial for those patients who are elderly, vulnerable, or suffering from a serious illness. Connecting these smart devices via the IoE, D2D, can allow doctors to interact with someone if a reading is outside the acceptable range. The doctor can then provide remedial advice and action.

Developments are constantly happening in the application area of healthcare and the IoE but other current smart devices that can help include:

- **Automated insulin delivery device:** This automatically monitors the blood sugar levels (glucose) of patients who have diabetes. The glucose level is monitored, and the correct amount of insulin is automatically provided to keep the readings within the acceptable range. This means that patients can be reassured that their blood sugar readings will stay stable.
- **Asthma monitor:** This predicts an asthma attack before it happens. The device takes readings and warns the patient if the readings show that an asthma attack is about to happen. The monitor can also keep track of inhaler use and can remind the patient to use it and request a new one if it's running low.
- **Swallowable sensors:** These sensors are like little tablets which are swallowed. This means that internal organ functions, for example heart, lungs, liver, can be monitored and treatment can be given based on these readings.

It is also possible that the smart devices can provide the wearer with an alarm which has been remotely triggered by medical staff. These alarms can be triggered to remind patients to, for example, take their medication or do some exercise.

The use of these smart devices and the constant readings mean that routine tests do not have to be carried out if the readings are within the acceptable range. This is because the readings sent via the IoE are monitored in real time. Any data collected from a patient can, if permission has been given, be used for healthcare research and treatments.

One of the most innovative uses of the IoE related to healthcare is the introduction of remote surgery. This means that the patient can be in one hospital, with the surgeon in a different hospital. Using robots and AR the surgeon is able to operate on the patient as they would if they were in the same operating theatre. It is also possible that the surgeon and patient can be in different countries.

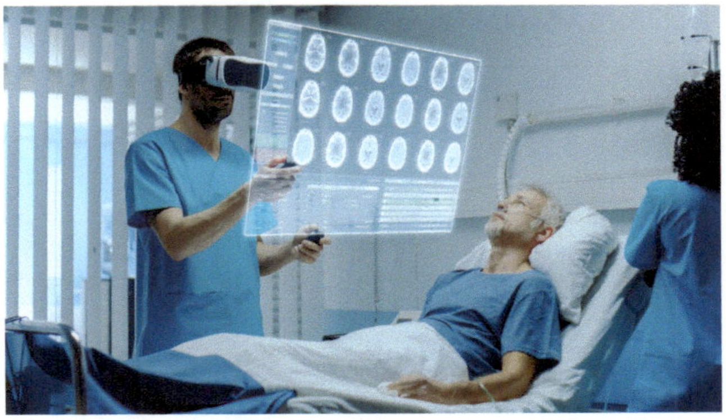

Figure 1.37 Devices sharing medical data through the IoE

The IoE allows hospitals to track and locate a range of equipment. Sensors are placed on the equipment, for example wheelchairs or oxygen machines, which send real-time data about their location. This can allow specialised equipment to be quickly and reliably located if needed in an emergency. Patient details can be stored on the cloud which would allow different hospitals and doctors' practices to access these. This means everyone involved in their care has up-to-date information including their medical history.

There are a number of advantages and disadvantages of using the IoE in healthcare. These are shown in Table 1.24.

As with other application areas of the IoE, the main security issue with the use of the IoE in healthcare is that of the security of the real-time data – data in transit. This real-time data includes sensitive patient data, including medical records and history. If this data was the target of a cyber-security attack, there would be impacts on the patients and medical staff. The impact of leaks of sensitive data, data destruction or manipulation could outweigh the benefits of IoE.

Synoptic links

The cyber-security threats are covered in Topic area 4, section 4.1 of this unit.

The impacts of a cyber-security attack are covered in Topic area 4, section 4.2 of this unit.

Prevention measures are covered in Topic area 4, section 4.3 of this unit.

Table 1.24 Advantages and disadvantages of using the IoE in healthcare

Advantages	Disadvantages
Remote monitoring of patients in real time using smart devices can diagnose illnesses, treat diseases and save lives in case of a medical emergency.	Security of data and privacy.
Smart sensors can analyse health problems and lifestyle choices. Alerts and recommendations can then be used to reduce the symptoms and keep the patient safe.	If there is a power cut, then devices will not work, and the real-time data will not be collected which could lead to loss of life in an emergency.
A patient's medical history is accessible meaning that wherever the patient is their medical history and records can be accessed.	There are no standards so devices produced by different manufacturers may not work well together. This can mean that there may not be complete integration between the smart devices which could reduce the effectiveness of the devices.
Smart devices help monitor a patient and provide the correct medication, for example insulin delivery devices.	The initial cost of the devices and integration is high. New cables, equipment and an increase in cloud storage area may be needed which can also add to the cost.
Equipment can be located quickly.	The smart devices may fail or be the victim of a cyber-security threat. This can prevent the devices and sensors working. If a remote operation is taking place, this could lead to loss of life if the connection and operating devices fail.
The collected real-time data can be used in research which can help in finding a cure for some diseases.	Scheduled software updates may not be installed by patients which means that the smart device may not work as intended or it may fail.

Manufacturing

Many manufacturing companies are now using the IoE in the manufacturing production process. Robots and sensors can be used to streamline processes and provide real-time data about the production process. Robots can also locate and replace tools and parts used in the production process using data sent and received from a storage location, usually the cloud. By doing this, the company can keep an accurate record of the number of parts used and how many are still in stock. This means that automatic ordering of parts can take place. The order will be based on the number of parts in stock and a pre-set number for re-ordering. The re-ordering will take place using D2D based on data.

Data is collected during the production and assembly process. This data allows the progress of the product on the production line to be tracked. Each product has a unique code. As it is being assembled, sensors identify the product using the code to collect data. This data provides information on the production rate which is monitored. Retailers are sent an automatic notification about products they are waiting for, informing them of when they will receive it.

Figure 1.38 Robots on a car production line

Many car manufacturers use robots and sensors when cars are on the production line. When a car is ordered, customers have a range of options that can be chosen. These options include, for example, the colour of the body and interior, lighting options or automatic boot opening. When a customer orders their new car, the details are automatically sent to the manufacturer. The options are programmed into a code which stays on the car during production. Each time the code is scanned and read by the sensors the options will be shown and, at the appropriate time in production, the options will be fitted to the car. When the car has been built, the code is read for a final time with a human carrying out quality control checks. The car is then transported ready for the customer to collect.

Robots can also move products around a warehouse or storage building. The location of any product will be stored in a database on the cloud. The robots are linked to the cloud and are able to access this data to enable them to locate, select and move the products – real-time data.

Amazon uses robots to move around the warehouse, locate items and carry products to the human packer. They also carry pallets of products to the appropriate location and stack them on the shelves. This reduces the need for people to walk around the warehouse looking for items that need packing for the customer. It also reduces the risk of the human employees injuring themselves by lifting heavy items.

Activity

Find the video 'Inside Amazon's Smart Warehouse' on YouTube. Watch the video and make notes about how the IoE is used in the warehouse. Include the advantages and disadvantages of using the IoE in the warehouse.

All the data collected can be analysed and used to inform future developments in production and the products.

Many manufacturers now sell spare parts for their products. When a spare part is despatched to a customer, a link to an AR app can be automatically sent to the customer's smartphone or other device in an email, sometimes as a QR code. The app can then be downloaded and used to show customers how to carry out repairs to their products.

Some manufacturers install **telematic** devices in their vehicles. These devices automatically send real-time data from sensors placed all over the vehicle to the manufacturer, D2D. This data will help the manufacturer improve the performance of the vehicles. It automatically alerts customers if a recall is required or the vehicle needs maintenance, for example a service or new tyres.

There are always developments in the use of the IoE in manufacturing. A power tool manufacturer, DeWalt, has begun trialling a connected battery system for its power tools. The system can monitor battery levels and warn the user when the battery needs to be recharged. The system can also shut down a power tool, for example a drill, if a thief attempts to remove it from a defined area.

The advantages and disadvantages of using the IoE in manufacturing are shown in Table 1.25.

Table 1.25 Advantages and disadvantages of IoE in manufacturing

Advantages	Disadvantages
Employee safety and productivity can improve.	Fewer jobs available on the production line.
The quality of the products manufactured will be consistent and to specified parameters.	Can be difficult, time consuming and expensive to convert a manual production line to IoE.
Faulty production elements can be identified and fixed with little, if any, break in manufacturing.	Employees will have to be retrained to manage an IoE production line so increasing costs.
Decisions can be taken based on analysed data.	If power or connectivity is lost then production will stop and no real-time data will be able to be sent.
Energy use can be reduced as those areas not being used can have lights and heating reduced.	Security of the data network and real-time data can be compromised meaning more cost will be needed for security.

One of the biggest threats to security in the manufacturing area is that of ransomware. Cyber-security criminals can attack a manufacturing company and hold the data and production lines to ransom until a, usually large, sum of money is paid.

Key term

Telematic Vehicle onboard communications and applications that communicate with one another via GPS receivers and other devices.

Security and prevention measures have to be used in the data storage area on the network that is used by the sensors and robots. The robots and sensors will also need to be protected. Customer data will also need to be protected during transmission between the manufacturing company, the retailer and customer.

Activity

Investigate other security issues that can affect the manufacturing application area. What would be the impacts on the company, retailers and customers of each of your issues? Discuss your findings with the rest of your group.

Synoptic links

Cyber-security threats are covered in Topic area 4, section 4.1 of this unit.

The impacts of a cyber-security attack are covered in Topic area 4, section 4.2 of this unit.

Prevention measures are covered in Topic area 4, section 4.3 of this unit.

Military/emergency services

The military and emergency services are there to help people whatever the situation. Developments in the IoE have helped provide a coordinated response to any emergency. The emergency services include:

- ambulance
- coastguard
- fire service
- mountain rescue
- police.

The military have been developing and using devices connected to the IoE such as drones. A drone is an aircraft without a pilot, crew or passengers on board. A drone is also known as an unmanned/un-crewed aerial vehicle (UAV).

A drone can be controlled (flown) by remote control through the IoE, by a human operator, by autopilot (self-navigation), or by a mixture of autopilot and human control.

Drones were originally developed by the military, but their uses have now expanded into commercial and personal use. The military developed drones for times when the use of traditional aircraft is too risky. Drones can provide the military and the emergency services with 24-hour, seven-days-a-week surveillance, known as 'the eye in the sky'. Some drones can stay in the air for up to 17 hours at a time, providing real-time video streams (D2D) back to the control centre.

To fly a commercial drone or a personal drone weighing over 250 g in the UK, the **Civil Aviation Authority (CAA)** requires users to register and take a test which must be passed before the user can legally fly. The CAA has also created a code, The Drone & Model Aircraft Code, which is legally binding.

Augmented reality (AR), mixed reality (MR) and virtual reality (VR) are used by the military and emergency services.

AR is used in in heads-up displays (HUD) showing real-time updates in front of the user's eyes on helmet glasses, the canopy of an aircraft cockpit or on the windscreen of an emergency vehicle.

MR and VR have been used to train personnel by using helmets with a screen inside, VR glasses and gloves fitted with sensors. VR and MR are computer-generated simulations of a three-dimensional image or environment. This can be interacted with in what appears to be a very real or physical way.

VR has been implemented by the military to train military personnel. VR can be used to transport military personnel into a wide variety of locations, situations and environments. Such examples currently in use include flight

Key term

Civil Aviation Authority (CAA) The organisation that regulates civil aviation in the United Kingdom.

simulations, battlefield simulations, vehicle simulations, fire and rescue drills and medical training. VR is totally immersive with a visual and sound-based experience available. It can replicate dangerous situations to train and prepare military personnel without putting them at risk. A key benefit to using VR for training (besides the decreased risk to the well-being of the personnel) is the reduction in costs.

Smart devices can help the emergency services. Vehicles can automatically send an alert of an accident which means a connected device in a smart city, such as traffic lights, can automatically divert the traffic away from the accident site and send real-time data to the emergency services about the accident site. Smart devices in a vehicle can also help emergency services to find a vehicle or missing person.

Land-based emergency vehicles include:

- ambulances
- fire engines
- police cars
- mountain rescue and coastguard 4 × 4.

Many of the emergency services use air-based helicopters. All the emergency services have access to helicopters that can help them. Helicopters can be used to rescue people, transport people to hospital or carry out surveillance.

In any of these situations, real-time data and images can be sent from the land-based vehicles or helicopters to a control centre or hospital. Connected wearable cameras can also be used by personnel to record, and live stream, images back to the control centre.

Smart fire alarm devices in buildings can alert the emergency services if an increase in temperature is identified – this could mean a fire. If the building is a smart building, then fire sprinklers will be activated by the devices and the fire service will be alerted. The fire service can use smart cameras which can identify any people trapped, while sending live-stream video back to the control room. Any smart devices that the people have, such as a smartphone, can also be used to quickly locate any people in the building by the device sending a signal to the emergency services. Emergency crew personnel can be tracked, with their location being streamed in real time back to the control centre, allowing them to be directed to incidents or even advised on different routes away from potential dangers.

The coastguard and mountain rescue can also use smartphones to quickly locate missing people. Smart devices can automatically send a distress signal to a control room alerting them of an emergency. This signal can be used to locate people in hazardous terrain such as at the bottom of a cliff or on a mountain. The benefit of this is that the signal will guide the emergency team to the location, irrespective of the weather conditions, to within one metre. It is also possible that medical data can be sent from the mountain rescue and coastguard to the ambulance services so that a smooth handover can take place.

Synoptic link

You learnt about the IoE and health earlier in this section.

The emergency services and the military can wear sensor devices that can detect, for example, poisonous gases in the air. The sensors will then alert the wearer and the control room so that remedial action can be taken, D2D.

Drones can also be used by emergency services including disaster relief and emergency services investigations. The drones can be flown above areas where it would be impossible for personnel to go. Drones can also cover more ground than a person on the ground. Some drones are fitted with thermal imaging cameras which means that, even in the dark, the heat of a person can be easily spotted. These images are sent back to personnel on the ground, D2D.

Police use a system called **Automatic Number Plate Recognition (ANPR)** in many of their police cars. This system checks the number plate of every vehicle that the police car sees. When a number plate is seen, the ANPR system can communicate with the **Driver and Vehicle Licensing Agency (DVLA)** to check who owns the vehicle and whether they have a current driving licence and insurance. The system can also check if the car is taxed and, if required, if it has a current MOT.

These checks are done almost instantly as the vehicle passes the police car, and if there is a problem with the vehicle then an alert is displayed on the screen of the ANPR device. This alert will then prompt the police to stop the vehicle to talk to the driver.

ANPR can also be used to restrict access to areas. For example, only police vehicles and the personal vehicles of police staff should park in the car park of a police station. ANPR can be used at an automatic barrier: if the number plate is recognised then the barriers open to allow access, if the number plate isn't recognised then the barriers do not open. This system can also be used in a congestion charge zone. As vehicles enter the charge zone the number plates are read by smart cameras. The owner of each vehicle is then automatically charged for entering the zone. This data can also be sent to the emergency services, so they are aware of the vehicles that have entered the zone.

The advantages and disadvantages of the military and emergency services using the IoE are shown in Table 1.26.

Key terms

Automatic Number Plate Recognition (ANPR) A system used by the police; it checks the number plate of every vehicle that the police car sees.

Driver and Vehicle Licensing Agency (DVLA) The government organisation that holds more than 49 million driver records and more than 40 million vehicle records.

Table 1.26 Advantages and disadvantages of the military and emergency services using the IoE

Advantages	Disadvantages
Training can be carried out with little, if any, risk to personnel.	Security of the devices, and the data being transferred.
Tracking of personnel can make sure their location is known at all times while on duty.	Lack of connectivity in remote areas in the UK and abroad.
Real-time data can be used to send appropriate, or more, resources.	Increased threats and the cost of security to reduce the chance of threats.
	If power or connectivity is lost, then devices will stop 'talking' to each other and safety can be reduced as no real-time data will be able to be sent.

Security is vital when the military and the emergency services are using the IoE. Sensitive data can be transferred by the military which, if accessed, could lead to incidents of national security, for example terrorist threats. When the emergency services are transferring data, this can include personal data.

Security has to be very high to protect not only the data but also the devices that are being used. If a threat occurs and devices are compromised, this could lead to a serious incident including loss of life or life-changing injuries.

Synoptic links

Cyber-security threats are covered in Topic area 4, section 4.1 of this unit.

The impacts of a cyber-security attack are covered in Topic area 4, section 4.2 of this unit.

Prevention measures are covered in Topic area 4, section 4.3 of this unit.

Smart devices

There is a huge range of smart devices available for use in the home and in a business. This range is increasing daily as new devices are invented that connect to the internet and each other.

Home

Homes can now contain many different smart devices, all of which can connect to the IoE and to each other, D2D. Some of these devices need no human interaction, others may need a human input such as a voice command. These are examples of H2D devices.

Figure 1.39 Home smart devices

Smart devices automate a range of functions that allow a home to run smoothly, improving comfort, convenience and security.

Smart alarm systems and security cameras can be installed in a home. These can alert the home owner, usually on an app, if something has happened, such as a break-in. It is possible that the home owner can speak into a microphone, and their voice can be outputted through a speaker in the alarm system or camera which may disturb the burglar or vandals. Some smart alarm systems can also send a silent alert to a police control room. The cameras will be constantly recording activity which can be stored on the cloud. These recordings can be used as evidence by the police if the person breaking in is caught and taken to court.

Some alarm systems have a feature that allows the alarm security company to remotely listen in to the house if the alarm is triggered. If they hear something, they can, through a speaker, ask for a password. There are two passwords – one if everything is okay and the other if help is needed. If they hear the password for help is needed then the security company continue to listen in and inform the police to go to the homeowner's aid. If no password is given, then the police are alerted to send assistance.

More and more people are installing smart doorbells. These usually include a camera as well as a traditional bell sound. If the homeowner is somewhere else in the home or out of the home and the doorbell is activated, again, the homeowner will be alerted via an HCI on an app which provides a live feed of the visitor. They can then see who has activated the doorbell. The homeowner can speak to the visitor via a connection between the receiving device and the doorbell.

Smart lighting, heating and plugs all contribute to energy management, energy efficiency and convenience. Lights, heating and plugs can be activated through voice commands to a digital assistant, through an HCI on an app or on pre-set timers activated through an app.

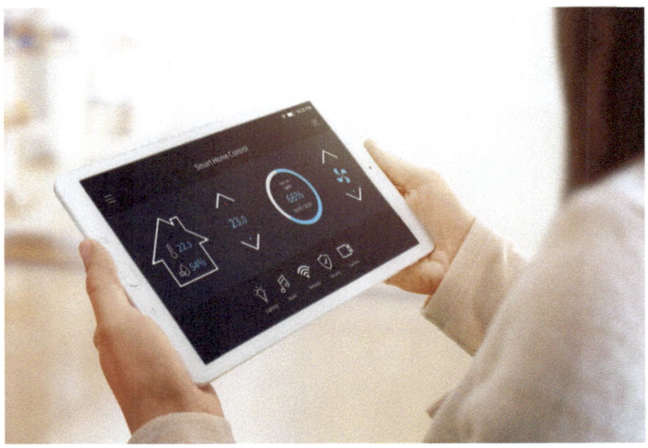

Figure 1.40 HCI for smart heating

Smart vacuum cleaners are also known as robotic vacuum cleaners. These can, like other smart devices, be activated through voice commends, through an HCI on an app or on pre-set timers.

Activity

Copy and complete this table to show the features of each smart device. Choose one smart device not already mentioned and complete the table for that device.

Smart device	How it is activated	Features	Connectivity
Fridge			
Lights			
Plugs			
Vacuum cleaner			

Digital assistant devices, such as Amazon Alexa, Google Home and Apple HomePod, are activated by voice. Among other things, they enable the user to:

- listen to music
- create 'to do' lists
- check a weather forecast
- learn first aid
- control smart devices in a house, such as lights and plugs
- check, and add events to, a calendar.

Figure 1.41 Amazon Alexa, a personal digital assistant

When a question is asked, the assistant will get real-time information from the internet to provide the answer.

Research

Investigate smart digital assistant devices. Make a list of features and tasks that they can perform.

Personal

Some smart devices are personal. You have already learnt about the range of health monitoring smart devices earlier in the section about health.

Research

Research the features available on different smart watches and fitness trackers. Create an infographic showing the results of your research.

Many people have a smartphone or tablet that allows them to download apps and interact, using an HCI, with their smart devices in the home. Smartphones also allow people to interact with their home smart devices while they are not at home, as long as there is internet connectivity.

Smart glasses are wearable computer glasses that add information alongside or to what the wearer sees. They can automatically provide information about something in the wearer's sight such as a product or location, and facial recognition of a person. The user can communicate with the system, for example with voice, signs or finger sweeps. The glasses can also control or retrieve data from other digital devices using wireless technologies like Bluetooth, Wi-Fi and GPS.

It is possible to use AR technology to live-stream digital images, using voice control through a digital assistant. This means that it is possible to connect sound-based AR, motion sensors and GPS data to produce three-dimensional real-time navigation and virtual street tours of attractions in a town, city or the countryside.

Synoptic link

Devices used with AR are covered in Unit R070, Topic area 1, section 1.3.

Amazon developed glasses frames which means that people who wear prescription glasses can now turn these into smart glasses. The glasses look like any normal glasses but Amazon Alexa's answers to questions and voice commands are heard through tiny speakers by the wearer's ears.

As with normal smart glasses the side of the glasses can be swiped to get more information, set reminders and control smart home devices. Most smart glasses include a filter facility which controls the notifications, for example emails or phone calls, the wearer gets.

It is also possible to connect smart glasses to home smart devices such as doorbells, cameras and alarm systems.

Figure 1.42 Interacting with a robotic arm using smart glasses

Business

Many of the smart devices used in the home are also used in business. How a business uses smart devices will depend upon the function of the business, for example a restaurant, shop or garage.

Many businesses advertise using AR installations, for example at bus stops or by scanning a QR code.

Activity

Find and watch the following AR installation video:

- Visa's AR campaign 'Try something new with Visa'

Synoptic links

Smart fire alarm systems are covered in the section on the emergency services earlier in Topic area 6, section 6.2 of this unit.

AR installations are covered in Unit R070, Topic area 1, section 1.1.

Digital assistant devices can be used in a business to carry out the same basic tasks as a home owner can use them for. If a business has many digital assistant devices, then they could be used to send messages to one or all devices.

Smart locks can be used to secure a building or specific rooms. Smart locks can lock and unlock a door using an instruction from a trusted digital device, for example a smartphone or tablet. Wireless technology is used to make the connection between the lock and the digital device. There is no physical key, which means there is no danger of the key becoming lost or falling into the wrong hands. An audit trail can be kept about who entered, and left, a room or building. Virtual keys can be sent, D2D, to authorised guests and visitors. Smart locks can be used in conjunction with a smart doorbell in a business or in a home.

Many businesses, such as retail and restaurants, take payment from their customers using debit and credit cards. When the customer is ready to pay, the card is inserted into, or tapped onto, the card reader. The card reader connects to the bank that issued the card, and the money is transferred from the customer's bank account to the business bank account. This is an example of D2D.

Some restaurants provide customers with a QR code. This means that when the QR code is scanned by the customers using, for example, their smartphones, the menu will appear. Customers may also be able to place an order for their food from the menu shown on their smartphone which will be sent to the restaurant kitchen.

A business can also make use of smart lights, plugs and heating controls in a similar way to the home. The heating controls, plugs and lights can be set to office hours. Smart alarm systems will be synced to a key holder who is alerted in case of a break-in or fire as well as the emergency services being alerted. In a building with lots of rooms, sensors can be installed to automatically switch off lights or heating if no movement is detected for a pre-set time period.

Some businesses that sell stock, for example a shop or take-away, can link their stock control to a till. This will mean that when an item is sold the quantity of that item is reduced in the stock levels. When the stock level of an item gets to a pre-set level an order can be automatically sent to the suppliers, this is D2D.

Activity

In groups of two, choose a different business area, for example a car repair garage or independent shop. Research the smart devices that can be used in the business area. Create a digital communication and present your findings to the rest of your class.

The advantages and disadvantages of smart devices connected to the IoE are shown in Table 1.27.

The security of smart devices is, as with other application areas, critical. Smart devices transmit data over the web. Some devices, for example cameras in smart doorbells, transmit unencrypted data. This data is very vulnerable to cyber-security threats such as hacking.

All smart devices use battery or mains power. If the batteries run out or there is a power cut, then the devices will not work as intended. This means that, for example, the smoke and burglar alarms can leave a house or building vulnerable. This could also leave people inside the house or building with no lighting or unable to get out because the smart lock isn't working.

Table 1.27 Advantages and disadvantages of smart devices connected to the IoE

Advantages	Disadvantages
All smart devices can be controlled from a central device, for example a smartphone or tablet.	The installation costs can be high.
New devices and appliances can be added.	A stable and reliable connection is needed.
Increased security of houses and buildings.	Vulnerable to data breaches and hardware failure.
Safer than sending a person to carry out dangerous tasks.	Technological problems, such as devices not talking to each other, can reduce efficiency.
Decreased energy costs.	Some people may be wary of smart devices and technology.
	Maintenance may be expensive in terms of time and money.

Synoptic links

Cyber-security threats are covered in Topic area 4, section 4.1 of this unit.

The impacts of a cyber-security attack are covered in Topic area 4, section 4.2 of this unit.

Prevention measures are covered in Topic area 4, section 4.3 of this unit.

Transport

Developments in the use of the IoE have impacted on a range of different transport methods. These methods include shipping, aeroplanes and autonomous vehicles (AVs). These AVs include driverless cars, trains and lorries. Smart cities also utilise the features of the IoE.

Activity

Massachusetts Institute of Technology (MIT) created a game to provide an insight into how autonomous cars should react when faced with a decision. Locate the game 'Moral Machine' on the W3 and play it. Compare your results with the rest of your group. Whose judgements were the best for society?

The IoE is not only used for AVs but it also enables vehicles, driven by humans, to connect to the internet and send/receive real-time data. Sensors built into vehicles are used to direct the vehicle using GPS positioning and receive real-time traffic conditions based on the route taken. Drivers can now receive information from vehicle-based sensors on apps about the performance of their car and their driving. For example:

- fuel consumption
- average fuel consumption
- tyre pressure
- distance before fuel needed
- distance before oil change needed.

Most cars have parking sensors and cameras which help the driver to safely manoeuvre the car and be alerted when the car is close to an obstacle, such as a child, dog or another car.

Figure 1.43 An AV car showing the sensors

Many cars send real-time data about their location to the manufacturer's cloud storage area. The journeys taken by the car can also be sent and stored on the cloud storage area. The real-time data about location can be used if the car is stolen. As the data is sent in real time, it is possible for the police to locate and retrieve a stolen car for the owner.

Many cars have an SOS button. The button can be activated by the driver if they have a problem or have been in an accident. When pressed, the car automatically links to a call centre via the IoE. It provides the location of the car and allows verbal communication between the call centre staff and the driver. This allows assistance to be sent to the car and driver and, if necessary, the emergency services can be alerted.

Figure 1.44 An SOS button on a car's dashboard

If the car is in an accident and the air bags have gone off, the SOS button will automatically alert the call centre so assistance and help can be sent to the location of the car. The call centre staff will attempt to speak to the driver as the communication link is activated.

The IoE applied to transport can become part of the smart city. As you have learnt, a smart city is a concept where everything is connected. This includes transport, traffic lights, street lights and pedestrian crossings.

Activity

Find the video 'V2V Communication' on YouTube. Watch the video and make notes about how the IoE is used in **vehicle-to-vehicle (V2V)** communication. Think about the advantages and disadvantages of using V2V on the road network.

For example, a road junction can include traffic lights, a pedestrian crossing and street lights. A car may use a Light Detection and Range (LiDAR) sensor to detect pedestrians. When these are detected, the car should start slowing down and braking to avoid an accident. This interaction is known as **vehicle-to-everything (V2X)** communication.

The number of cars waiting at traffic lights can be determined by a sensor signal either sent from the cars or through sensors built into the road. This is an example of D2D. This signal can also tell the traffic lights where on the road junction the cars are waiting. This data will allow the traffic lights to change to green where the most cars are waiting.

Sensors on the AV and traffic lights can 'talk' to each other. This means that when the traffic light turns green, a 'go' signal can be sent to the car and the cars can automatically begin to move. When the traffic light turns red, a 'stop' signal can be sent to the car and the cars can automatically begin to slow down and stop at the traffic lights.

Activity

Investigate how the IoE can be used to track shipping containers on their journey. Create a digital communication showing your findings. You should use a range of different elements in your communication.

Other types of vehicles also have sensors that are linked via the IoE to manufacturers and smart device developers. Trains have sensors which allow controllers to track their progress on their journey. This enables controllers to keep passengers up to date about any delays in their journey and how late the train will be at each station stop.

Key terms

Vehicle-to-everything (V2X) The wireless transmission of data between vehicles, traffic infrastructure, networks and devices.

Vehicle-to-vehicle (V2V) The wireless transmission of data from vehicle to vehicle to increase safety while driving.

Planes have many sensors. These include sensors about the fuel, weight of the plane and flying height (altitude). These sensors not only help the pilots fly the plane but also send real-time data back to the airline and manufacturer. This data will help identify the life of a part and can inform future developments in plane design and manufacture.

Activity

Driverless buses are being developed and trialled. Investigate the IoE devices that have made this possible. Create an infographic to show your findings.

Speed cameras on motorways and roads use an ANPR system. As a vehicle passes a speed camera, the camera takes a measurement of its speed. If the vehicle is travelling at or below the speed limit, then no action is taken. If the speed limit is being broken, however, the camera takes a picture of the number plate. The number plate is then looked up using the DVLA database and a speeding notice is sent to the registered owner of the vehicle. This is all done automatically using D2D.

Figure 1.45 ANPR used on a motorway

The advantages and disadvantages of using the IoE in transport are shown in Table 1.28.

One of the disadvantages of using the IoE in the transport application area is that of security, as security in the transport application area is very important. If the connectivity between the smart devices, sensors and vehicles is

Table 1.28 Advantages and disadvantages of using the IoE in transport

Advantages	Disadvantages
It is safer to use an AV because digital devices do not get distracted or tired.	Extra costs in terms of creating and maintaining the infrastructure for road use.
Better public transport management as data is collected about the progress of the journeys and if any problems have been identified.	Increased costs of vehicles because of research and development costs.
Better service for passengers using, for example, a train or bus, as data can be used to see how many passengers use the service which means that changes can be made such as more frequent services.	A stable connection is needed to send and receive data between devices and vehicles.
More cost effective as the collected data can be used to identify problems so maintenance can be carried out; as this is safer, this means that fewer accidents will happen meaning the costs of dealing with accidents are reduced.	Increased threats and the cost of security to reduce the chance of threats.
Data can be used to identify trouble spots in terms of congestion meaning action can be taken to reduce these areas.	If power or connectivity is lost, then devices will stop 'talking' to each other and safety can be reduced as no real-time data will be able to be sent. Major accidents could happen leading to loss of life or serious injuries.

compromised through a threat this could lead to loss of life or serious life-changing injuries. The threats include hacking, malware and a denial of service attack. The threats can be targeted at the smart devices, the data when it is in transit or the vehicles, or any combination of these.

Synoptic links

Cyber-security threats are covered in Topic area 4, section 4.1 of this unit.

The impacts of a cyber-security attack are covered in Topic area 4, section 4.2 of this unit.

Prevention measures are covered in Topic area 4, section 4.3 of this unit.

Smart device security

You have learnt about the security issues for each application area. Security is very important in the IoE, mainly because of the connectivity between the smart devices and the amount of real-time data that is transferred D2D.

Smart devices and their apps will ask permission to link to other apps, camera, microphone, connected locks and personal data. Sometimes users are told that this permission is essential to carry on using the smart device and tailoring it to meet their needs. However, if the app gets hacked then there is a strong possibility that the smart device will no longer work, and data could be accessed from the linked apps.

Most smart devices have a default password. This is a weak password and may be the same for all of that type of smart device. The default password may be easily available on a website, so default passwords should be changed to a strong password.

Synoptic links

Cyber-security threats are covered in Topic area 4, section 4.1 of this unit.

Prevention measures are covered in Topic area 4, section 4.3 of this unit.

If hackers manage to access a smart device, then there is a strong probability that other connected smart devices will be accessed. This means that these devices can be used to distribute malware and a denial of service attack (DoS).

Many IoE smart devices and apps use very little data. This can mean they can be difficult to update and install any patches issued by the manufacturer. This lack of updating can mean that cyber-security prevention measures, such as firewalls, anti-virus software and encryption, may not work as intended, leaving the device open to a threat.

Some older smart device apps were not developed for cloud connectivity. This means they are probably not compatible with the newer security features such as encryption. Smart devices should be updated or replaced regularly to ensure they are kept up to date with the latest developments in cyber-security.

Another issue is that there are no common security standards for smart devices. This means that each manufacturer has slightly different protocols and guidelines. This lack of standardisation between smart devices makes it harder to secure connected devices from different manufacturers, so leaving them open to a cyber-security threat. This problem can also mean that D2D communication can be harder.

Test your knowledge ✔

6 Identify one health reading that can be monitored by a fitness tracker.
7 What are smart glasses?
8 What is meant by V2V?
9 What does ANPR stand for?
10 What is a default password on a smart device?

Practice questions ✔

1 When do smart meters send data to an energy company? [1 mark]
2 Explain how the IoE can be used when a patient is being taken to a hospital in an ambulance. [2 marks]
3 Explain why the default password on a smart device used in healthcare should be changed. [2 marks]
4 Discuss how a digital assistant can be used in a home. [9 marks]
5 Explain **one** advantage and **one** disadvantage of using the IoE in the transport application area. [4 marks]

Unit R060

Data manipulation using spreadsheets

About this unit

Every day, you create data. For example, you count your daily steps, post 'likes' on social media, and buy and sell items using the internet. Organisations manipulate this data and turn it into useful information that they can use. Spreadsheet applications are commonly used to do this.

In this unit, you will learn to develop the skills required to plan and develop a spreadsheet solution that manipulates data for an organisation.

Topic areas

In this chapter you will learn about:

1. Planning and designing the spreadsheet solution (TA1)
2. Creating the spreadsheet solution (TA2)
3. Testing the spreadsheet solution (TA3)
4. Evaluating the spreadsheet solution (TA4)

How will I be assessed?

You will be set an assignment which will provide you with a scenario, problems to solve and a data set to use. You will then need to use the skills that you have learnt to plan, design, create, test and review a spreadsheet solution to solve the problems set out in the assignment.

The assignment will cover the following performance objectives:

PO2 – Apply knowledge and understanding

PO3 – Analyse and evaluate knowledge, understanding and performance

PO4 – Demonstrate and apply skills and processes relevant to the subject area

Topic area 1 Planning and designing the spreadsheet solution

Getting started

The first step when creating a spreadsheet solution is to plan and design the solution. Time spent doing this will increase the chances that the solution is both successful and meets the client's requirements.

Selecting the correct tools to plan and design the solution is also important. This reduces the chances of crucial pieces of information or steps being missed out.

The **Human Computer Interface (HCI)** is a key part of *any* website.

Choose a travel website that allows people to book a holiday. Draw what you see on the screen when you try to find a holiday.

Highlight, with annotations:

- data entry methods (dropdowns, text boxes, and so on)
- messages that help you enter data
- images/graphics that are used.

1.1 Design tools

You learnt about design tools in Unit R050, Topic area 1.

Flow charts

Flow charts can be used in different ways when planning and designing a spreadsheet solution. They can break the problem down into smaller steps to see what will be needed to create the solution. The flow chart can then be used to keep track of how the project is developing.

Flow charts can also be used to analyse how the data will flow through a system. This will allow system developers to see:

- what data is entered into the system
- how it can be entered into the system
- how it will need to be processed
- how it can be outputted from the system.

Figure 2.1 shows the flow diagram of how the data flows through a system when a new user signs up to a social media account.

Key term

Human Computer Interface (HCI) An HCI allows communication between the user and a digital system.

Mind maps

Mind maps (also called spider diagrams) can be used to generate ideas and link concepts together.

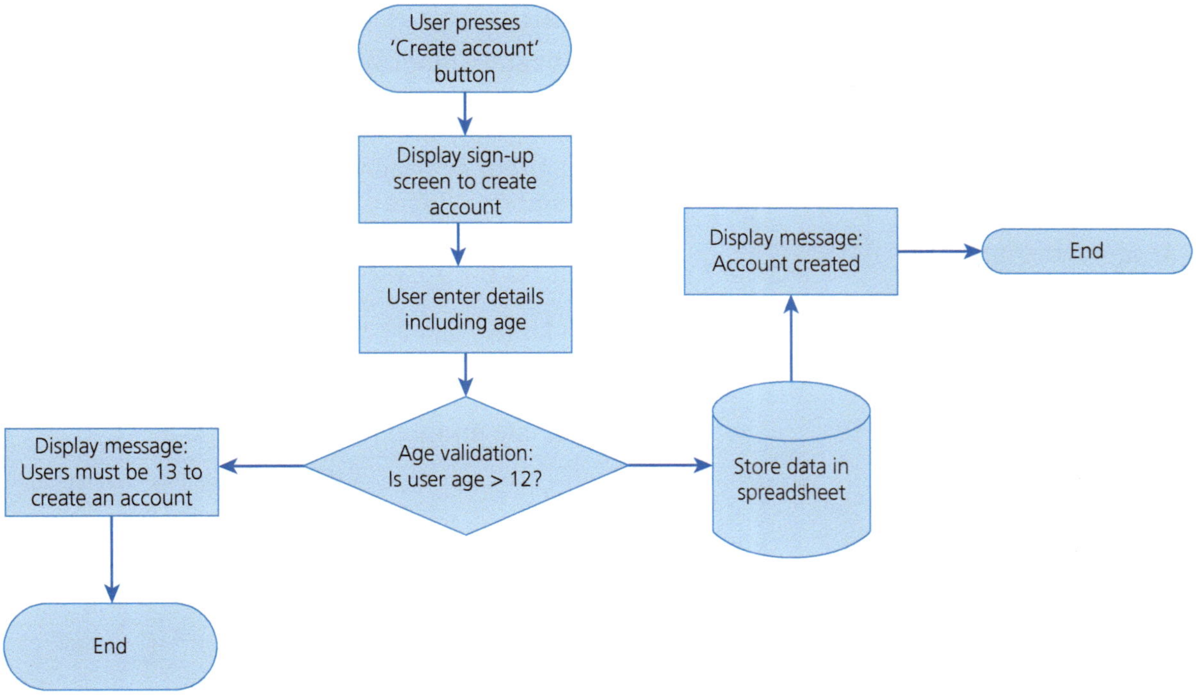

Figure 2.1 Social media sign-up flow chart

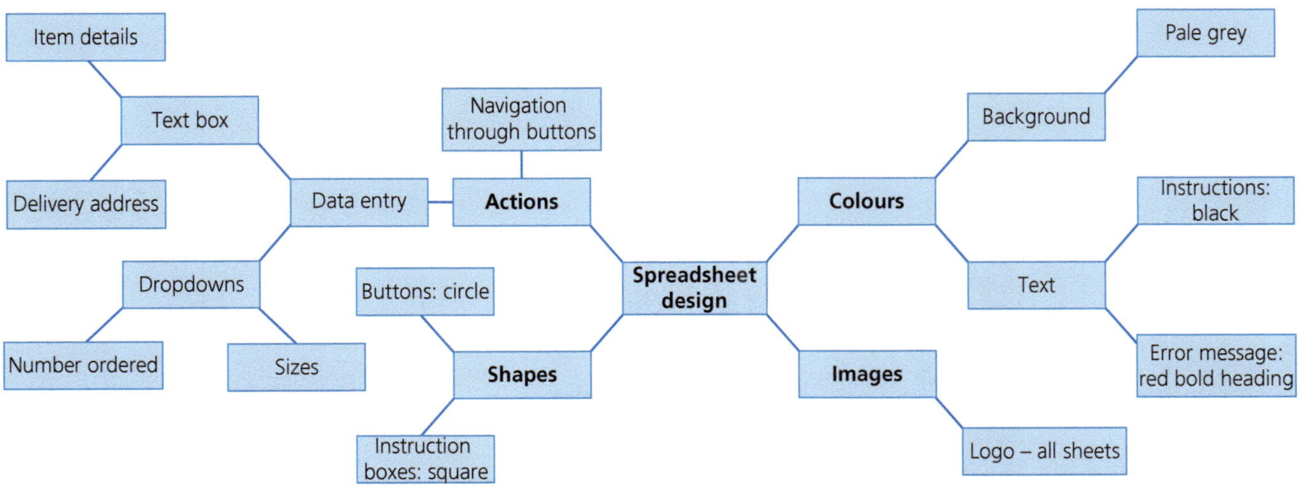

Figure 2.2 Mind map of HCI navigation considerations

Figure 2.2 shows a mind map created when beginning to consider how to create the navigation on a screen-based HCI.

Storyboards

Storyboards are a sequence of images placed together to represent a series of steps.

Storyboards can be used to show how the interaction in a spreadsheet solution would take place and how it would appear. They allow the user to clearly see what will happen using images instead of trying to understand it by reading words only.

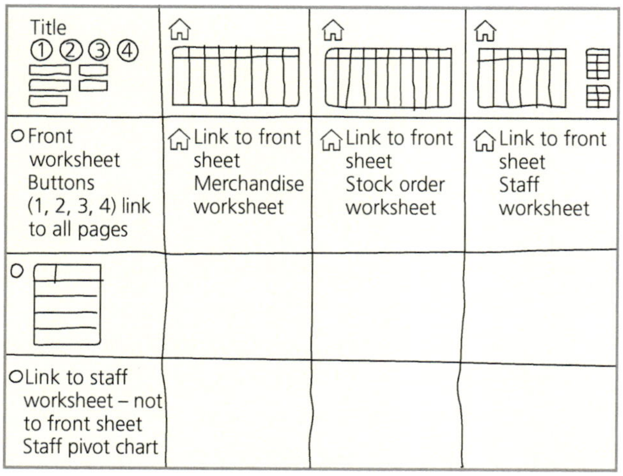

Figure 2.3 Example of a simple storyboard for a spreadsheet solution

Visualisation diagram

Visualisation diagrams can be used to design and show how a spreadsheet, screen or HCI will look. They are used to communicate ideas to the client or programmer using images and annotations. Visualisation diagrams can also be used to show how the data will look when it is output from the system.

When planning a spreadsheet solution, a visualisation diagram can be used to design the interfaces and outputs and help ensure that critical information is not missed out.

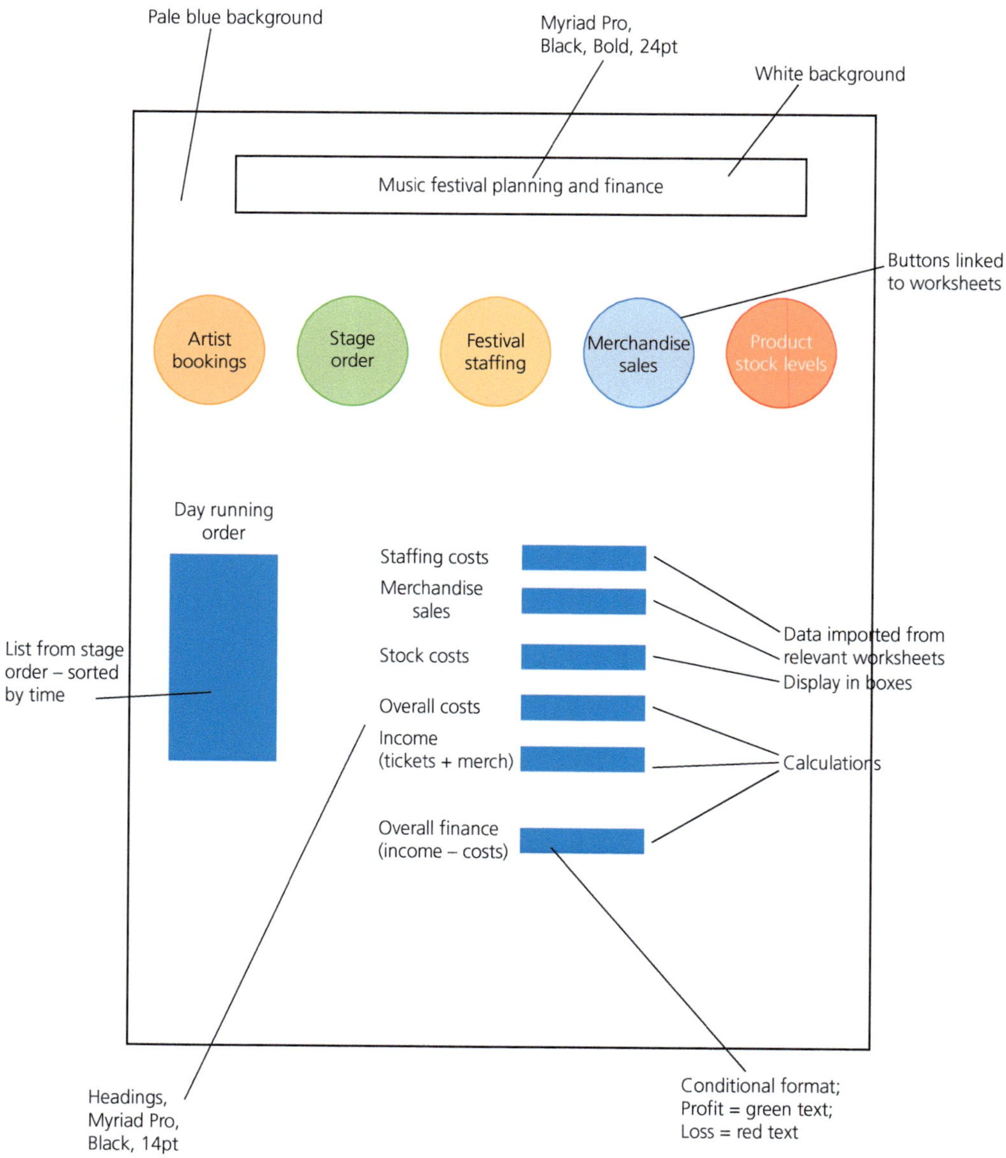

Figure 2.4 Example of a visualisation diagram of HCI for a spreadsheet solution

Wireframe

A wireframe is a blueprint for a screen, spreadsheet or output document. A wireframe shows the possible layout that could be used without detail being shown. It looks like a series of empty shapes on top of each other. The wireframe can be used to see if the design is appropriate for the audience and purpose.

> **Test your knowledge** ✔
>
> 1 What can a flow chart be used for?
> 2 Which design tool is used to link concepts together?
> 3 What does a storyboard contain?
> 4 Identify **two** uses for a visualisation diagram.
> 5 What is a wireframe used to show?

1.2 HCI design conventions and principles

Functionality

The first step to designing a spreadsheet solution is to consider what the system needs to do. From the client brief, the developer needs to consider what will need to happen in the system to make it work. They will need to consider:

- what data will go into the system
- what will happen to the data in the system (how it will be processed)
- how the information will be output from the system.

One way of doing this is to create a series of flow charts showing how data travels through the system. An example of this is shown in Figure 2.1, where the flow of data entered in the sign-up process for a social media account is shown moving through the system as it is processed and finally displayed on a screen.

When considering the functionality of the system, a developer must consider several aspects.

Calculations

Developers need to consider the calculations that will take place inside the system to convert input data into usable output information. Spreadsheets can carry out calculations – from simple addition, subtraction, multiplication and division, to complex multi-step functions.

The specifics of the cell references used in the calculations do not need to be considered just yet – these can be looked at when the spreadsheet solution is built. At this stage of development, considering what calculations need to take place, and when they take place, is vital to the functionality of the system being developed.

Sorting

Data may be entered into the system in an order that is not easy to use or read. This is especially true with large data sets. So, the developer must consider how to sort the data into a logical and usable order, for example alphabetical order, numerical order, size order. Spreadsheet software can sort the data into ascending or descending order based on the lists that it is stored in. This is important when considering the output information and how it will be displayed to the end user. Decisions need to be made such as: will sorting be carried out automatically by the system, or will the end user sort the data manually?

Filtering

Filtering allows only certain data to be shown to the end user when they require it. Filtering can be applied using criteria that are decided by the end user. One of the advantages of filtering is that filters can be added and removed without changing the underlying data. Developers must consider what data needs to be filtered when designing a spreadsheet system, for example only red shirts or only customers who have paid in full.

User aids

Using a combination of data entry messages and data validation tools means that an efficient, intuitive and easy-to-use interface can be created.

Data entry messages

Instructions can appear on screen to explain how to enter data into the system. These can be text written onto the spreadsheet itself, or text rollovers that appear when the user goes to enter data. To aid accessibility, audio explanations may also be included. Deciding what messages are needed, and in what format, is an important aspect of HCI design.

Data validation tools

Data validation ensures that data is entered in the format required for the system to work correctly. These tools can be combined with data entry messages that explain how the data has to be entered or where the data has been entered incorrectly.

> **Test your knowledge**
>
> **6** Identify **five** different calculations that a spreadsheet can do.
> **7** Why is sorting data important?
> **8** Explain what happens when you apply filters to a spreadsheet.
> **9** Identify **three** different data entry messages that could appear on a screen.
> **10** Why is data validation used?

Types of outputs that clearly present information for an organisation

Once the data in a spreadsheet system has been manipulated, it will be output as information. How the information is output from the system depends upon the organisation's requirements and the media that will be used to present the information, such as audio, screen or paper.

The layout of the output chosen should communicate the information effectively. Table 2.1 includes some of the factors to consider when deciding what to use when designing the system output.

> **Key term**
>
> **House style** A set of rules set by an organisation covering how all its documents are formatted. This can cover: colours, font sizes and style, logo style, text alignment.

Table 2.1 Document factors to consider when presenting information

Factor	Questions to think about
Page size	What size document will the content be displayed on, for example A5, post card, screen?
Print area	Will the document be printed? If it will be printed, how much space is needed at the edge of the paper so that information is not cut off? How does the content fit inside the guidelines? Will the worksheet be printed? Does it fit onto one page?
Margins	How much space is needed on the edge of the document? Do the margins need to be changed to fit all the information onto the output document? How much space is needed between elements in the document, for example between a graph and a table in a report?
Header/ footer	Is there information that needs to appear at the top and bottom on every page, slide or screen? Will these be automatic fields?
Orientation	What orientation (landscape or portrait) will the output appear in? This will affect where information can be placed on the output.
Scaling	Will the user be able to zoom in or out of a document if it is a digital version? Does anything need to be made smaller to fit onto the page/screen? Do the cells on the worksheet need to be expanded to show all the information that they contain?
House style	Does the organisation that the system is being built for have a **house style**? Is there a specific style the organisation wants to use? How can you incorporate that into your designs? Are there logos that need to be used?
Font styles and sizes	Information needs to be easy to read so the font style and size needs to be easy to read. Will headings need to have different font styles, sizes, emphasis, and so on?
Colours	If there is no house style, what colours will be used? What colour will the output background be? What colour will the information be? Are there accessibility guidelines that need to be followed, for example colour blindness, high contrast colouring?

Charts

Charts and graphs can be created as an output to visualise the numerical output from the manipulated data. Charts and graphs may help users visualise numerical data in a way that looking at large tables of figures may not. The system developer will need to consider what type of chart and graph to use to present the data. This will depend upon what will be shown and where it will be shown.

Some of the factors to be considered are shown below.

- Does a trend over time need to be shown?
- Does a final figure need to be shown?
- Does a comparison between figures need to be shown?
- Does a breakdown of percentages need to be shown?
- Does the data need to contain 'live' updates, or will the data be static?
- Will the output be in colour or greyscale?
- Will the chart be on a screen or paper?
- Will the end user be able to zoom in on the chart or graph?

Once the type of chart or graph has been decided on, there are conventions and principles that need to be applied to make the chart or graph effective. These include:

- title
- labels
- key
- scale
- distinct colours for different data.

Without the use of these conventions and principles the chart or graph can be difficult to read, leading to possible misinterpretation of the information.

Activity

Create a three-column table.

Column 1: List the different types of graphs that could be made using spreadsheet software.

Column 2: Explain what each graph type can be used to do, for example comparing product sales or showing trends.

Column 3: Provide a specific example of where you have found the graph being used.

Lists

Lists are a simple way of outputting the data from a spreadsheet. However, to make the list user friendly the system developer needs to consider a range of factors.

- What will the list be used for?
- How long will the list be? Is it a complete list of all the data or only some of the data? Does it need to be filtered?
- Does the list contain one column? Or does it require more columns of data based on the first column?
- Does the list need to be sorted? What criteria will be used?
- Does the list need to be in alphabetical order?

Once these factors have been considered, then there are conventions and principles that need to be applied to ensure that the list is effective and communicates the information properly. These include:

- title
- labels.

Table 2.2 shows fares collected by taxi drivers working for a local business.

Looking at List A it is very difficult to see who has collected the most fares because the data is not in an order. In List B, the data has been sorted based on the Total column with the largest number at the top and the smallest at the bottom. This means that it is much easier to see that Eve has collected the highest fares this week while Mark has collected the lowest and is not making that much money for the business.

Table 2.2 Using a sort on data for taxi driver fares

List A			List B	
Driver	**Total**		**Driver**	**Total**
Kareem	£255		Eve	£848
Jasmine	£344		Ling	£444
Eve	£848		Jasmine	£344
Mark	£72		Kareem	£255
Ling	£444		Sam	£132
Sam	£132		Mark	£72

Invoices

Some businesses need to send bills to customers after goods or services have been provided. The document used to do this is called an invoice, which will contain data from the spreadsheet system. An invoice can be output directly from the spreadsheet system with a worksheet being set up to be populated with the data. Another method of creating an invoice is by using a separate software application to create an invoice template and then mail merging the data from the spreadsheet onto the invoice template. The systems developer will need to decide on the best method of doing this when designing the system.

Activity

In pairs or small groups, find three examples of invoices from the internet, your school or someone you know. For each invoice, identify the information and data included. Then compare the invoices and create a final list that identifies the items that are consistently included on all three invoices.

Reports

Some organisations will want the data to be used in a report. A report is a formal document about a topic that can vary in length from a single page to multiple pages. Data from the spreadsheet can be included in the report in a variety of ways, such as:

- graphs
- charts
- tables
- lists.

A report should be logical in structure and include headings and subheadings. This will make it easier for the reader to understand the information included in the report so there is no miscommunication. A report explains the information shown in the graphs, charts, and so on that are included.

Worksheets

The worksheets in spreadsheet software are also a possible output of information and how these are set up needs to be considered. The information once processed needs to appear in a logical and clear way so that the end user can clearly see the results produced by the system. Data and information need to be clear and easy to read.

Worksheets can display data in a variety of ways. The system developer needs to make the decision about which is the best way to meet the client and end-user needs, presenting the data in a clear and logical way. Some examples of methods to display data in the worksheet include:

- figures in cells
- typed comments
- graphs on the worksheet
- PivotCharts
- tables of specific groupings
- conditional formatting of cells and values.

Using the worksheet as an output has the advantage that no other software is required, so a level of complexity is removed. If a worksheet is going to be used as a printed output, then titles, scaling, margins, and so on need to be considered. (See the questions to think about in Table 2.1.)

Test your knowledge

11 What does the term 'print area' mean?
12 What does house style mean?
13 List **three** things that should be included on a graph or chart.
14 What type of graph is the best to show data changing over time?
15 Why are sorted lists more useful than unsorted lists?

HCI

Purpose

A clear and logical HCI will make a spreadsheet system simple to use for the end user. This can result in fewer data entry errors and greater **user adoption**. Most users will not be concerned with what happens with the processing and calculations in the spreadsheet system; their concern will be how easy the system is to use when they need to enter data and output information. The key to this is creating a navigation system that is clearly set out and logical to use. One key aspect to this is to think about the end-user journey through the system. What will they need to do to complete their tasks? What is the purpose of the system as a whole? Beginning at this point will make it easier for a system developer to design an effective HCI navigation system.

Navigation

When planning a new HCI, the developer needs to consider how users will move around the spreadsheet solution. This means thinking about:

- how they will move forward through the system
- how they will get to all the different aspects of the solution (such as data entry locations, information output locations, changing output settings, and so on)
- how they will move backwards through the system (to the home screen).

Then, they need to consider how these navigation points will be communicated to the user. For example: will there be buttons, arrows or other elements used to indicate the navigation aspects of the solution?

User perceptions

When planning a new HCI, the system developer needs to consider the range of experiences of the users. Some users will have used several different computer systems in the past and will find using a new HCI relatively simple. Some end users, however, will not have this experience, and the

Key term

User adoption The number of users who start to use a system because it suits their needs.

Table 2.3 Accessibility considerations

Interface aspect	Consideration
Typed content	A large font size is easy to read. Stylised or decorative fonts can be difficult to read. Spacing between lines should be enough to clearly separate the lines of text. Do not put text over images as it can be difficult to read.
Contrast and colour	Always use the highest contrast possible: a dark font on a light background or a light font on a dark background. Some users may be colour blind, so colour choice is important.
Audio	Audio messages can be created to explain parts of the system to the user. Subtitles be created for audio content.
Data entry	Use a microphone through speech-to-text software to enter data. Use drop-down menus to make data entry easy. Ensure elements on the screen are large enough to be selected easily.

system developer will need to design the HCI to include elements that will make it easier for users to learn and use the new system. These will include items such as colours, messages and icons.

Accessibility

The HCI needs to be designed so that as many people as possible can use the system. To do this, the system developer will need to consider users who may have extra physical, visual, audio or speech needs (see Table 2.3). Accessibility can also refer to the end user's skill level and how much have they used a spreadsheet system previously.

Colour

Colours can play an important part in helping a user navigate a system. Accessibility requirements need to be considered but there are ways that colours can be used to emphasise pieces of information needed to use the HCI.

Look at how colours have been used in this book to emphasise different pieces of information. Think about how the colours used have been changed and combined for emphasis.

Table 2.4 Choosing colours

Colour	Possible use
Red	Eye catching, use for warnings, caution, error messages.
Blue	Calming, use for backgrounds or text instructions.
Green	Positive feel, use to show where user actions are needed, GO!
Yellow Orange	Sunny and warm, confirming messages when system data entered or processed correctly.
Black	Neutral, easy to read against light backgrounds, message content.
White	Stands out against dark backgrounds.

Colours can help users but using too much colour can have a negative effect and make the interface difficult to use meaning key parts can be missed. Using lots of light text on dark backgrounds, such as white on black, can be very tiring on the eyes.

Layout

Do not clutter the interface: less is more. This is a simple thing for the system developer to consider but has a huge impact on the effectiveness of an HCI. Spreading out the elements on the interface allows the end user to find them on the screen easily – this can be done by using **white space** between the elements.

Another aspect of layout is the order in which the HCI requires actions to take place. Using the end-user journey concept, the system developer should consider the first things that the end user will need to do when they enter the system; these should be placed towards the top of the screen. This is important because the top of the screen loads first and we read from top to bottom. This means you automatically look to the top of the screen when you first open the system.

The layout can be designed using a wireframe, allowing elements to be moved around easily without the need to add in detail.

Learnability

The HCI should be simple to use and get easier to use each time an end user operates the system. As the end user uses the system repeatedly, they should learn how it works. This means any tasks they need to carry out on a regular basis should become intuitive and quicker. This benefits them by reducing their workload. Learnability is linked to memorability – the past experiences of the end user affect how they use a new HCI.

Memorability

End users will have a range of experiences of different computer systems and websites. However, there are consistent methods of how users interact with computer systems which can be adopted when designing a new HCI. This consistency makes it easier for the end user to learn and use new systems. These include the use of buttons and symbols to indicate actions that need to take place. Buttons on the computer screen should be designed and created to mimic a button or a switch on a wall or computer. This can be done using borders and shadows which indicate to the user that it is a button and they need to press it.

Key term

White space Empty space used to separate elements on a screen or document.

Messages

When designing a new HCI, the system developers should not presume users will understand what they require them to do. Messages on the screen help a user by explaining and/or showing them what they need to do. Using short messages, either text or audio based, can help the end user operate the system independently. This makes them more comfortable using the system and improves the quality of information that they receive, as they will make fewer mistakes entering and manipulating data.

Test your knowledge

16 What is the purpose of an HCI?
17 Why are user perceptions important?
18 Why is white space used?
19 Why is memorability important?
20 Why are messages important in an HCI?

Research

Open a spreadsheet software and make notes about all the ways that you as a user are helped to use that software.

Think about:

- messages provided (including rollovers)
- colour
- icons/images
- learnability
- memorability.

Open another piece of software, such as a word-processing package or art package. (It would help if it is from the same suite of software as the spreadsheet.) Repeat what you did for the spreadsheet software above.

Create a two-slide presentation that explains what you found about how the HCIs have been designed to help the user.

Assignment practice

Task 1

The headteacher of your school wants a new spreadsheet system to monitor the spending of the different departments in school. The spreadsheet will need an HCI that allows the headteacher to select different departments and see:

- the percentage of their budget that they have spent
- what they have bought in the last month.

The school logo will need to appear on the screen as well as the name and email address of the Head of Department of the department being viewed.

Create a visualisation diagram for the new spreadsheet HCI. This should provide enough detail for the headteacher to understand clearly what the screen will look like.

Topic area 2 Creating the spreadsheet solution

The spreadsheet software used in this topic area is Microsoft Office Excel and Google Sheets: both are the latest standard versions as of August 2021. Both applications are updated by the parent companies on a regular basis. The specific steps and interface look may change, however the underlying usage and principles will not. These principles can also be used in other spreadsheet software such as Apache OpenOffice Calc.

Getting started

Using the internet find two examples of spreadsheets used by different organisations.

List the following.

- The formulae they have used in the spreadsheet.
- The worksheet names used.
- The different formatting, such as colours, fonts and sizes used.

2.1 Use spreadsheet tools and techniques to create the solution

Spreadsheet software contains a range of tools and techniques that can be used to manipulate and present data to produce an effective solution for a client.

Data handling and manipulation

Naming worksheets

A spreadsheet consists of several **worksheets** which by default are named 'Sheet1', 'Sheet2', and so on. These worksheets form a **workbook**. Changing the names of the different worksheets is a simple process that will allow you to label each worksheet with a name that tells the user what information or data it contains. Renaming a worksheet makes the process of linking worksheets easier because you can find each worksheet in the workbook more easily.

Figure 2.5 Naming different worksheets

Key terms

Spreadsheet A software application for organising, analysing and storing data in tables.

Workbook A collection of one or more worksheets into a single file.

Worksheet A single table of cells within a spreadsheet application.

Naming cells

A cell in a spreadsheet can be named. In Figure 2.6, the cell Q23, where the final total for all wages is added up, has been named 'Total'. This is done by typing the required name into the box at the top left of the spreadsheet.

A group of cells can also be named. This makes it easier to refer to them in a formula rather

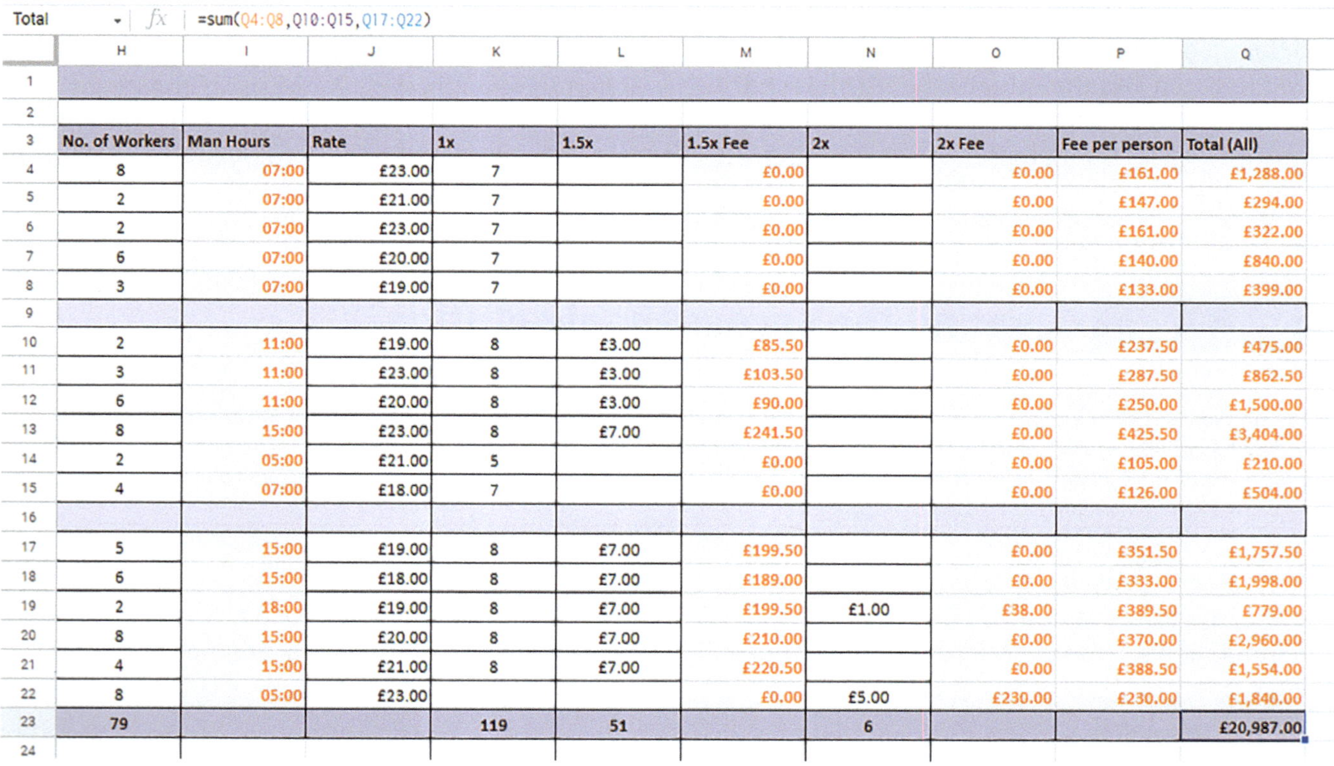

Total | =sum(Q4:Q8,Q10:Q15,Q17:Q22)

	H	I	J	K	L	M	N	O	P	Q
1										
2										
3	No. of Workers	Man Hours	Rate	1x	1.5x	1.5x Fee	2x	2x Fee	Fee per person	Total (All)
4	8	07:00	£23.00	7		£0.00		£0.00	£161.00	£1,288.00
5	2	07:00	£21.00	7		£0.00		£0.00	£147.00	£294.00
6	2	07:00	£23.00	7		£0.00		£0.00	£161.00	£322.00
7	6	07:00	£20.00	7		£0.00		£0.00	£140.00	£840.00
8	3	07:00	£19.00	7		£0.00		£0.00	£133.00	£399.00
9										
10	2	11:00	£19.00	8	£3.00	£85.50		£0.00	£237.50	£475.00
11	3	11:00	£23.00	8	£3.00	£103.50		£0.00	£287.50	£862.50
12	6	11:00	£20.00	8	£3.00	£90.00		£0.00	£250.00	£1,500.00
13	8	15:00	£23.00	8	£7.00	£241.50		£0.00	£425.50	£3,404.00
14	2	05:00	£21.00	5		£0.00		£0.00	£105.00	£210.00
15	4	07:00	£18.00	7		£0.00		£0.00	£126.00	£504.00
16										
17	5	15:00	£19.00	8	£7.00	£199.50		£0.00	£351.50	£1,757.50
18	6	15:00	£18.00	8	£7.00	£189.00		£0.00	£333.00	£1,998.00
19	2	18:00	£19.00	8	£7.00	£199.50	£1.00	£38.00	£389.50	£779.00
20	8	15:00	£20.00	8	£7.00	£210.00		£0.00	£370.00	£2,960.00
21	4	15:00	£21.00	8	£7.00	£220.50		£0.00	£388.50	£1,554.00
22	8	05:00	£23.00			£0.00	£5.00	£230.00	£230.00	£1,840.00
23	79			119	51		6			£20,987.00
24										

Figure 2.6 Naming a cell

than having to include all their cell references. In Figure 2.7, the cells in R4 to S10 are called 'StaffRates'.

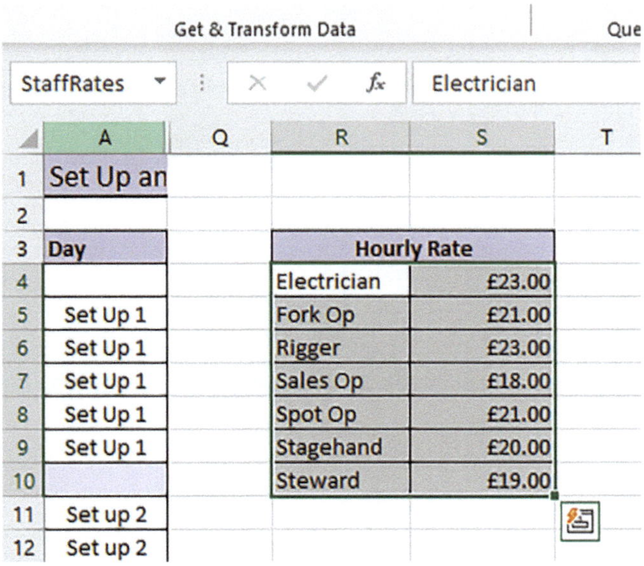

Figure 2.7 Naming a group of cells

Data types

Synoptic link

Look back at Unit R050, Topic area 3, section 3.2 for the details about the data types.

A range of data types can be used within a single worksheet to ensure that data is presented in a meaningful way so that there is no miscommunication of information. The data types selected would also depend upon what needs to happen to the data in the system: is it just being displayed or will it be used in a process?

For example, the price of an item could be displayed as text, which is meaningful to us as humans. However, displaying a price this way would not allow a calculation to be carried out on it – for example, multiplying by number sold to get the profit. Displaying the price as a numerical data type, ideally as Currency, would be both meaningful to us as humans and allow the figure to be used in a calculation.

Figures 2.8 and 2.9 show a range of data types applied to the worksheets.

Activity

Copy and complete this table to show how each data type could be used in the areas shown. (Use the internet to find examples.)

	Hotel website	Travel agent website
Boolean		
Currency		
Integer		
Text		
Alphanumeric		

Entering different data types

Different data types can be entered by using the keyboard and mouse. The data type that a cell displays depends upon the formatting that is applied to that cell. In Figure 2.9, the data entered in Column B for Start Time is entered as a number using a keyboard or keypad. The cell is formatted using the Time format option to display the number as part of a 24-hour clock.

Importing different data types

Data can be imported into a spreadsheet from different sources. Importing data can speed up data entry when creating a spreadsheet instead of having to enter all the data manually. How data is imported depends upon the software package being used and the version of the software package. As software is updated, the detail of the process may change or look different but the feature will still be there.

In Google Sheets there is an import wizard in the File section of the menu bar. By using this wizard, you can select the data source, including dragging and dropping the source file from your computer.

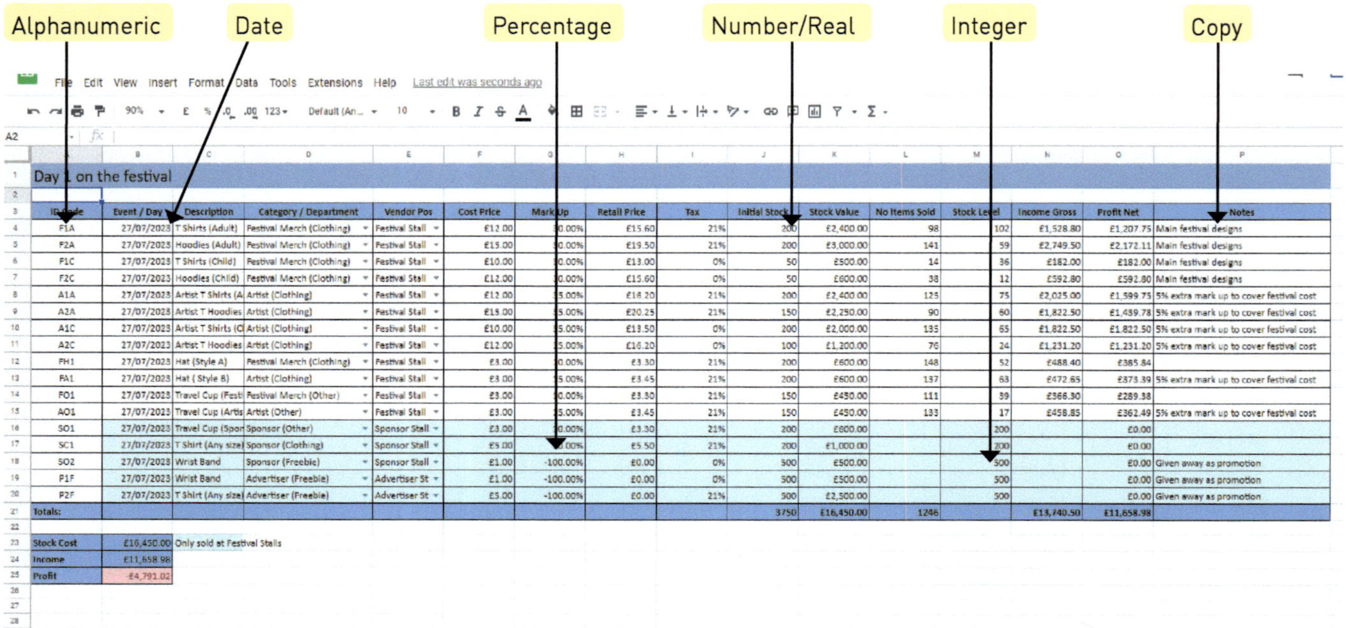

Figure 2.8 Different data types being used in a spreadsheet (Google Sheets view)

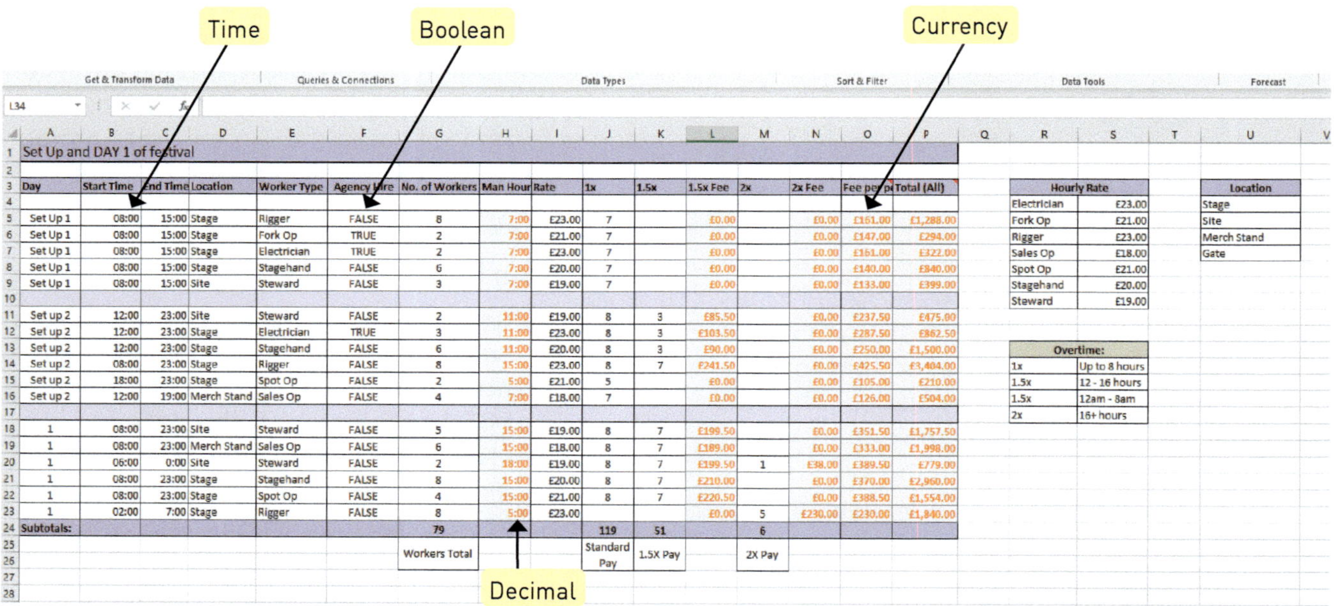

Figure 2.9 Different data types being used in a spreadsheet (Microsoft Excel view)

Figure 2.10 shows a **CSV file** being imported. The wizard then provides you with an option of selecting how the text in your file is separated. You can let the wizard select the most appropriate option for the file or if you know how the data is separated you can choose the option. This is shown in Figure 2.11.

Key term

CSV file A plain text file where the fields are separated by commas and the records are separated by carriage returns/enter key.

Figure 2.10 Importing data into Google Sheets (Google Sheets view)

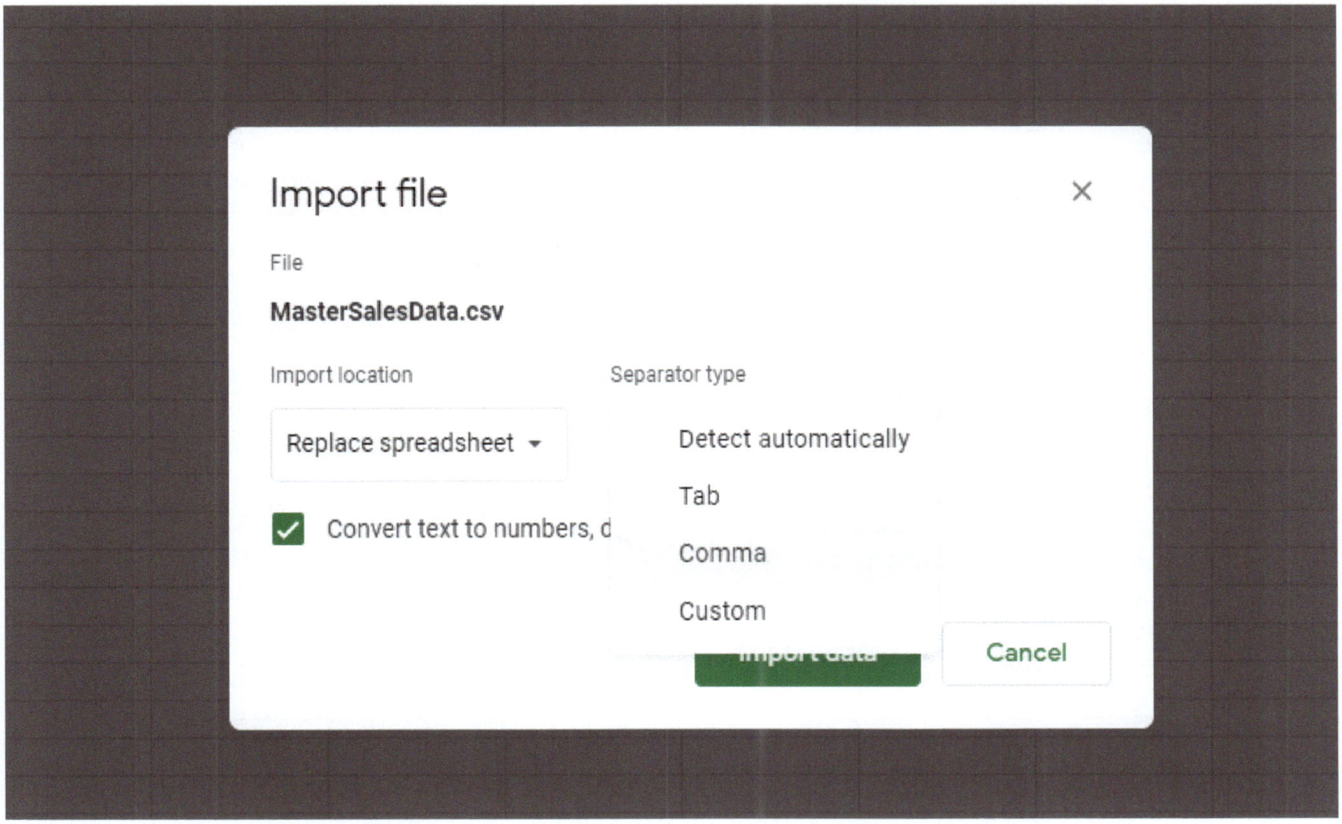

Figure 2.11 Selecting the Comma separator option on the wizard (Google Sheets view)

In Microsoft Excel, the Data option allows you to select the data source, in this case a CSV file.

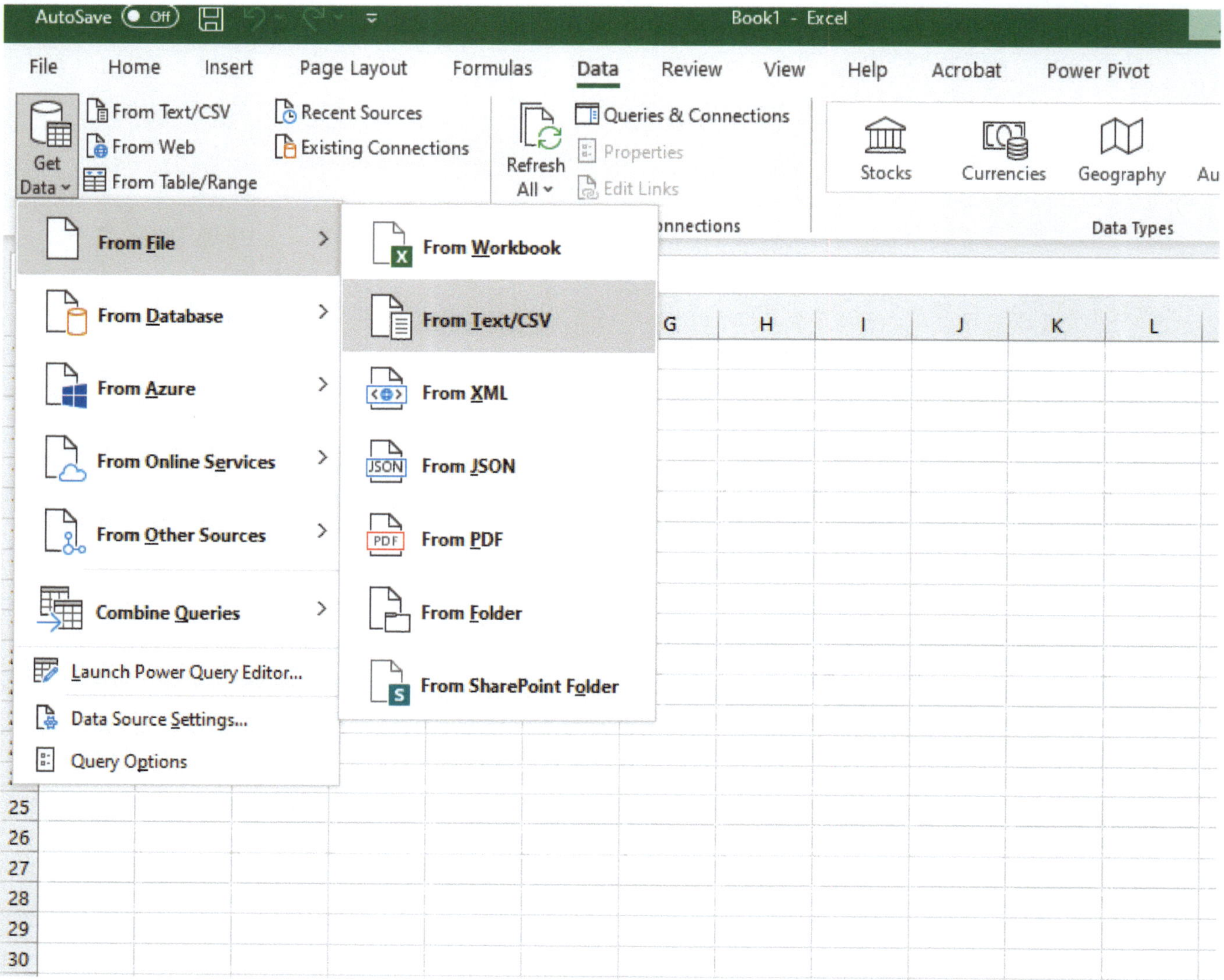

Figure 2.12 Selecting a data source to import (Microsoft Excel view)

Once the user has selected the file, some versions of Excel show you a preview of how it will look once imported. There are options available to change the import process and settings if you are not satisfied with it at this stage.

Key terms

Delimiter These are the separators between the values in text files. These can be commas, spaces or semi-colons.

Text file A plain text file used for importing into a spreadsheet. A text file uses tabs or spaces as delimiters for the fields. It uses carriage returns/enter key to separate the records.

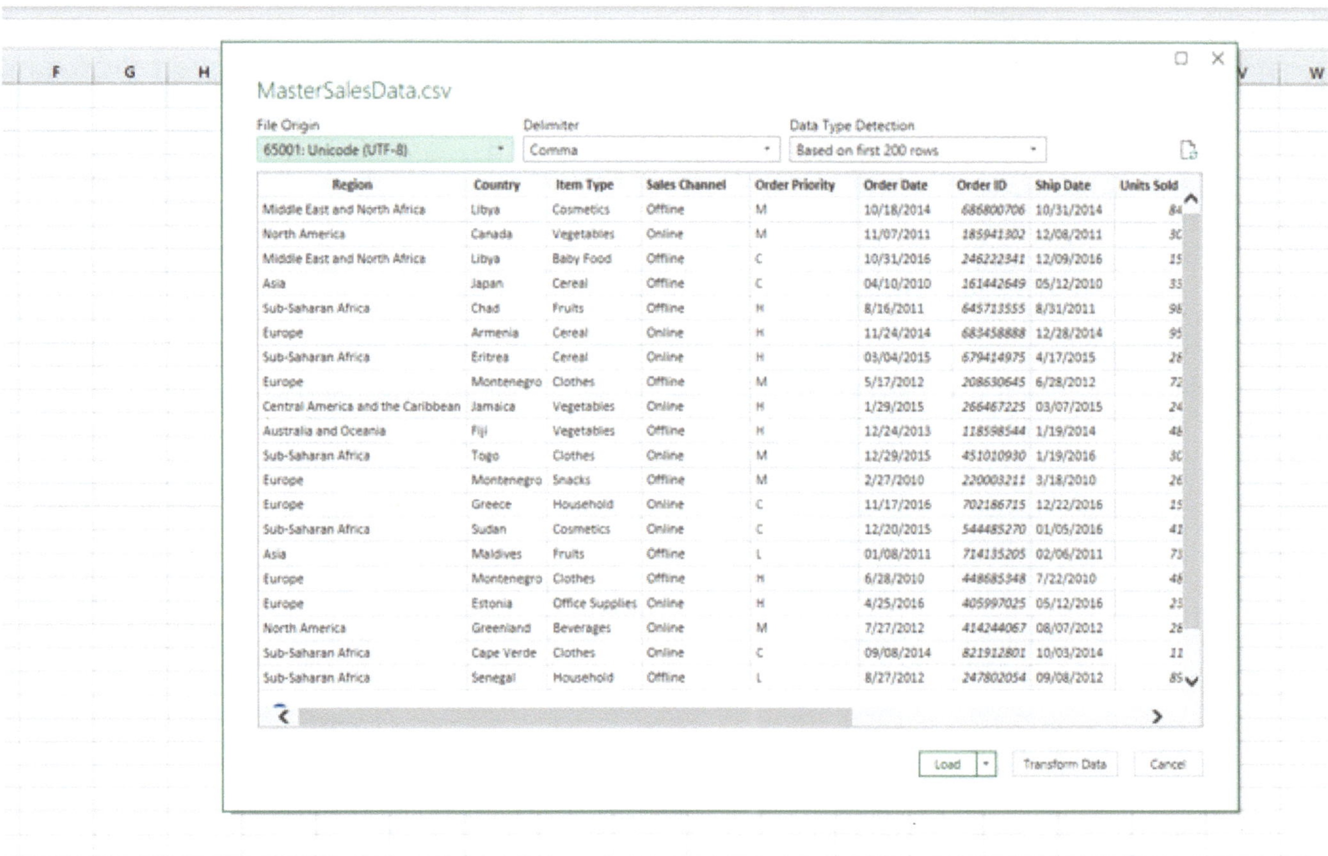

Figure 2.13 Preview of imported data (Microsoft Excel view)

Data validation

Synoptic link

You learnt about the different data validation tools in Unit R050, Topic area 3, section 3.2.

The system user will often be required to input some of the data into a spreadsheet solution, even when most of the data has been imported from an existing file. Ensuring that the data is input correctly is important, and there are various data validation tools that can be used to aid this. Table 2.5 shows a range of data validation techniques that can be used in a spreadsheet. Each technique works differently but they all help to reduce the number of data entry errors.

Activity

Create a worksheet that uses the data validation techniques listed to enter the following data.

Data entry	Validation technique
Make	List from Ford, Renault, Skoda
MOT due in next month	Radio button Yes, No
Fuel type	List from Unleaded, Diesel, Hybrid, Electric
Registration	Must be between four and seven characters

Cell formatting

The cells on a worksheet are, by default, borderless (the grey outline to a cell only appears on screen) and set to use the default text font size and colour set by the user's computer. This means that all worksheets look the same when the spreadsheet solution is developed.

Table 2.5 Examples of validation tools in spreadsheets

Lookup (method 1)	
Lookup data in an already populated list. In this example, the Vendor Pos column in the spreadsheet looks up the data from a list in cells F40 to F42. This is also an example of a Limited Choice drop-down list. (Microsoft Excel view)	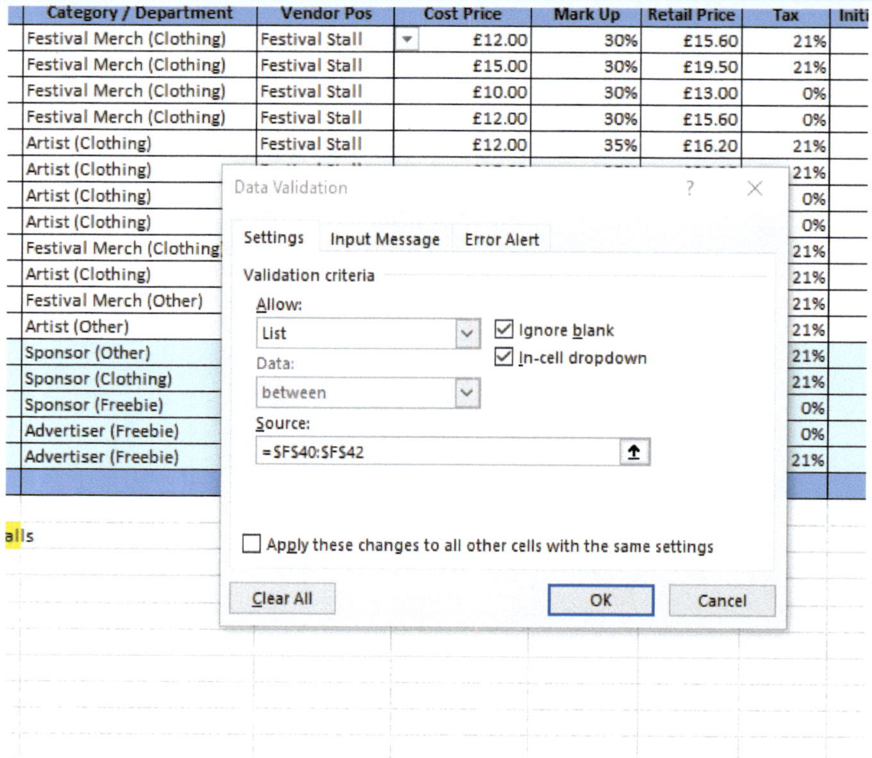
Lookup (method 2)	
Using a formula to insert data based on a provided value. Column I uses a VLOOKUP formula to input the rates. As long as the correct Worker Type is entered into Column E the rate of pay will automatically be entered into Column I. (Microsoft Excel view)	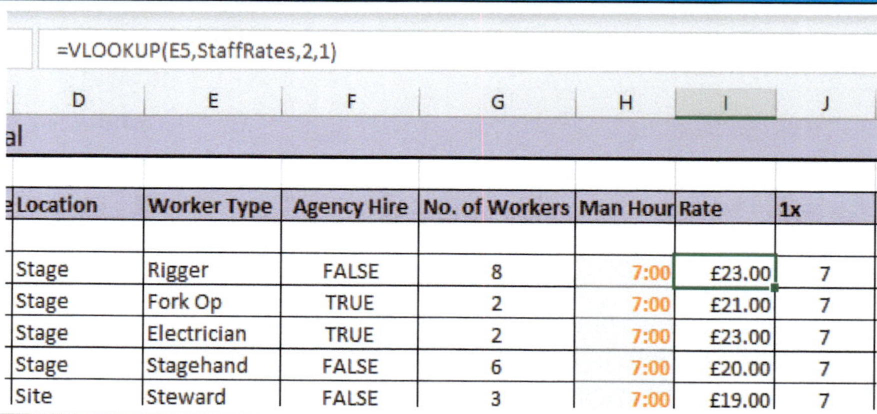

Range check

The hours worked in Column J can only be set between 0 and 8 (hours).

If 8.5 hours were entered a warning would appear.

(Google Sheets view)

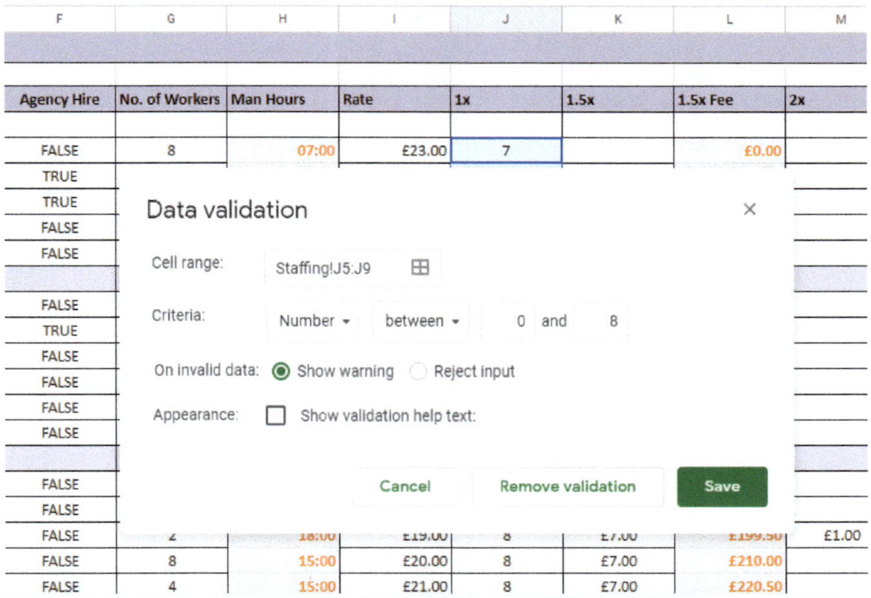

Text length

The data entered in Column A must be a 3-character code.

(Microsoft Excel view)

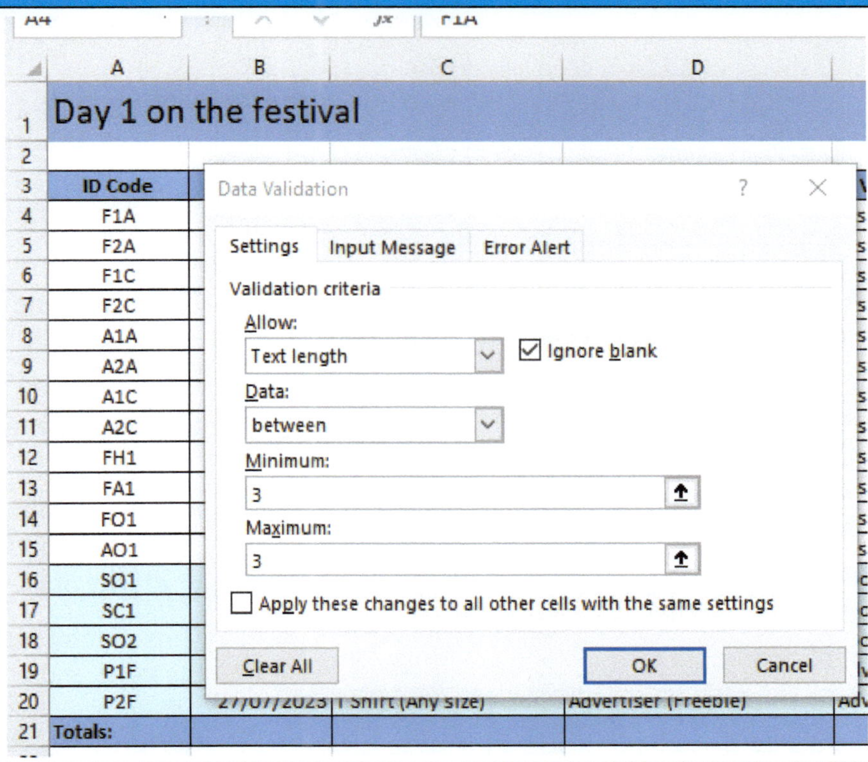

Limited choice

The data entry in column G ('Booked') is limited using a Tick box list.

This is also an example of the Boolean data type (True or False).

(Google Sheets view)

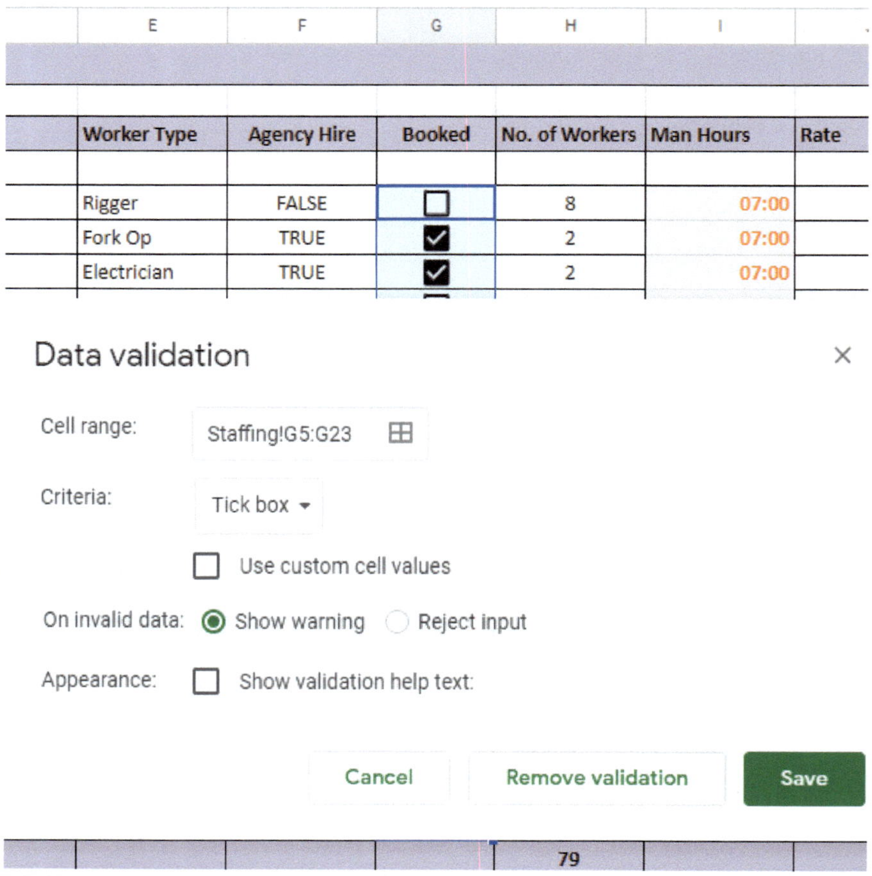

The cells and the content they contain can all be formatted so that the worksheets are easier to look at rather than large white pages of numbers. There are many options that can be applied to the cells. The images in this section of the book show the use of:

- borders
- cell colours
- data type format
- font alignment
- font colours
- font size
- text wrapping.

The formatting used in each cell, worksheet and workbook will need to be considered based on factors such as:

- who is the target audience of the spreadsheet solution?
- what device will they be using to access the spreadsheet on?
- clarity of viewing.

These factors all need to be considered to make the cells and spreadsheet fit for purpose.

Conditional formatting

Some cells can be formatted so that how they appear changes based on the data that they contain.

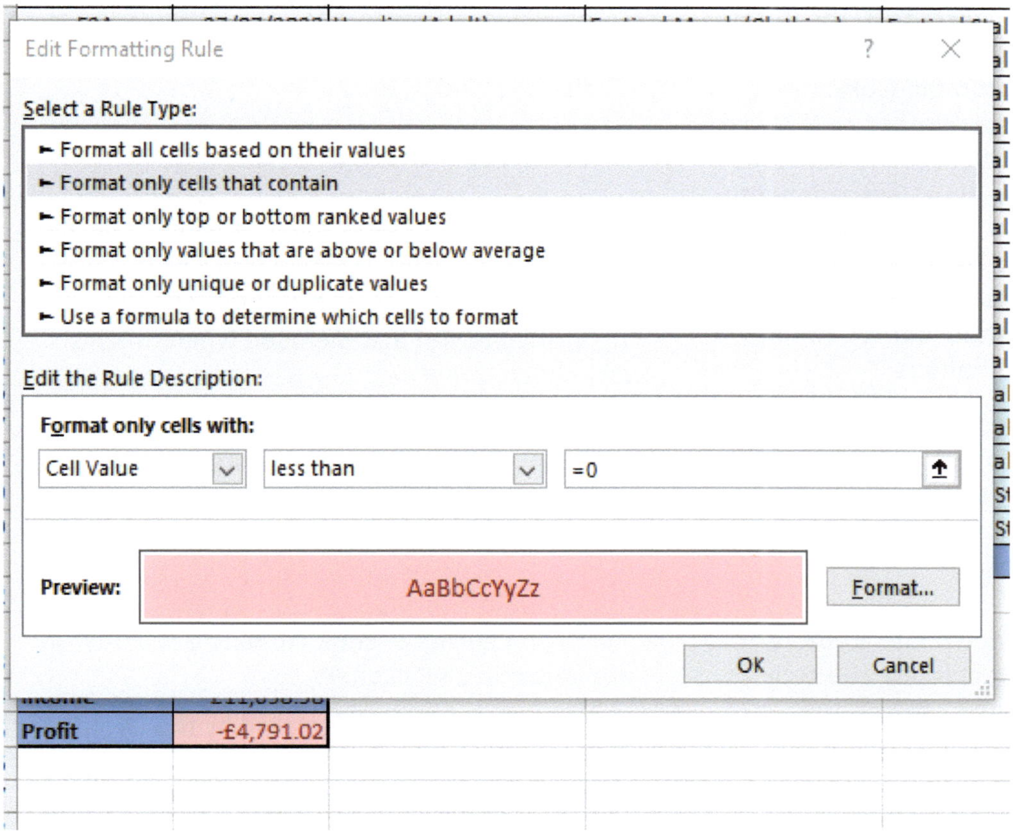

Figure 2.14 Conditional formatting (Microsoft Excel view)

In Figure 2.14 the cell displaying the profit figure is formatted so that if the number displayed is 0 or below the cell will have a light red background with red text. This shows easily to the user that there is not enough money being made and that the business is running at a loss.

Cell references

Spreadsheets are made up of cells, with each cell being given an address in the form of a letter and number. This is called the cell reference. The very first cell in a spreadsheet has the cell reference A1. All other cells take their reference off this starting point; that is, A2, A3, B1, CC1, HZ1600.

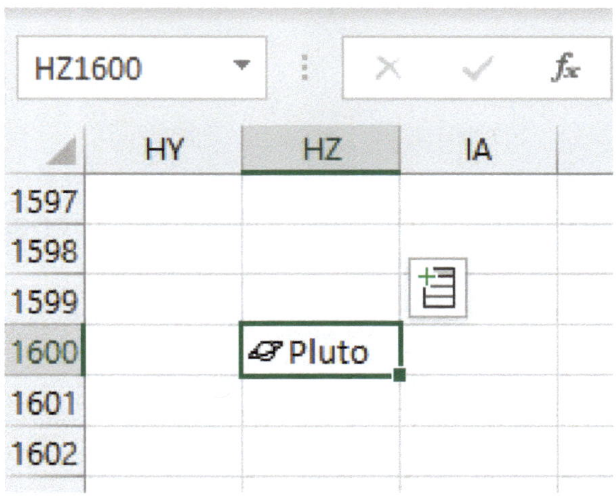

Figure 2.15 Cell reference HZ1600 contains the word Pluto (Google Sheets view)

The cell reference has two parts to it, the letter indicating the **column** on the worksheet and the number indicating the **row** on the worksheet. The value in a cell such as a number or text can change, however the cell reference is constant and does not change. This allows spreadsheets to be developed that carry out processes such as calculations or lookups, based on a cell containing the data, not the actual data itself. This means that a spreadsheet can be used repeatedly when the data changes.

Cell references can be used in a **formula**, a **function** or as reference point for a link within a spreadsheet workbook. The cell reference can be referred to either relatively or absolutely.

Relative references

When you copy a formula down into a different row or across to a different column, the cell references used will change based on the position of the new cell relative to the data.

Figure 2.16 shows how the formula used in Column M always references the data in the cells in Columns J and L on the same row. The formula in M4 subtracts the data in L4 from J4. Then as the formula is copied down Column M, the row references change so that when the formula is in Row 12 the formula uses the data in cells L12 and J12.

Absolute references

Sometimes a formula or cell will need to refer to a specific cell regardless of where the formula is being used. This uses an absolute cell reference – the cell reference stays absolutely the same. This principle can also be used when linking worksheets together.

To create an absolute cell reference the $ sign is placed inside the cell reference. (See the Lookup (method 1) example in Table 2.5.)

Key terms

Column A series of cells running vertically/up and down in a worksheet.

Formula A calculation created by the user that uses cell references and operators.

Function A tool or calculation that is pre-built into the spreadsheet application.

Row A series of cells running horizontally/ across in a worksheet.

J	K	L	M	N
Initial Stock	Stock Value	No Items Sold	Stock Level	Income Gross
200	=F4*J4	98	=J4-L4	=L4*H4
200	=F5*J5	141	=J5-L5	=L5*H5
50	=F6*J6	14	=J6-L6	=L6*H6
50	=F7*J7	38	=J7-L7	=L7*H7
200	=F8*J8	125	=J8-L8	=L8*H8
150	=F9*J9	90	=J9-L9	=L9*H9
200	=F10*J10	135	=J10-L10	=L10*H10
100	=F11*J11	76	=J11-L11	=L11*H11
200	=F12*J12	148	=J12-L12	=L12*H12

Figure 2.16 Relative cell references in Columns K, M and N (Microsoft Excel view)

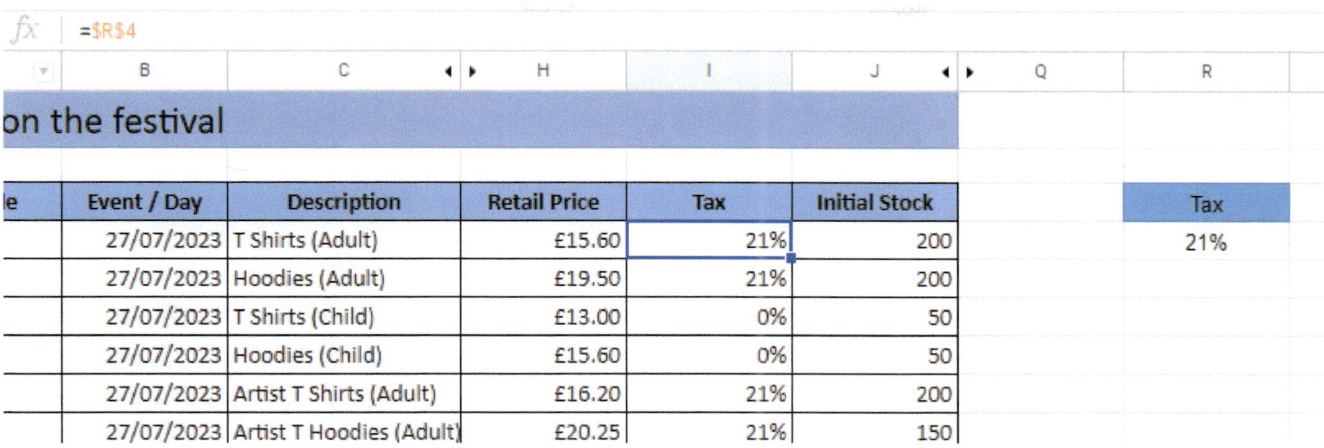

Figure 2.17 Absolute cell references in Column I (Google Sheets view)

The example in Figure 2.17 shows that cells in Column I use the **value** in cell R4 where tax is charged. If the tax level changes, the only cell that needs to be edited is R4, as whatever is entered here will appear in all the relevant cells in column I.

The formula bar at the top (*fx*) contains the formula =$R$4. The $R value forces the cell to look only in Column R and the $4 value forces the cell to look only in Row 4.

Named references

A group of cells can be used or referenced in a formula. In the VLOOKUP example for data validation earlier in this section (Table 2.5), the group of cells called StaffRate is referenced using absolute cell referencing.

Multi-sheet referencing

Cells can also be referenced across a different worksheet. It is less confusing when you do this if you have named the worksheets appropriately.

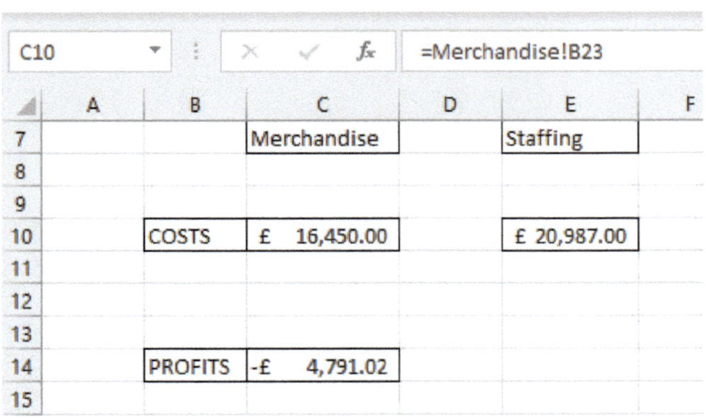

Figure 2.18 Multi-sheet referencing (Microsoft Excel view)

In Figure 2.18, the data displayed in C10 is pulled from the cell B23 in the Merchandise worksheet.

Formulae

Formulae are used to create calculations in a spreadsheet solution. In Figure 2.16, formulae have been created to multiply and subtract figures.

Table 2.6 Useful formulae

Operator symbol	Use	Example
+	Addition	=C3+D3
-	Subtraction	=D2-S2
/	Division	=A3/3 or =A3/D1
*	Multiplication	=A1*2 or =A2*C2
=	Equals	Tells the software to calculate everything after it.

Parentheses ( ) are used in formulae and functions to group together parts of the calculation that need to be done before other parts. This follows the same **BODMAS** principle you have probably used in your Maths lessons since primary school.

Key terms

BODMAS An acronym to remember the order in which calculations are carried out (**B**rackets, **O**rders, **D**ivision, **M**ultiplication, **A**ddition, **S**ubtraction).

Value A specific piece of data contained in a cell.

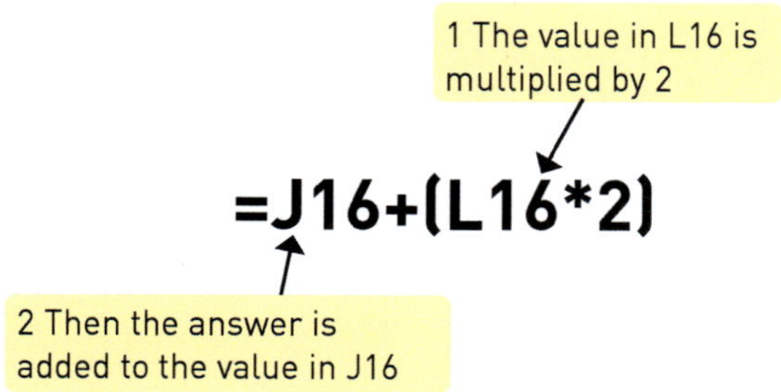

Figure 2.19 Example of parenthesis use in a spreadsheet

Relational operators

Some spreadsheet solutions will require that comparisons are carried out – for example, is the data in cell A3 more than the data in A4? To do this, a relational operator can be used.

Table 2.7 Relational operator symbols

Operator symbol	Use	Example
=	Are values equal?	=A2=B5
>	Is one value greater than the other?	=A5>B7
<	Is one value less than the other?	=D5<G5
=>	Is the value equal to or greater than?	=F4=>H5
<=	Is the value equal to or smaller than?	=G2<=F5
<>	Is the value not equal to?	=G3<>H6

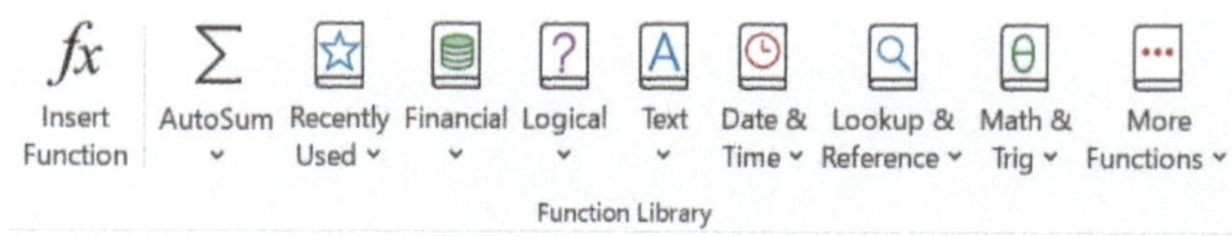

Figure 2.20 Function bar (Microsoft Excel view)

Functions

Spreadsheet software uses functions, readymade calculations that can be used to speed up the creation of a spreadsheet solution. These functions fall into groups which some software programs group together to make it easier for the user.

Arithmetic functions

SUM

This adds together all the numerical values in a cell **range** and displays the answer.

Key term

Range A group of cells containing data used in a formula or function. First and last cells in the range are separated using a colon ':' (B22:B32).

Activity

Create a worksheet using the following data and headings.

Item	Stock Level	Price (Cost)	Stock Value	Items Sold	Price (Retail)	Income	Profit
Coats	200	30		100	44.99		
Shirts	300	20		169	25.00		
Shoes	400	24		285	31.00		
Trousers	200	15		88	22.50		
						Total Profit	

- Format the cells to display the data in an appropriate format.
- Write the formulae in correct cells to complete the table's calculations.
- Save this worksheet with a meaningful name. (You will add to the worksheet later.)

MIN

This displays the smallest numeric value in a range of cells.

MAX

This displays the largest numerical value in a range of cells.

AVERAGE

This displays the arithmetic mean (average) for a range of cells. It adds all the values together and divides it by the number of values counted.

Stock Value	No Items Sold
£2,400.00	98
£3,000.00	141
£500.00	14
£600.00	38
£2,400.00	125
£2,250.00	90
£2,000.00	135
£1,200.00	76
£600.00	148
£600.00	137
£450.00	111
£450.00	133
£600.00	
£1,000.00	
£500.00	
£500.00	
£2,500.00	
£16,450.00	1246

No sold	=sum(L4:L15)
Min sold	=min(L4:L15)
Max sold	=max(L4:L15)
Average sold	=average(L4:L15

Figure 2.21 Arithmetic functions for Column L shown in the bottom four rows (Google Sheets view)

SUBTOTAL

This function allows calculations to be carried out on a small sub-set of data in a spreadsheet. The function makes use of a table of other pre-defined functions in the form of a list. The range of data does not need to be in one block.

Number in list	Function
1	AVERAGE
2	COUNT
3	COUNTA
4	MAX
5	MIN
6	PRODUCT
7	STDEV
8	STDEVP
9	SUM
10	VAR
11	VARP

This example AVERAGES all the values in the cell range B2 to XX2:

=SUBTOTAL(1,B2:XX2)

This example will find the smallest (MIN) value in the cell range B2, G2, F3 to J3 and H7:

=SUBTOTAL(5,B2,G2,F3:J3,H7)

This example totals (SUM) all the values in the cell range B2 to XX2:

=SUBTOTAL(9,B2:XX2)

Figure 2.22 SUBTOTAL examples

SUMIF

This is similar to COUNTIF (see below) but only works on numbers by adding up (SUM) all the values in the range that meet the criteria specified.

In Figure 2.23, if the user typed in

```
=SUMIF(I4:I24,">20")
```

at the bottom of the Rate column, the function would add together all the cells that contain values

Set Up and DAY 1 of festival

	Day	Start Time	End Time	Location	Worker Type	Agency Hire	No. of Workers	Man Hour	Rate	1x	1.5x	1.5x Fee	2x	2x Fee	Fee per p	Total (All)
4																
5	Set Up 1	08:00	15:00	Stage	Rigger	FALSE	8	7:00	£23.00	7		£0.00		£0.00	£161.00	£1,288.00
6	Set Up 1	08:00	15:00	Stage	Fork Op	TRUE	2	7:00	£21.00	7		£0.00		£0.00	£147.00	£294.00
7	Set Up 1	08:00	15:00	Stage	Electrician	TRUE	2	7:00	£23.00	7		£0.00		£0.00	£161.00	£322.00
8	Set Up 1	08:00	15:00	Stage	Stagehand	FALSE	6	7:00	£20.00	7		£0.00		£0.00	£140.00	£840.00
9	Set Up 1	08:00	15:00	Site	Steward	FALSE	3	7:00	£19.00	7		£0.00		£0.00	£133.00	£399.00
10																
11	Set up 2	12:00	23:00	Site	Steward	FALSE	2	11:00	£19.00	8	3	£85.50		£0.00	£237.50	£475.00
12	Set up 2	12:00	23:00	Stage	Electrician	TRUE	3	11:00	£23.00	8	3	£103.50		£0.00	£287.50	£862.50
13	Set up 2	12:00	23:00	Stage	Stagehand	FALSE	6	11:00	£20.00	8	3	£90.00		£0.00	£250.00	£1,500.00
14	Set up 2	08:00	23:00	Stage	Rigger	FALSE	8	15:00	£23.00	8	7	£241.50		£0.00	£425.50	£3,404.00
15	Set up 2	18:00	23:00	Stage	Spot Op	FALSE	2	5:00	£21.00	5		£0.00		£0.00	£105.00	£210.00
16	Set up 2	12:00	19:00	Merch Stand	Sales Op	FALSE	4	7:00	£18.00	7		£0.00		£0.00	£126.00	£504.00
17																
18	1	08:00	23:00	Site	Steward	FALSE	5	15:00	£19.00	8	7	£199.50		£0.00	£351.50	£1,757.50
19	1	08:00	23:00	Merch Stand	Sales Op	FALSE	6	15:00	£18.00	8	7	£189.00		£0.00	£333.00	£1,998.00
20	1	06:00	0:00	Site	Steward	FALSE	2	18:00	£19.00	8	7	£199.50	1	£38.00	£389.50	£779.00
21	1	08:00	23:00	Stage	Stagehand	FALSE	8	15:00	£20.00	8	7	£210.00		£0.00	£370.00	£2,960.00
22	1	08:00	23:00	Stage	Spot Op	FALSE	4	15:00	£21.00	8	7	£220.50		£0.00	£388.50	£1,554.00
23	1	02:00	7:00	Stage	Rigger	FALSE	8	5:00	£23.00			£0.00	5	£230.00	£230.00	£1,840.00
24	Subtotals:						79			119	51		6			
25							Workers Total			Standard Pay	1.5X Pay		2X Pay			

Hourly Rate	
Electrician	£23.00
Fork Op	£21.00
Rigger	£23.00
Sales Op	£18.00
Spot Op	£21.00
Stagehand	£20.00
Steward	£19.00

Overtime:	
1x	Up to 8 hours
1.5x	12 - 16 hours
1.5x	12am - 8am
2x	16+ hours

Location
Stage
Site
Merch Stand
Gate

Figure 2.23 Column J use of SUMIF in J24

greater than 20. In this example, it would be all the cells containing £21.00 and £23.00.

Counting functions

COUNT

This counts the number of cells in a range that contain a numerical value. If a cell is blank or contains text, it ignores the cell. It does not add the values together, it only counts how many cells in the range contain a numerical value.

This is a really useful function for checking that data has been entered. The data in a column or row can be counted and if the total is not the same as the number of rows/columns used, then there is a data entry error: something is missing.

COUNTIF

This counts the number of cells that contain a specified value. This value can be a number or word.

```
=COUNTIF(range, value)
```

In Figure 2.23 if the user typed

```
=COUNTIF(F5:F24,"true")
```

at the bottom of the Agency Hire column, the function would count all the cells where 'True' appeared. In this case, three.

Logical functions

IF

The IF function is used to make a decision or choice based on a test. The test can be as simple as checking if a cell contains a value or is empty. The IF function can also be used to trigger an answer based on the criteria used.

1 If the value in D6 is greater than 60

=IF(D6>60,"Pass","Fail")

2 Display 'Pass' in the cell; if 60 or less, display 'Fail'

Figure 2.24 Structure of an IF statement

AND

This function allows for a comparison of values to be used to output a value. In this function all of the comparisons must be correct for a 'true' value to be displayed as the answer.

In Figure 2.25, the stock order is completed, so nothing else needs to happen on the system once it has been ordered, paid for and shipped.

OR

This function allows for comparison of values where only one of the values compared has to be 'True'.

For the status of an order in Column J to be 'Completed' all three columns G, H and I must meet the criteria in the formula.

If any of them are not met, the order is still 'Pending'.

Only the second order down has all the criteria met and has a completed status.

=IF(AND(G6="Ordered",H6="Paid",I6="Shipped"),"Completed","Pending")

	G	H	I	J
'alue	Ordered from Supplier	Supplier Paid	Stock Arrived	Status
£2,400.00	Ordered	Unpaid	Shipped	Pending
£3,000.00	Ordered	Paid	Shipped	Completed
£500.00	Ordered	Unpaid	Shipped	Pending
£600.00	No	Unpaid	Open	Pending

Figure 2.25 AND function combined with an IF function (Microsoft Excel view)

For the status of an order in Column I to be 'Shipped' only one or both of Columns G and H must be 'True'.

To be correct Column G must = 'Ordered'

To be correct Column H must = 'Paid'

The top three rows all have one or both of these criteria met.

```
=if(OR(G6="Ordered",H6="Paid"),"Shipped","Open")
```

G	H	I	J
dered from Supp	Supplier Paid	Stock Arrived	Status
Ordered	Unpaid	Shipped	Pending
Ordered	Paid	Shipped	Completed
Ordered	Unpaid	Shipped	Pending
No	Unpaid	Open	Pending

Figure 2.26 OR function with an if function (Google Sheets view)

With all of these logical functions a spreadsheet can be created that will provide answers such as a grade or order status with minimal user input. This reduces the workload of the user and reduces the chances of errors occurring in the data.

Lookup and reference functions

LOOKUP

This function finds the value required in the first column and displays the value next to it in the same row. It does not need to be in the next column, you can tell the software which column to look in.

```
=lookup("Hat (StyleA)",C4:C20,D4:D20)
```

C	D
Description	Category / Department
T Shirts (Adult)	Festival Merch (Clothing)
Hoodies (Adult)	Festival Merch (Clothing)
T Shirts (Child)	Festival Merch (Clothing)
Hoodies (Child)	Festival Merch (Clothing)
Artist T Shirts (Adult)	Artist (Clothing)
Artist T Hoodies (Adult)	Artist (Clothing)
Artist T Shirts (Child)	Artist (Clothing)
Artist T Hoodies (Child)	Artist (Clothing)
Hat (Style A)	Festival Merch (Clothing)
Hat (Style B)	Artist (Clothing)
Travel Cup (Festival)	Festival Merch (Other)
Travel Cup (Artist)	Artist (Other)
Travel Cup (Sponsor)	Sponsor (Other)
T Shirt (Any size)	Sponsor (Clothing)
Wrist Band	Sponsor (Freebie)
Wrist Band	Advertiser (Freebie)
T Shirt (Any size)	Advertiser (Freebie)

Artist (Clothing)

Figure 2.27 LOOKUP function (Google Sheets view)

In Figure 2.27 the value 'Hat (Style A)' is looked up in Column C and the value in Column D is then displayed showing which category/department it is.

VLOOKUP

This function looks for the required value in a column and returns the value next to it from a specified column.

Activity

In an earlier activity, you created and competed the following table in a worksheet.

Item	Stock Level	Price (Cost)	Stock Value	Items Sold	Price (Retail)	Income	Profit
Coats	200	30		100	44.99		
Shirts	300	20		169	25.00		
Shoes	400	24		285	31.00		
Trousers	200	15		88	22.50		
						Total Profit	

Using extra columns on the worksheet add in the headings, data and functions from Columns G, H, I and J in Figures 2.25 and 2.26 for each of the items of stock.

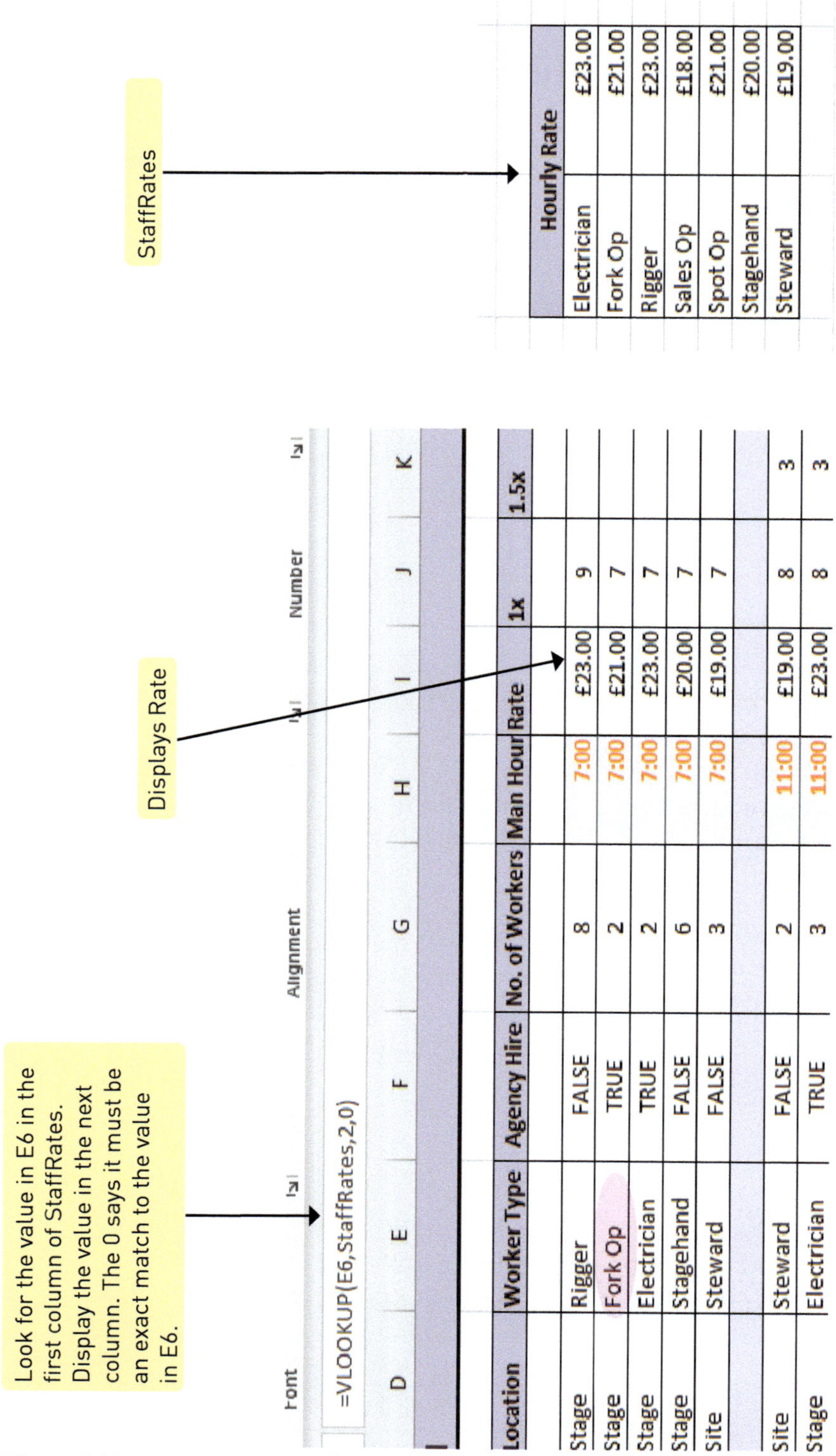

Figure 2.28 VLOOKUP function (Microsoft Excel view)

In Figure 2.28, the VLOOKUP looks for the value required in a name range of cells called 'StaffRates'. When copying this to other cells in the column, the name cell range will be correct in each row. It is less complicated to create than using absolute cell references.

The values in the cells searched must be in alphabetical order. In 'StaffRates' the first worker type is Electrician and the last is Steward.

HLOOKUP

This function does the same as the VLOOKUP, but the data being referenced would be in a horizontal table.

Look for the value in E6 in the first row of the cell range $S$21 to $Y$22. Display the value in the row column. The 0 says it must be an exact match the value in E6.

=HLOOKUP(E6,$S$21:$Y$22,2,0)

F	G	H	I	J	K
Agency Hire	Booked	No. of Workers	Man Hours	Rate	1x
FALSE	☐	8	07:00	£23.00	7
TRUE	☑	2	07:00	£21.00	7
TRUE	☑	2	07:00	£23.00	7
FALSE	☐	6	07:00	£20.00	7

Horizontal data

Hourly Rates						
Electrician	Fork Op	Rigger	Sales Op	Spot Op	Stagehand	Steward
£23.00	£21.00	£23.00	£18.00	£21.00	£20.00	£19.00

Figure 2.29 HLOOKUP function (Google Sheets view)

This is a formula that speeds up entering a series of values that depend upon on a criterion. If the criteria changes, such as change of worker in the example, then the rates paid will automatically update with no user input.

These LOOKUP functions save a user looking row by row through the data to find the values required and updating the data by hand. In Figures 2.28 and 2.29, if the hourly rates for all the workers is increased by £2.00 a user will only need to change the values in the 'StaffRates' and "$S$21:$Y$22" cells. The data in the spreadsheet will update automatically. If the spreadsheet solution contains thousands of rows and columns of data, for example a spreadsheet of Amazon's products and prices, consider how quickly the system can be updated using these functions.

> **Activity**
>
> In pairs create a step-by-step user guide explaining how to use the different LOOKUP functions.

DATE and TIME functions

Including dates and times in a spreadsheet are useful for several reasons.

DATE

This function constructs a date using cell references.

=DATE(Year,Month,Day)

=DATE(B2,C2,D2)

B	C	D	E
Year	Month	Day	Combined
2021	12	22	22/12/2021

Figure 2.30 DATE function (Google Sheets view)

The data has to be entered in the order year, month and finally day, before the function outputs it in the correct date format.

TIME

This function constructs time using cell references.

```
=TIME(Hour,Minute,Second)
```

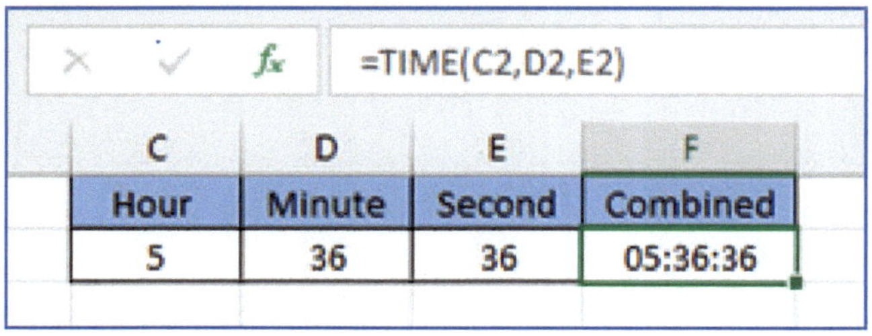

Figure 2.31 TIME function (Microsoft Excel view)

There are other DATE and TIME functions that can be useful in a spreadsheet.

Table 2.8 Useful DATE and TIME functions

=NOW()	Displays the current data and time
=NOW()+7	Displays the date and time seven days in the future
=NOW()-3	Displays the date and time three days ago
=TODAY()	Displays today's date
=TODAY()-7	Displays the date seven days a go
=TODAY()+14	Displays the date in 14 days' time
=EDATE(TODAY(),12)	Displays the date one year from today
=EDATE(TODAY(),-24)	Displays the date two years ago

Solving formula errors

Using formulae and functions in a spreadsheet is not always straightforward, and errors can appear. These errors appear as codes in cells of the spreadsheet.

When a user is entering the data, seeing an error appear in a cell can be quite stressful, especially if the user does not know what it means.

The IFERROR() function can help with this. When setting up a spreadsheet solution, the developer can use the IFERROR() function to display a help message to guide the user through the steps to fix the error.

```
=IFERROR(S12*T12,"You have not
entered a number in the cells needed.
Please check.")
```

Sorting

Synoptic link

You learnt about the importance of sorting in Topic area 1, section 1.2 of this unit.

The data contained in a worksheet can be sorted into ascending or descending order using any of the columns within the data. How this is done is software application specific.

In Microsoft Excel, the quickest way is to click in the column that you want to sort and then go to the Data menu and click on the A-Z or Z-A icons.

- A-Z: sorts the data into alphabetical order, or lowest to highest if the column contains numbers.
- Z-A: sorts the data into reverse alphabetical order, or highest to lowest if the column contains numbers.

You can also use the Sort option in the Data menu. This provides options to sort the data more specifically.

The data can also be sorted by more than one set of values.

Table 2.9 Troubleshooting formulae and functions

Error	Explanation	Solution
#DIV/0	One of the cells included in the division operation contains a 0 or is empty.	Review the cells in the formula and check the values in them. Update the values where needed.
#NAME?	Name is not recognised. Range of cells may have been named originally but has now been deleted. The name of the range does not have "" around it in the formula.	Update the name for a new range of cells. Check that the formula has been entered correctly.
#NULL!	Cell range has been typed incorrectly. =SUM (D8 D10)	Update the cell reference used in the formula: =SUM(D8:D10)
#REF!	Invalid cell reference. The cell looked for in the formula no longer exists/has been deleted.	Update the cell reference being looked at.
#VALUE!	Wrong argument is used. Incorrect operator or function called.	Check that there is no text in any cell being used for a mathematical calculation.

In Figure 2.34, the data in the spreadsheet will be sorted first by the final Profit Net column and then the Cost Price. This will place the data for the whole sheet in order of the largest Profit Net at the top and the lowest at the bottom. If there are any products making the same profit, they will be ordered by the Cost Price, the one that costs the most above the one that costs the least. The result of this sort is shown in Figure 2.35.

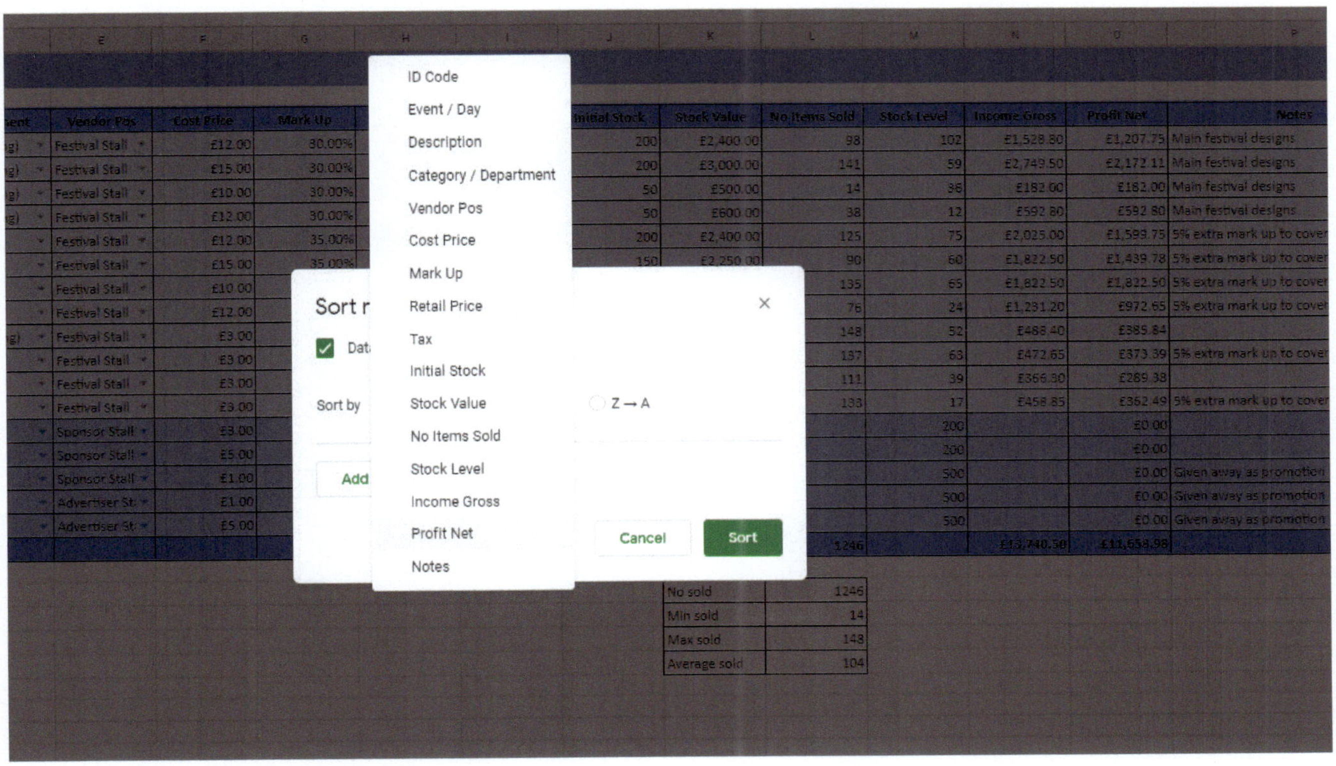

Figure 2.32 Sorting options (Google Sheets view)

Tax	Initial Stock	Stock Value	No Items Sold	Stock Level	Income Gross	Profit Net	Notes
21%	150	£450.00	111	39	£366.30	£289.38	
21%	150	£450.00	133	17	£458.85	£362.49	5% extra mark up to cover festival cost
0%	50	£500.00	14	36	£182.00	£182.00	Main festival designs
0%	500	£500.00		500		£0.00	Given away as promotion
0%	500	£500.00		500		£0.00	Given away as promotion
0%	50	£600.00	38	12	£592.80	£592.80	Main festival designs
21%	200	£600.00	148	52	£488.40	£385.84	
21%	200	£600.00	137	63	£472.65	£373.39	5% extra mark up to cover festival cost
21%	200	£600.00		200		£0.00	
21%	200	£1,000.00		200		£0.00	
21%	100	£1,200.00	76	24	£1,231.20	£972.65	5% extra mark up to cover festival cost
0%	200	£2,000.00	135	65	£1,822.50	£1,822.50	5% extra mark up to cover festival cost
21%	150	£2,250.00	90	60	£1,822.50	£1,439.78	5% extra mark up to cover festival cost
21%	200	£2,400.00	98	102	£1,528.80	£1,207.75	Main festival designs
21%	200	£2,400.00	125	75	£2,025.00	£1,599.75	5% extra mark up to cover festival cost
21%	500	£2,500.00		500		£0.00	Given away as promotion
21%	200	£3,000.00	141	59	£2,749.50	£2,172.11	Main festival designs
	3750	£16,450.00	1246		£13,740.50	£11,658.98	

Figure 2.33 Result of sort (Google Sheets view)

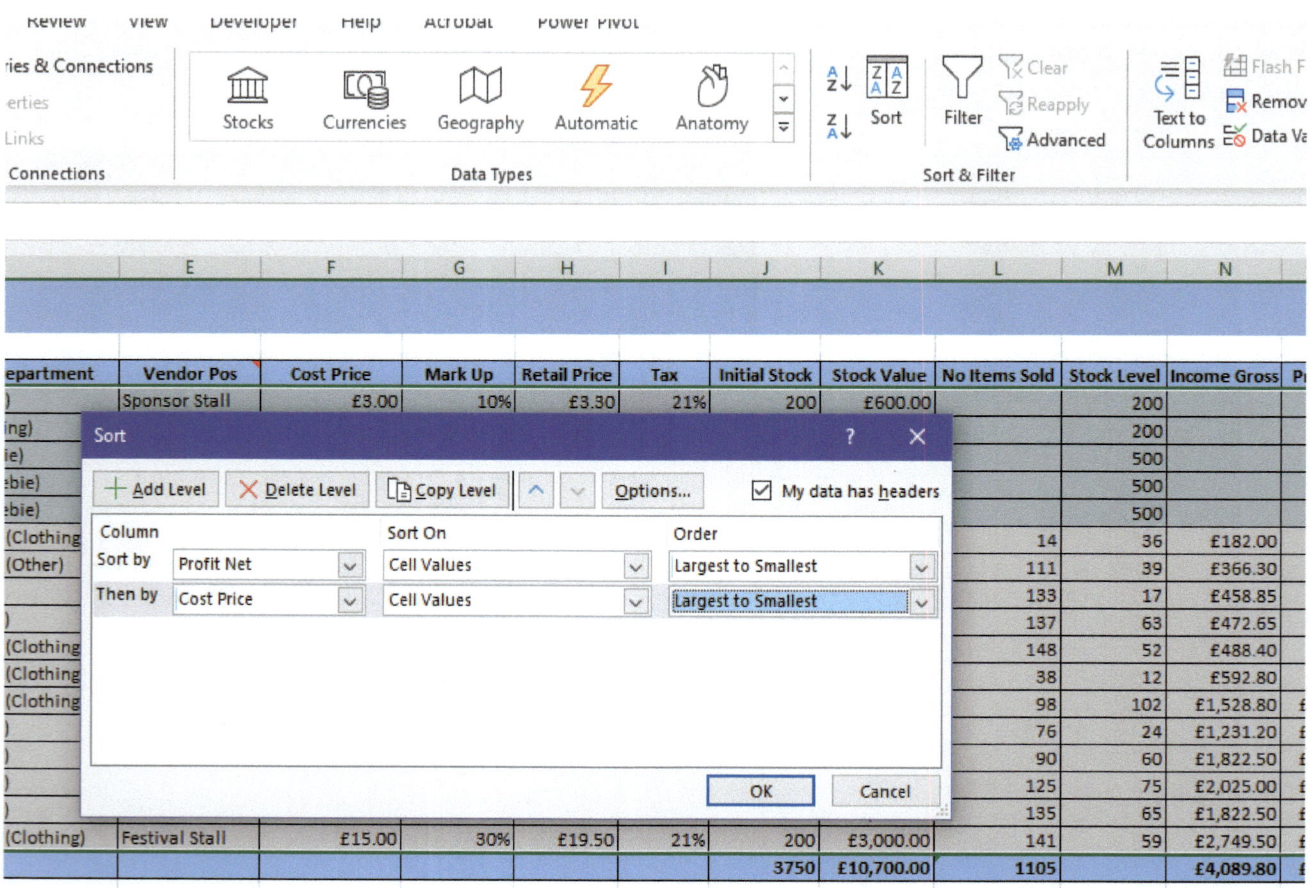

Figure 2.34 Sorting using multiple columns (Microsoft Excel view)

The box at the top right of the pop out has been ticked, stating that the highlighted data has headers – titles to the columns which will not be included in the sort.

E	F	G	H	I	J	K	L	M	N	O	
Vendor Pos	Cost Price	Mark Up	Retail Price	Tax	Initial Stock	Stock Value	No Items Sold	Stock Level	Income Gross	Profit Net	
stival Stall	£15.00	30%	£19.50	21%	200	£3,000.00	141	59	£2,749.50	£2,172.11	M
stival Stall	£10.00	35%	£13.50	0%	200	£2,000.00	135	65	£1,822.50	£1,822.50	5
stival Stall	£12.00	35%	£16.20	21%	200	£2,400.00	125	75	£2,025.00	£1,599.75	5
stival Stall	£15.00	35%	£20.25	21%	150	£2,250.00	90	60	£1,822.50	£1,439.78	5
stival Stall	£12.00	35%	£16.20	0%	100	£1,200.00	76	24	£1,231.20	£1,231.20	5
stival Stall	£12.00	30%	£15.60	21%	200	£2,400.00	98	102	£1,528.80	£1,207.75	M
stival Stall	£12.00	30%	£15.60	0%	50	£600.00	38	12	£592.80	£592.80	M
stival Stall	£3.00	10%	£3.30	21%	200	£600.00	148	52	£488.40	£385.84	
stival Stall	£3.00	15%	£3.45	21%	200	£600.00	137	63	£472.65	£373.39	5
stival Stall	£3.00	15%	£3.45	21%	150	£450.00	133	17	£458.85	£362.49	5
stival Stall	£3.00	10%	£3.30	21%	150	£450.00	111	39	£366.30	£289.38	
stival Stall	£10.00	30%	£13.00	0%	50	£500.00	14	36	£182.00	£182.00	M
onsor Stall	£5.00	10%	£5.50	21%	200	£1,000.00		200		£0.00	
vertiser Staff	£5.00	-100%	£0.00	21%	500	£2,500.00		500		£0.00	Gi
onsor Stall	£3.00	10%	£3.30	21%	200	£600.00		200		£0.00	
onsor Stall	£1.00	-100%	£0.00	0%	500	£500.00		500		£0.00	Gi
vertiser Staff	£1.00	-100%	£0.00	0%	500	£500.00		500		£0.00	Gi
					3750	£16,450.00	1246		£13,740.50	£11,658.98	

Figure 2.35 Result of sorting on multiple columns (Microsoft Excel view)

Filters

Synoptic link

You learnt about the importance of filtering in Topic area 1, section 1.2 of this unit.

Filtering is another method of displaying selected data in a spreadsheet solution. A filter is applied to a column of data.

To be able to filter information, the Filter tool needs to be activated on the Data tab. Once the Filter option is available the criteria can be selected. More than one criterion can be filtered at a time, and a filter can be applied across more than one column in a worksheet at a time. Figure 2.36 shows a simple filter being applied based on one criterion ('Sponsor Stall') in one column.

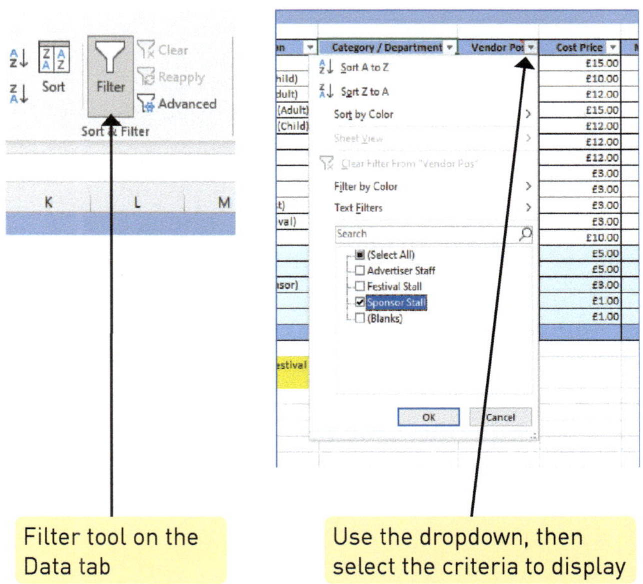

Figure 2.36 Filter use (Microsoft Excel view)

Filters can also be applied based on relational operators. In Figure 2.37 the relational operator of <1000 is applied to the Stock Value section of the worksheet.

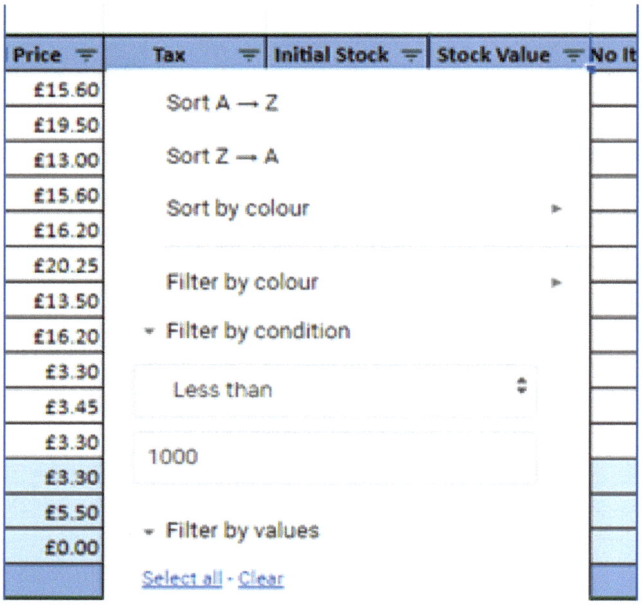

Figure 2.37 Relational operator filter (Google Sheets view)

Security measures

> **Synoptic link**
> You learnt about the importance of cyber-security in Unit R050, Topic area 4.

Ensuring **data integrity** is an important consideration when developing a spreadsheet solution. If the data is not accurate and correct, then the spreadsheet solution will output incorrect information. Data validation is one method of ensuring the integrity of the data, ensuring that the data can only be entered in the correct format in the correct locations. There are other methods and tools that can be applied to the spreadsheet that will help ensure both the integrity of the data and the structure of the spreadsheet solution that has been created.

> **Key term**
> **Data integrity** Making sure that the data has nothing missing (is complete), that it is error free and up to date. This will mean that the data is reliable for use in its specific context.

A cell or group of cells in a spreadsheet can be locked to ensure that the content cannot be changed. This is a good tool to use to protect the formulae and functions in spreadsheets. This will stop a user altering the formulae and functions when they enter the data into the system.

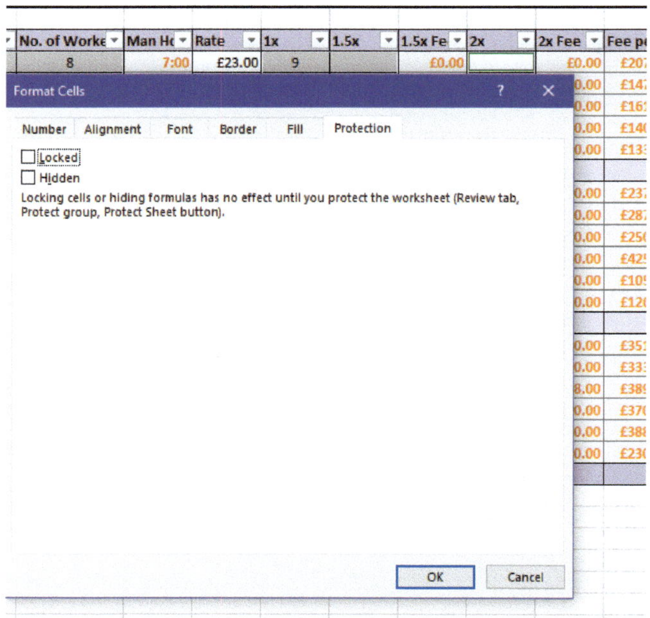

Figure 2.38 Unlocked cells (Microsoft Excel view)

By default, the cell 'Locked' option for the cell format is ticked so that once a worksheet has been password protected all the cells are locked. This means that to allow editing in a cell, where the user had to enter data, the protection needs to be removed. Figure 2.38 shows all the cells in the worksheet highlighted where data will be entered by a user, and the Locked cell option has been unticked. This will allow users to enter data once the worksheet has been password protected.

The worksheet can then be protected (locked from incorrect editing) by adding a password to the worksheet and only allowing the unlocked cells to be edited (Figure 2.39). Users can still access the data in the locked cells but they cannot alter the formula. An error message will appear that informs the user that they have tried to do something that they are not allowed to do.

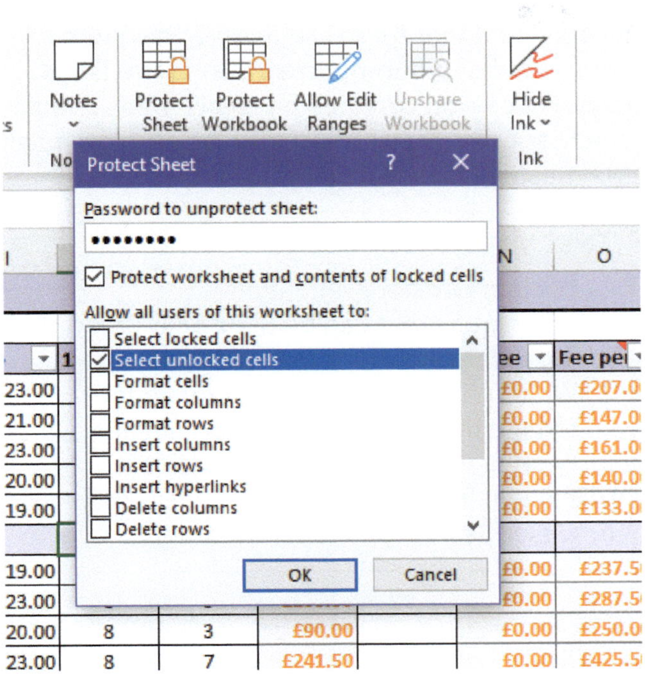

Figure 2.39 Protecting a worksheet (Microsoft Excel view)

Locking the cells and protecting a worksheet reduces the chances of the data being edited incorrectly. However, the data can still be viewed by anyone who has access to the computer system where the spreadsheet solution is stored.

Some spreadsheet applications allow the workbook to be protected. This is done by encrypting the workbook and requiring a password to open the workbook. Other application software protects the workbooks by the Share setting.

Modelling tools

What-if and Goal Seek

Spreadsheet applications can be used to analyse data and experiment with different situations that could be applied to the data.

What-if analysis allows you to find out what would happen to the results of any calculations if you changed some of the data used. In Google Sheets there is a Goal Seek tool that is an extension that has to be installed. (In Microsoft Excel, Goal Seek is in the What-If section of the Data tab.)

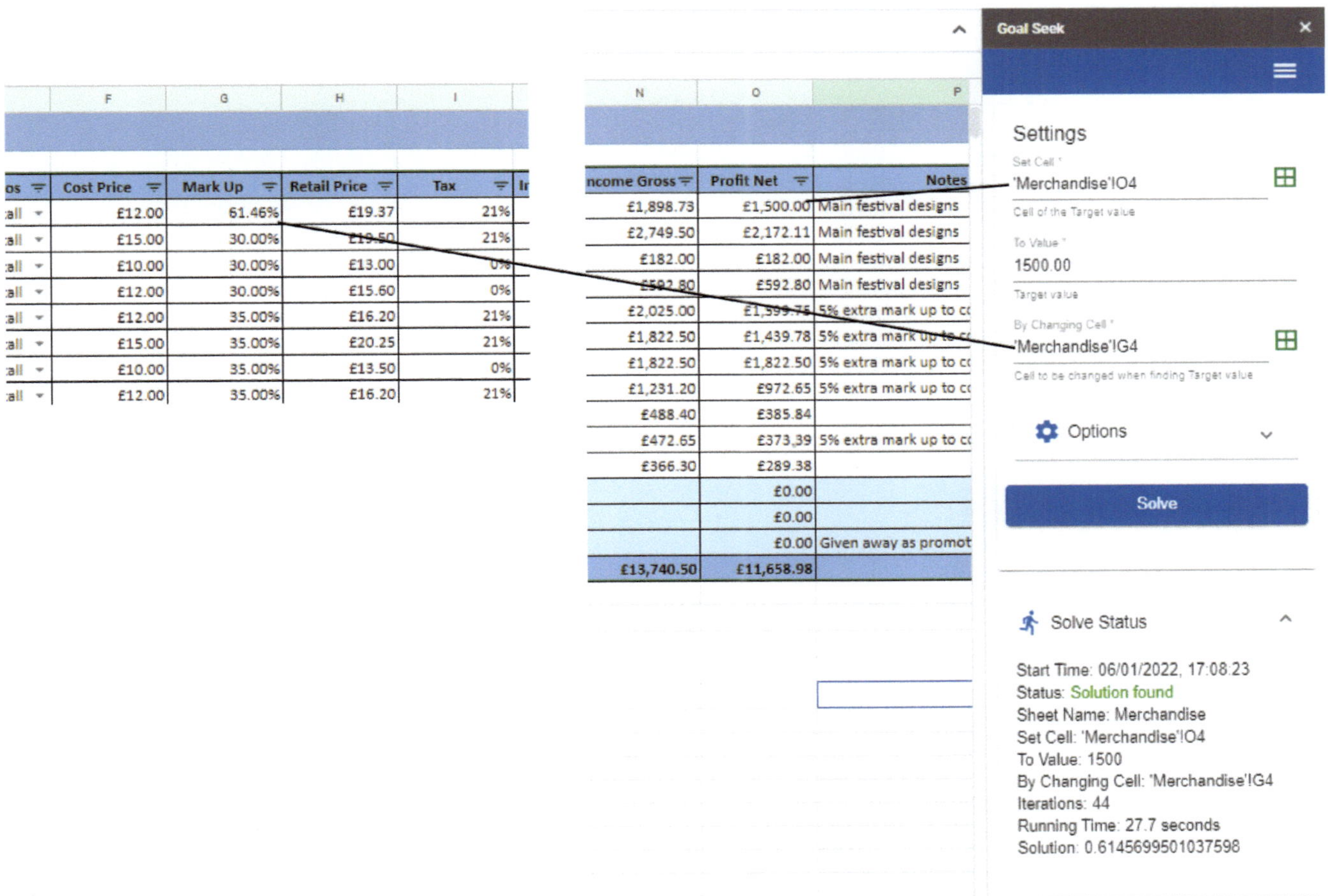

Figure 2.40 Goal Seek (Google Sheets view)

Figure 2.40 shows a Goal Seek running where the question has been asked, how much does the 'Mark Up' in G4 need to be if the Profit Net in O4 is to be £1500. The answer is 61.46%. That would require an Adult T-Shirt to be sold for £19.37. A decision could then be made whether to increase the price of the Adult T-Shirt to reach that profit figure.

PivotTables

PivotCharts and Tables are powerful (but complex) tools that can be used to analyse the data by rearranging it in a way that it is easy to understand.

Figure 2.41 shows the original data in the Staff worksheet. By creating a PivotTable it becomes easier to see that most of the workers employed during the music festival work in the Stage location and that there are only 12 Stewards being used at different times during the three days. A decision can then be easily made about whether more Stewards should be employed for the music festival.

Test your knowledge

1 Explain **two** data validation techniques that can be used on a spreadsheet.
2 What function would you use to enter today's date and time in a spreadsheet?
3 What is the purpose of filtering data?
4 Explain how to lock a spreadsheet cell.
5 Describe how Goal Seek works.

Location	Worker Typ	Agency Hi	No. of Worke
Stage	Rigger	FALSE	8
Stage	Fork Op	TRUE	2
Stage	Electrician	TRUE	2
Stage	Stagehand	FALSE	6
Site	Steward	FALSE	3
Site	Steward	FALSE	2
Stage	Electrician	TRUE	3
Stage	Stagehand	FALSE	6
Stage	Rigger	FALSE	8
Stage	Spot Op	FALSE	2
Merch Stand	Sales Op	FALSE	4
Site	Steward	FALSE	5
Merch Stand	Sales Op	FALSE	6
Site	Steward	FALSE	2
Stage	Stagehand	FALSE	8
Stage	Spot Op	FALSE	4
Stage	Rigger	FALSE	8
			79

Original data in the worksheet

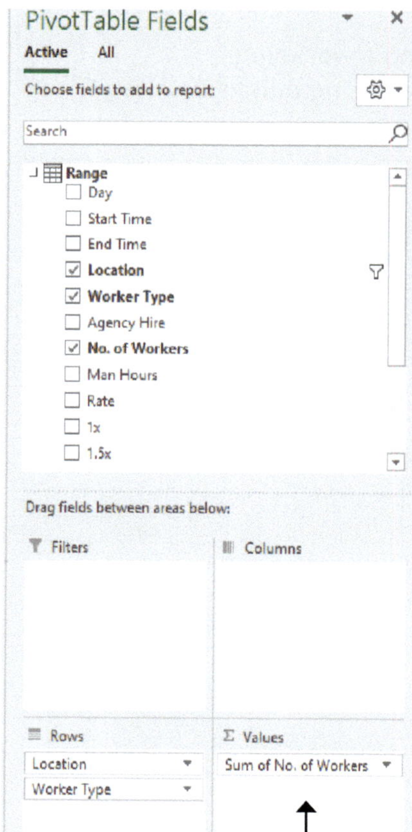

Setting up the PivotTable by selecting the required fields

2		
3	Row Labels	Sum of No. of Workers
4	⊟Merch Stand	
5	Sales Op	10
6	⊟Site	
7	Steward	12
8	⊟Stage	
9	Electrician	5
10	Fork Op	2
11	Rigger	24
12	Spot Op	6
13	Stagehand	20
14	Grand Total	79
15		
16		

PivotTable showing where the workers are required

Figure 2.41 Using a PivotTable (Microsoft Excel view)

Techniques to generate the outputs

Designing the data manipulation aspect of a spreadsheet solution is only part of the process. Consideration needs to be given to how the data will be outputted as information for different audiences. There are several methods that can be used to create outputs which are fit for purpose:

- Creating and formatting a variety of charts and graphs.
- Creating output documents that follow the house style and page layout properties as planned and designed.
- Ensuring the information in the rows and columns headings is visible or hidden as needed.

Synoptic links

You learnt about the different types of digital communications in Unit R050, Topic area 5, section 5.1.

You learnt about the different types of outputs in Topic area 1, section 1.2 of this unit.

Charts/graphs

One of the main outputs of spreadsheets is charts or graphs. There are many different types of charts and graphs that can be created in spreadsheet software. Choosing the most appropriate chart or graph for the information being shown is the important part.

Column	
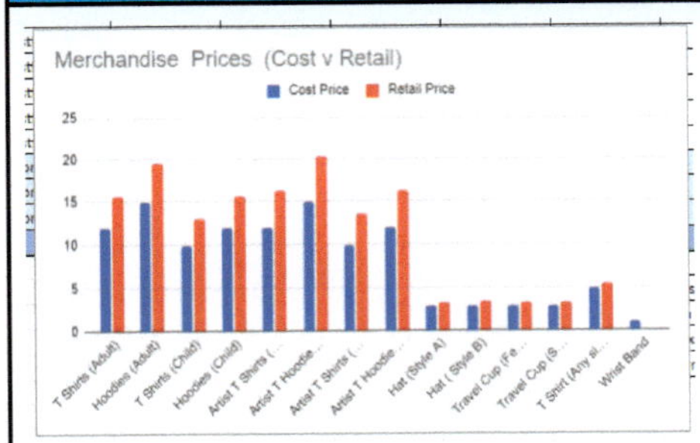	Data that is arranged in columns or rows in a worksheet can be plotted in a column chart. Categories typically go along the horizontal axis. Values typically go along the vertical axis. Allows comparisons between different categories.
Line	
	Data that is arranged in columns or rows in a worksheet can be plotted in a line chart. Categories typically go along the horizontal axis evenly. Values typically go along the vertical axis. Allows trends to be seen more easily.
Pie	
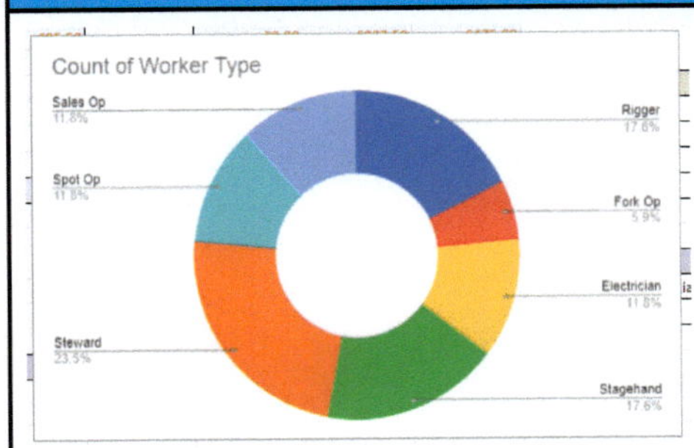	Data that is arranged in a column or row on a worksheet can be shown in a pie chart. Allows breakdown/proportion of overall to be seen more easily.

Bar

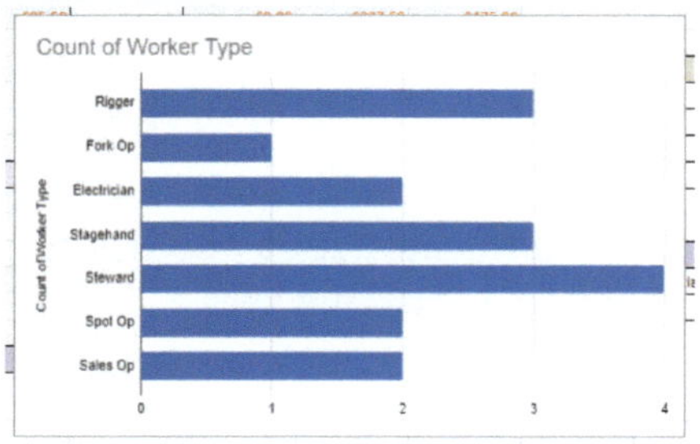

Data that is arranged in columns or rows in a worksheet can be plotted in a bar chart.

Categories typically go along the vertical axis.

Values typically go along the horizontal axis.

Allows comparisons between different categories.

Area

Data that is arranged in columns or rows in a worksheet can be plotted in an area chart.

Categories typically go along the horizontal axis.

Values typically go along the vertical axis.

Allows contribution over time of different elements to be seen. Differences between the elements can be seen.

Scatter

Data that is arranged in columns and rows in a worksheet can be plotted in a scatter graph: X value in one column/row, Y value in the column/row next to it.

Allows statistical data to be shown at regular intervals.

Combined

Data that is arranged in columns or rows in a worksheet can be plotted in a combined (Combo) chart.

Contains more secondary vertical axis.

Allows relationship between different data to be seen.

Radar

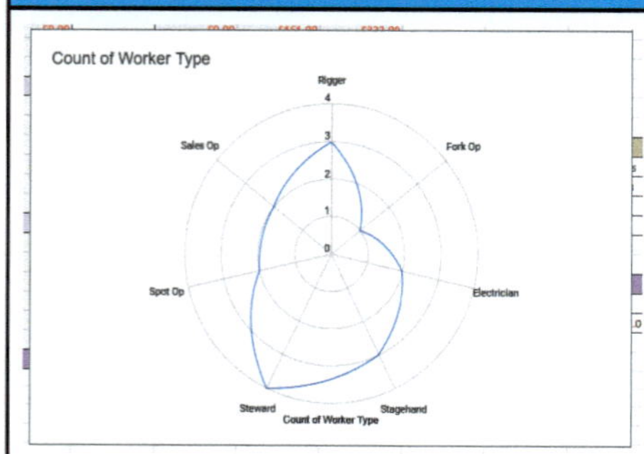

Data that is arranged in columns or rows in a worksheet can be plotted in a radar chart.

Allows the aggregate (collective) values to be compared.

Activity

Collect age and shoe size data from at least 10 people who you know.

Enter the data into a spreadsheet and create a combined chart/graph to show the data visually.

Page layout properties

When information from a spreadsheet solution is presented to an audience it is essential that all the information needed can be seen easily by the audience. One of the easiest ways that some of the information can be lost or missed is by not setting up the layout of the spreadsheet document correctly.

The layout of a print can also be edited again in the Print menu where scaling can be applied to allow all the worksheet to appear on the single page.

Adjusting row and column settings

Data can be unreadable on a worksheet if it is too large to fit in the cell. This will result in words being cut off in the cell or, in the case of numerical data, the cell will display as ##########. Data is there but it cannot be displayed. Double clicking on the line between the letters (columns) or numbers (rows) will force the application to resize automatically to present all the data in the cells.

Test your knowledge

6 What chart/graph type would be best used to show trends over time?
7 What chart/graph type would be best used to show the breakdown of an overall figure?
8 What is a combined chart?
9 What is the print area?
10 Describe what margins are.

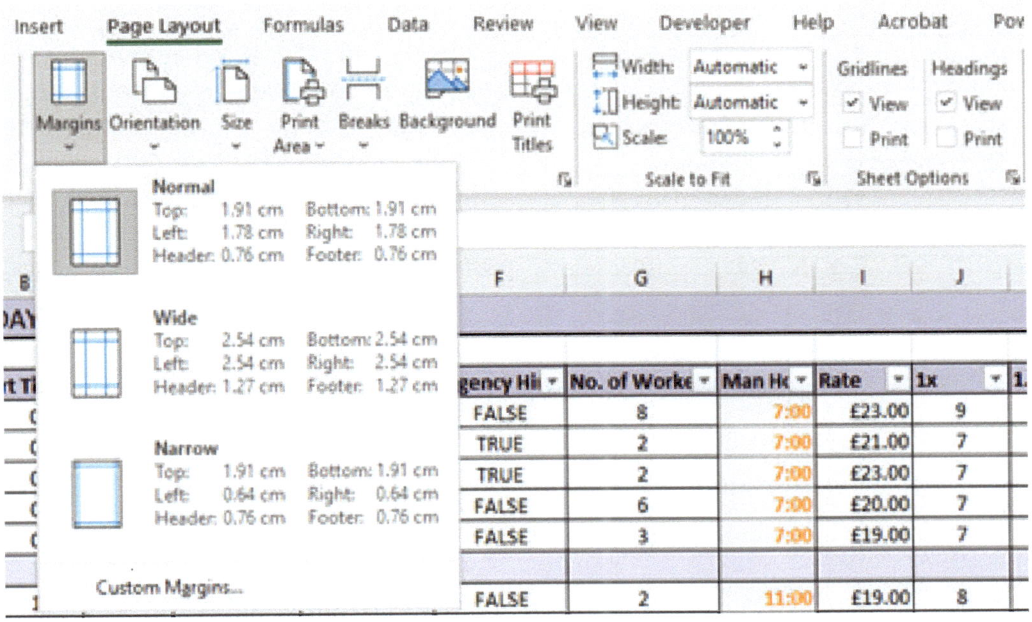

Figure 2.42 Page layout settings (Microsoft Excel view)

Table 2.10 Page layout properties

Page layout property	Description of use
Margins	Gap between edge of paper and printable area.
Orientation	Portrait or landscape. Portrait is the default setting, but landscape is better for worksheet printing.
Size	The size of paper being printed on.
Print Area	The specific section of the worksheet that is printed. The whole worksheet does not need to be printed.
Breaks	Splits the worksheet up between sheets of paper when printed. Can be used to fit sections across pages.
Background	Adding a background image to a printed worksheet. Will it make the content harder to view?
Print Titles	If a worksheet is printed across more than one page, headings for columns and rows can be selected to appear on each page. This makes the data/information clearer to understand.
Width	The number of pages that the worksheet displays horizontally.
Height	The number of pages that the worksheet displays vertically.
Scale	The size on a page. Default at 100% of its design, but this may be too big to fit on one page when printed.

User interface

Synoptic links

You learnt about the HCI considerations in Unit R050, Topic area 2, section 2.1.

You learnt about the HCI considerations in Topic area 1, section 1.2 of this unit.

Creating a spreadsheet solution requires a user interface to be developed. A user interface can also be called a Human Computer Interface (HCI). This contains elements and processes that will make the solution easier and more intuitive for the user.

Buttons

Buttons are used to trigger an action or event. You use them every day to turn things on and off – such as lights and mobile devices. Creating and adding them to a spreadsheet solution helps users navigate and use the spreadsheet system, especially one that goes across multiple worksheets.

Buttons can be created within spreadsheet application software or in other application packages – these can then be imported. Shapes can be inserted to create buttons with clear text content indicating their use. These buttons can then be hyperlinked to different parts of the spreadsheet solution.

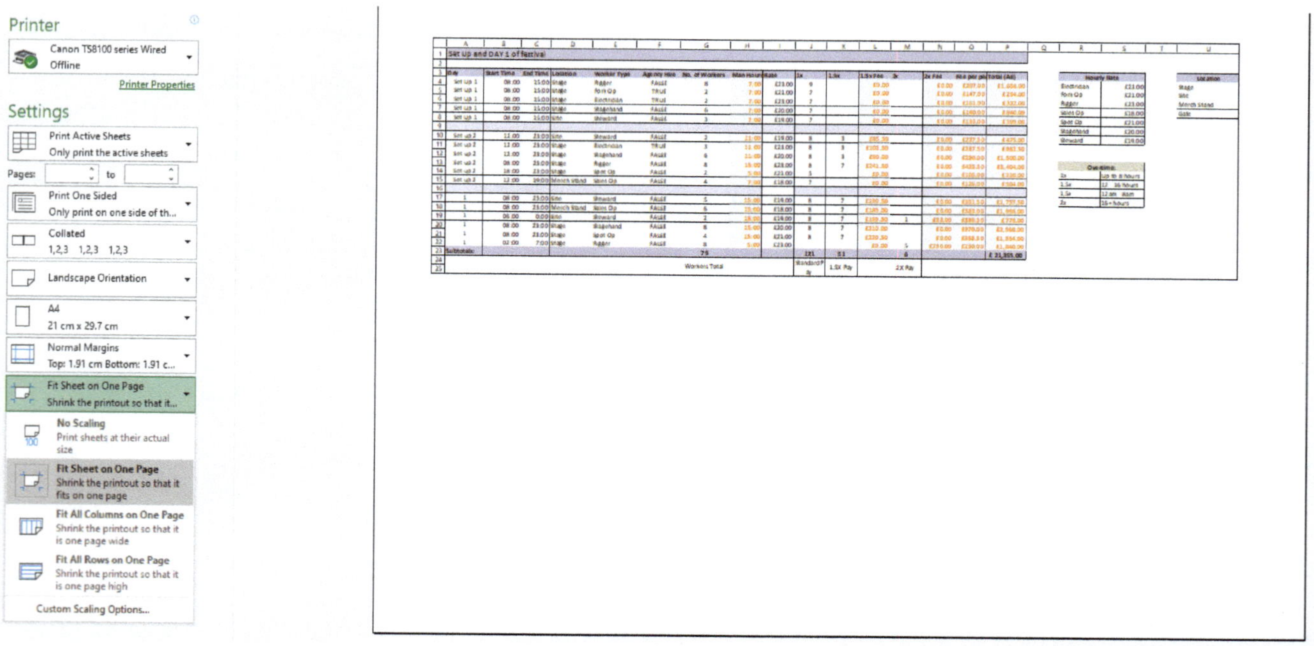

Figure 2.43 Print options (Microsoft Excel view)

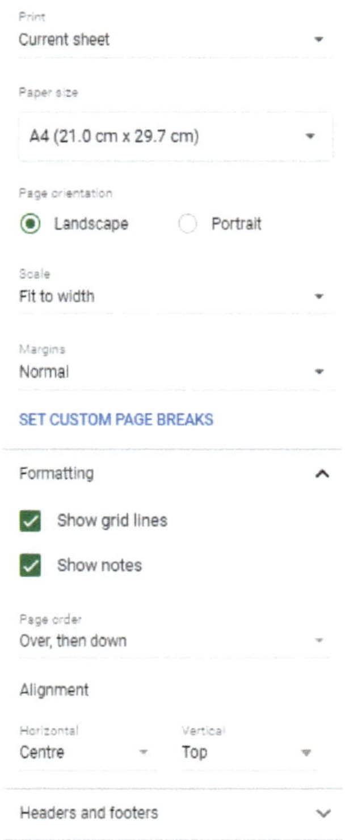

Figure 2.44 Print options (Google Sheets view)

In Figure 2.45, a green circle has been inserted and a hyperlink to the 'Stock Ordering' worksheet has been attached. This provides the user with a clear method of navigation in the spreadsheet solution.

Activity

Create a workbook with four worksheets named: Cover, Shoes, Shirts and Trousers. Link the pages together using buttons and hyperlinks.

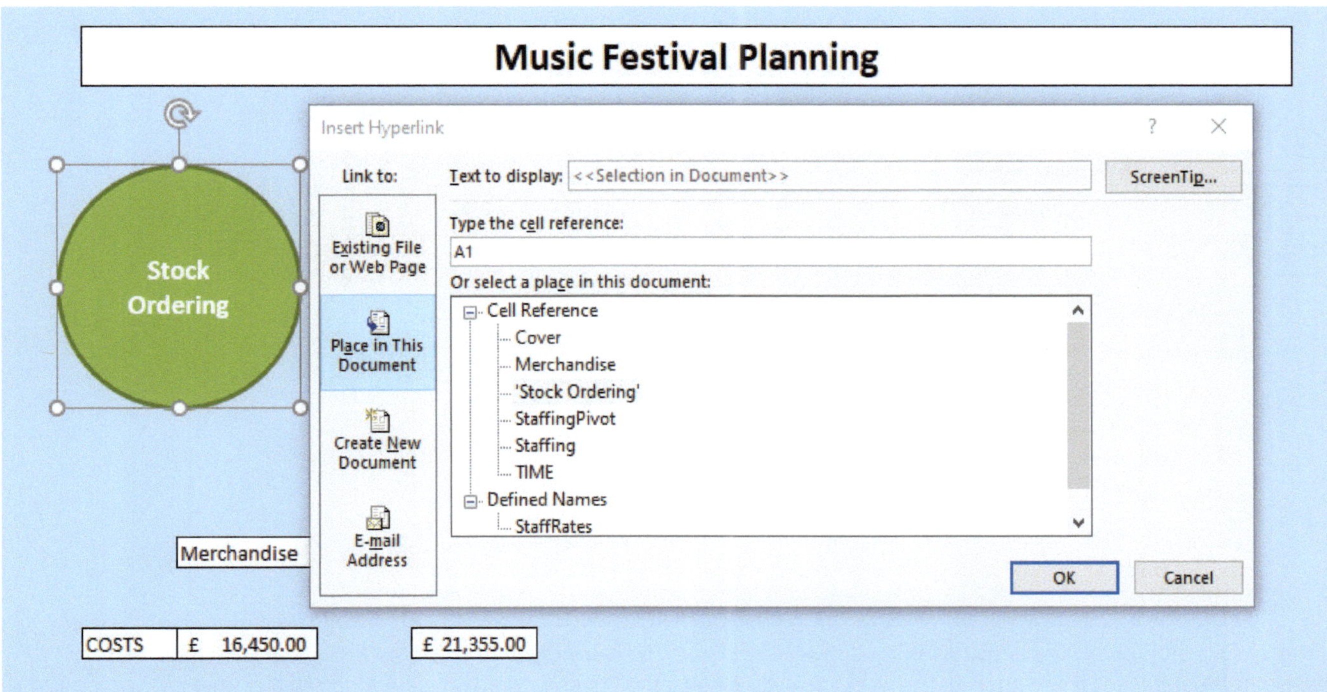

Figure 2.45 Button creation (Microsoft Excel view)

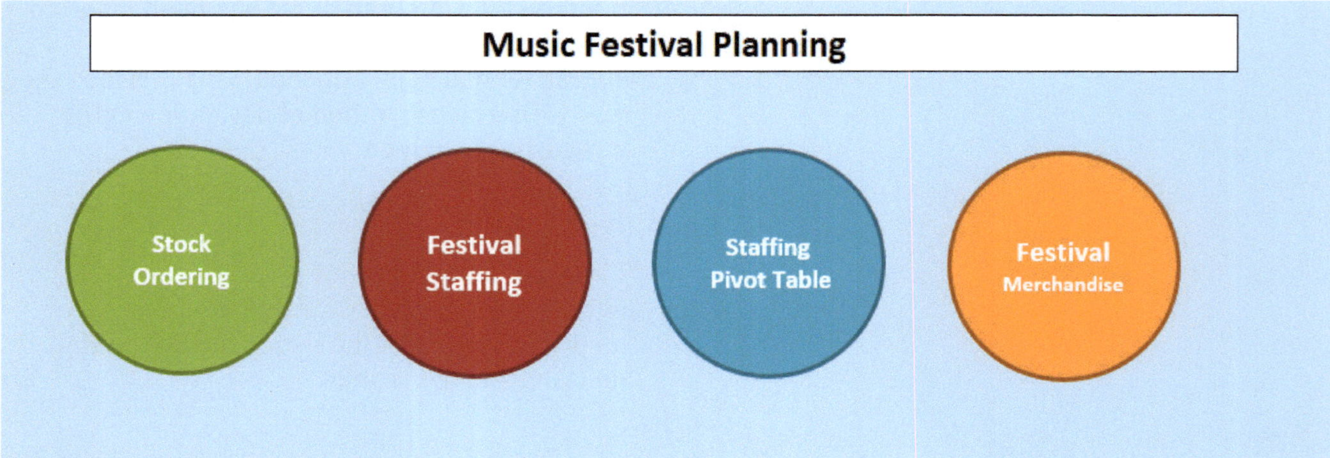

Figure 2.46 Button-based user interface (Microsoft Excel view)

Hyperlinks

Hyperlinks are used in all websites to link pages, or parts of pages, together. Hyperlinks can also be used in spreadsheets to link worksheets together to create a user interface. In Figure 2.48, the hyperlink is attached to the button for the Festival Merchandise worksheet.

Hyperlinks can be attached to text as well as to images or shapes, as in Figure 2.47. Once the hyperlink has been attached, the format of the text can be edited, and the text can be changed from the default hyperlink format which is underlined in blue.

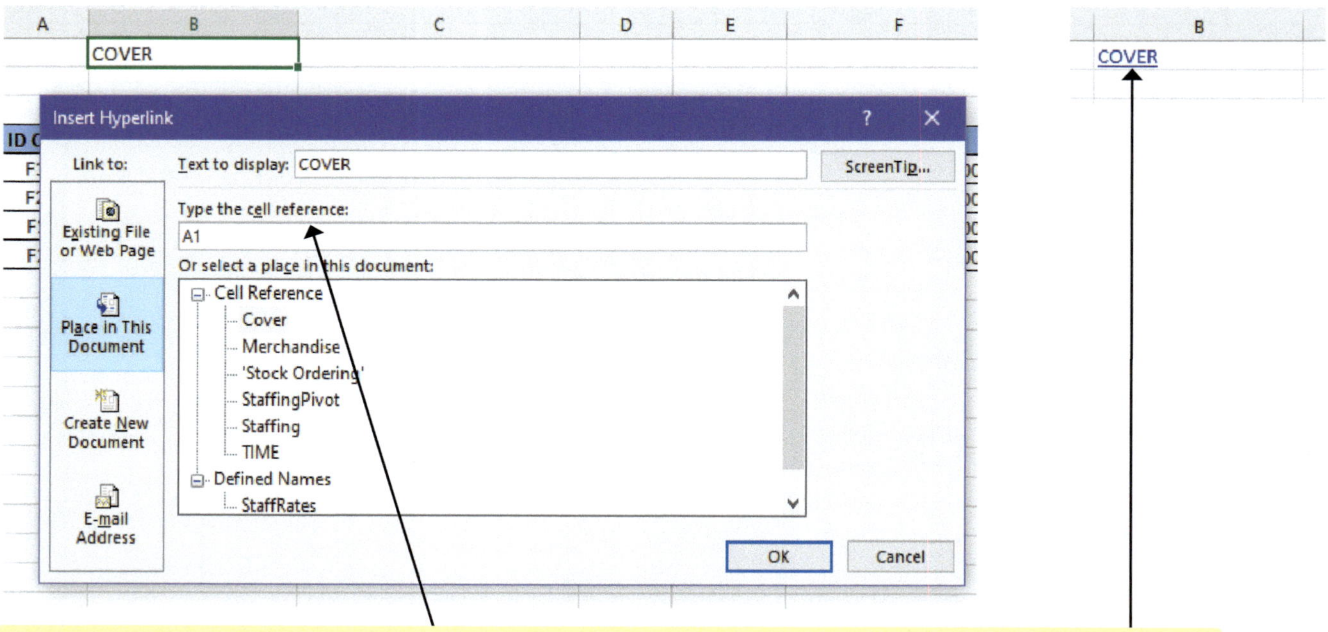

The text in cell B1 is linked to cell A1 in the Cover worksheet. The word Cover is now blue and underlined, as it has a hyperlink attached. When clicked, the workbook will display the Cover worksheet, selecting cell A1.

Figure 2.47 Text hyperlink (Microsoft Excel view)

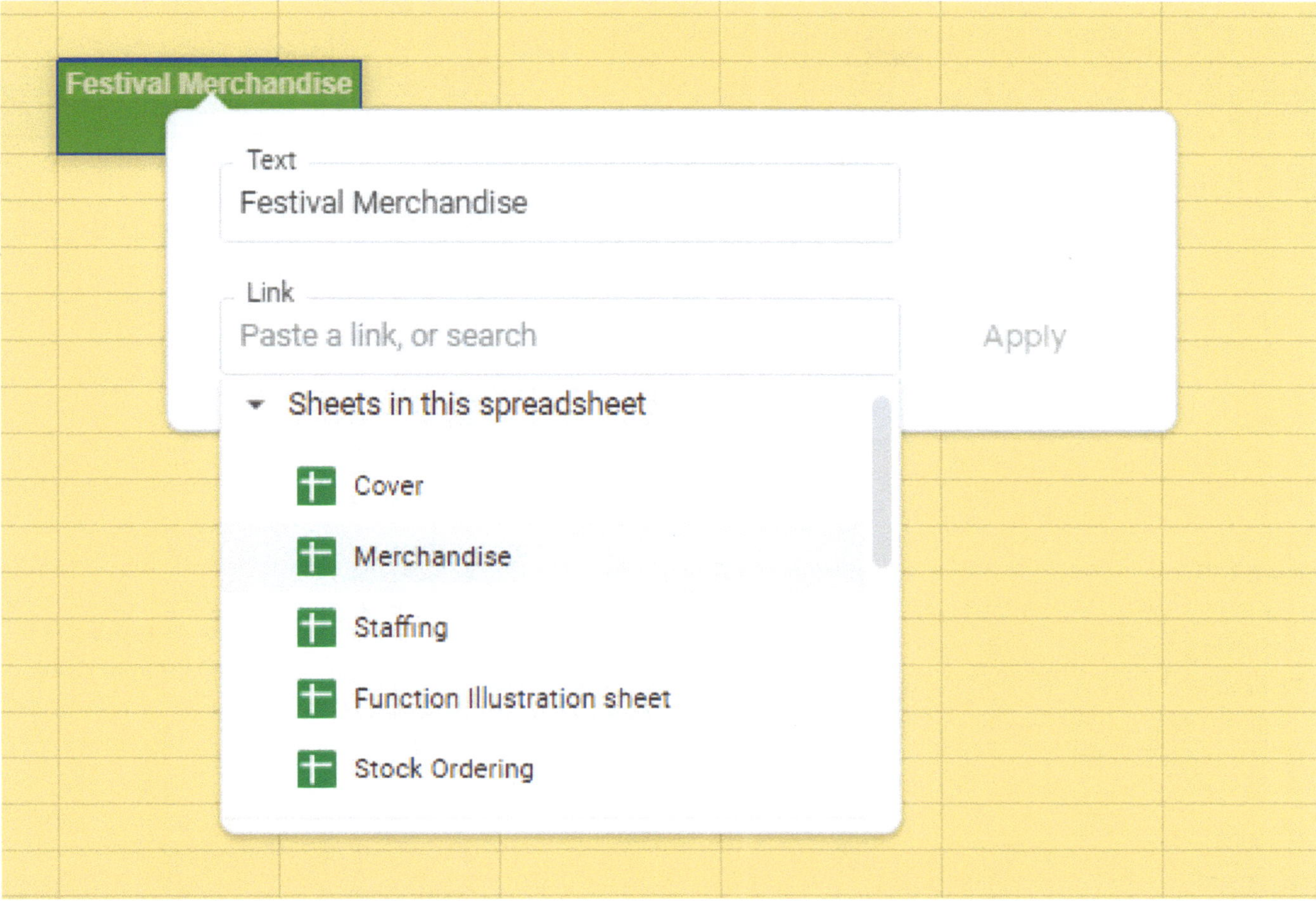

Figure 2.48 Hyperlink creation (Google Sheets view)

Forms

Forms can be used to make data entry easier for users. There are different types of forms, such as the Microsoft Forms that you can use for surveys or quizzes. These collect data and then store it in a worksheet. You can define where these forms store the information (that is, into an existing workbook), but you need to set up the worksheet using Microsoft Forms rather than setting up the worksheet first and then linking it to the form. (This may change with different versions of Microsoft Office.) This is the same when working with Google Sheets and Google Forms.

Forms can also be used within spreadsheet applications, but these may require an extension to be added to the software application.

Figure 2.49 shows a data entry form in Excel; the fields requiring user input are formatted white. The other fields, which match the grey format of the form itself, are either calculation or function based. These do not need the user to enter any data. This stops any unwanted data entry being made and protects the integrity of the data. The form has picked up the validation techniques used to format the cells in each of the columns of the worksheet.

When the user presses the 'New' button (see Figure 2.49) the data that is entered by the user will fill in the next empty row of the worksheet.

Forms contain different controls that can be used to help users enter data and increase the integrity of the data.

These include:

- combo box
- check box
- spin button
- list box
- option button
- group button
- scroll bar.

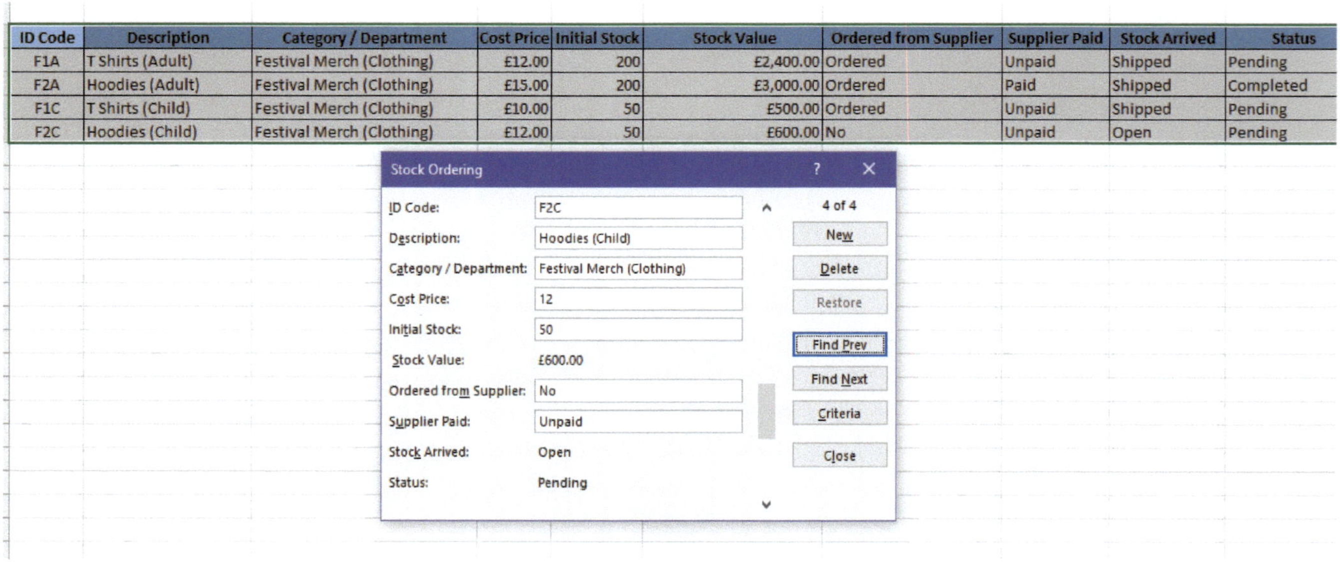

Figure 2.49 Data entry form in a spreadsheet (Microsoft Excel view)

Activity

For each of the Form controls listed create a set of flash cards that explains how it is used in a form.

Macros

Macros allow the automation of a series of actions, compiling them together into a single process. This process can then be triggered by a user interaction such as opening the software application or pressing a button on the interface.

Macros can be created for a range of different tasks including printing specific worksheets, running combined calculations, and opening workbooks on a specific worksheet.

Macros use **Visual Basic for Applications (VBA) code**, but you do not need to know the specifics of the code to create a macro. Spreadsheet applications allow you to record the steps in the process and then convert it into the VBA code and save it as a macro. These recorded macros can then be attached to user interactions.

To enable these macros to be used, the spreadsheet must then be saved as a Macro-Enabled Workbook (Excel) and in Google Sheets you may need to grant permissions for the macros to be run.

```
/** @OnlyCurrentDoc */

function PrintOrderStatus() {
  var spreadsheet = SpreadsheetApp.getActive();
  spreadsheet.getRange('A4:J8').activate();
};
```

Figure 2.50 Macro code (Google Sheets view)

Figure 2.50 shows the recorded code to print a restricted selection of cells in a worksheet. Figure 2.51 shows the code being attached to a button in Google Sheets.

Key term

Visual Basic for Applications (VBA) code
A programming language that can be used within spreadsheet software programs.

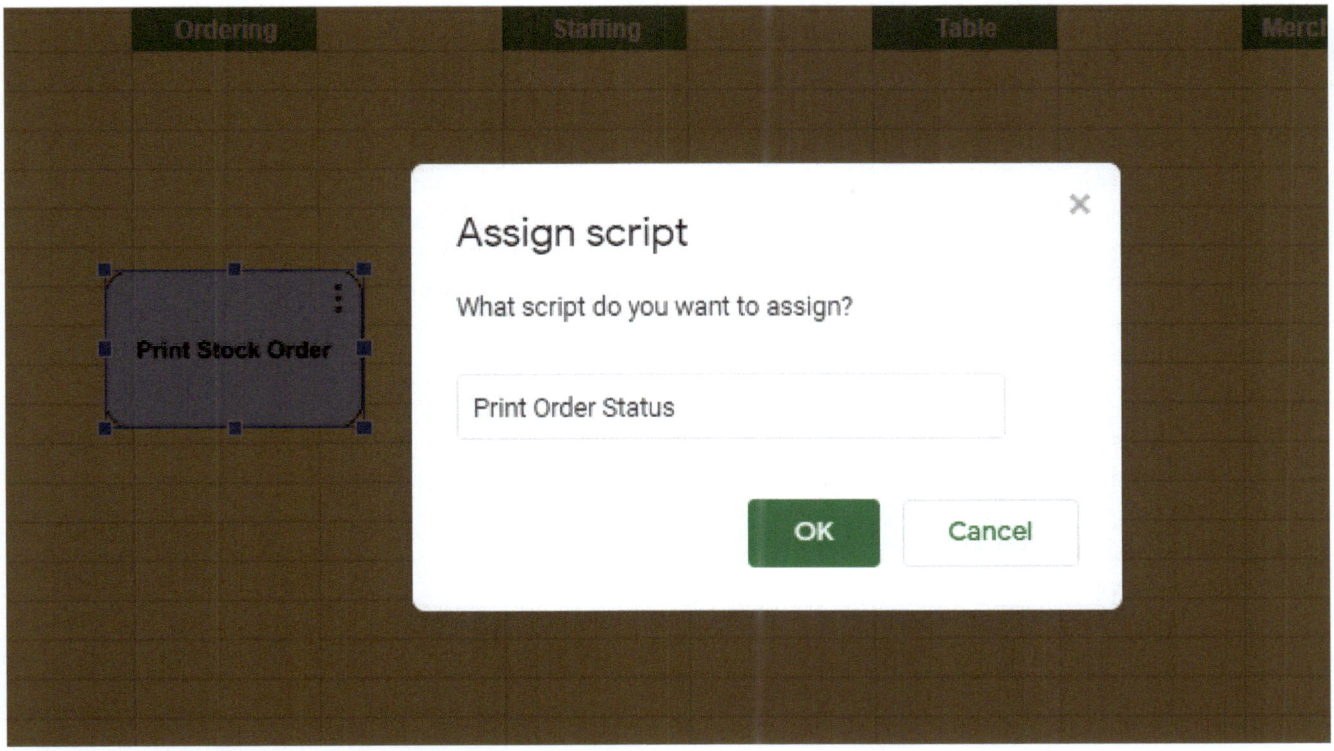

Figure 2.51 Code assigned to a button (Google Sheets view)

Activity

In pairs, create a New User Guide to explain how to create macros that can be used to automate the following processes.

- Open a workbook at a specific worksheet.
- Navigate from a worksheet back to the cover/front worksheet of a workbook.
- Print a completed worksheet with all the data appearing on a single page – landscape orientation.

Test your knowledge

11 What is a button?
12 Why is a form useful?
13 What is a hyperlink?
14 What is a macro?
15 Why is a macro useful?

Assignment practice

Task 2

You now need to develop the spreadsheet for the headteacher using the work you did in Assignment practice task 1. Here's a reminder of the scenario:

> The headteacher of your school wants a new spreadsheet system to monitor the spending of the different departments in school. The spreadsheet will need an HCI that allows the headteacher to select different departments and see:
>
> - the percentage of their budget that they have spent
> - what they have bought in the last month.
>
> The school logo will need to appear on the screen as well as the name and email address of the Head of Department of the department being viewed.

Create the spreadsheet solution that meets the headteacher's requirements. The solution must contain:

- a user interface (HCI)
- worksheets for each department
- a summary of data for the headteacher displayed in a suitable way.

Topic area 3 Testing the spreadsheet solution

Getting started

Developing a spreadsheet solution is at times a complex and time-consuming process. There are many aspects of the development where issues can arise. The worst situation to be in is to get to the end of the development and find the solution that has been developed does not work fully or meet the needs of the user.

To reduce the chances of the system not working as intended and increase the chances of the system meeting the needs of the user, testing is carried out continually during the development process.

Testing needs to cover all aspects of the spreadsheet solution. This ranges from the technical functions such as the formulae and functions used in calculations, through to the HCI and its ease of use.

Using the internet, find a spreadsheet used by a business or charity. Identify the parts of the spreadsheet that you think would need to be tested to check that they work properly.

Next to each part that you think would need to be tested describe how you think you could test it.

Synoptic link

You learnt about testing in Unit R050, Topic area 3, section 3.5.

3.1 Test the user interface and the technical aspects of the spreadsheet solution

Types of test data

When a spreadsheet solution is developed, testing should be carried out using the three different types of test data.

To test the validation applied in Figure 2.52 using the three different types of test you could carry out the following tests.

Key terms

Extreme data Data that is on the boundary between valid and invalid data for a spreadsheet solution.

Invalid data Data that is unacceptable for the spreadsheet solution.

Valid data Data that is acceptable, sensible and reasonable for the spreadsheet solution.

Table 2.11 Test data types

Type of data	Data used	Explanation of choice
Extreme	0 and 8	These are the two numbers at the limits of acceptable values. These should be accepted.
Invalid (Erroneous)	−2, 9, 20, AA,	These values are outside the acceptable values – too low or too high or the wrong data type. These should not be accepted.
Valid	1, 3, 7	These three numbers are within the normal range of data that would be expected in this column. These should be accepted.

Activity

Column K on the worksheet in Figure 2.52 only accepts data for people working between 9 and 16 hours.

Create a table like Table 2.11 and identify and describe the test data that you would use to test the data validation rule in Column K.

Synoptic link

Testing is covered in Unit R070, Topic area 4.

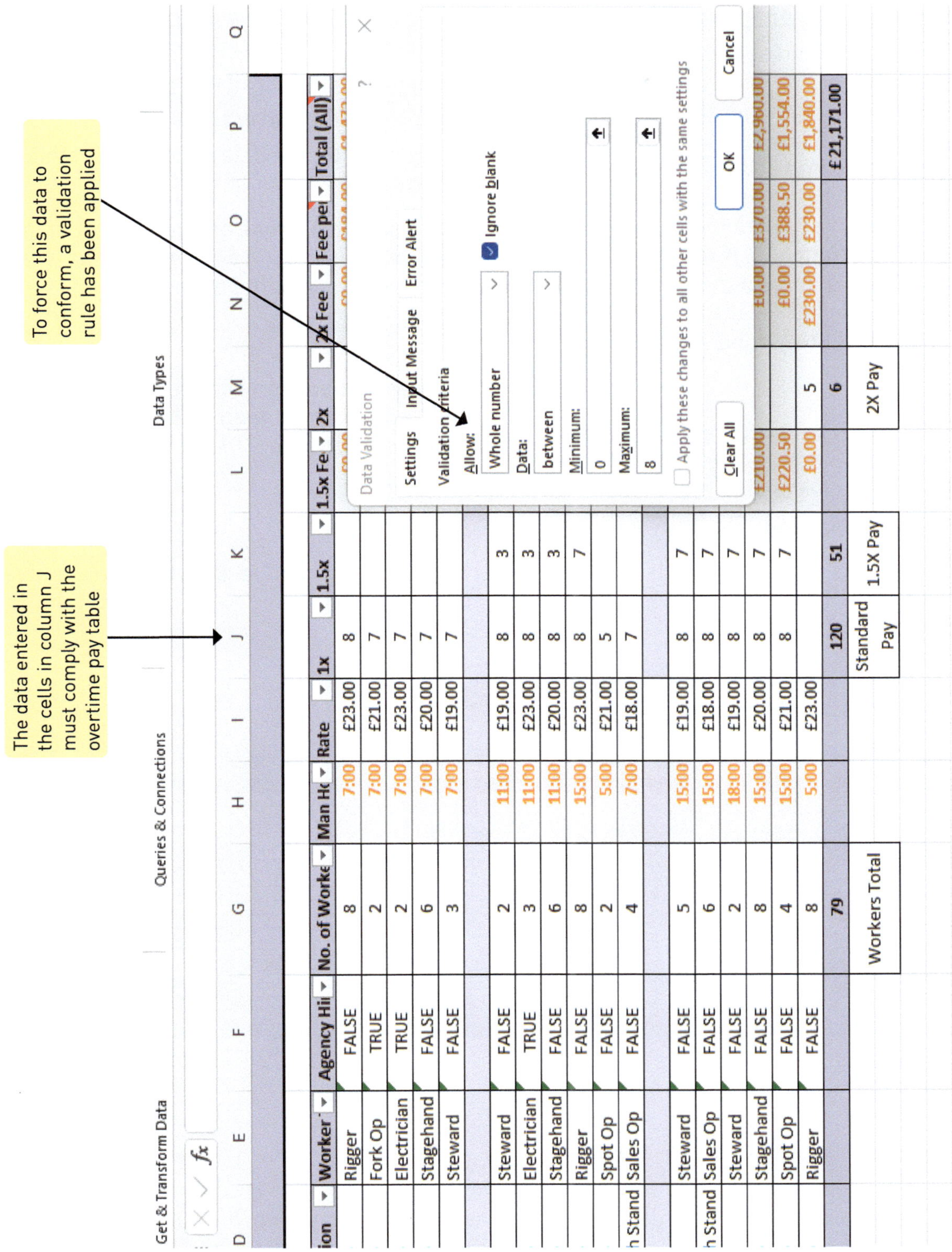

Figure 2.52 Testing validation (Microsoft Excel view)

Testing during development

The spreadsheet solution should be tested continually throughout development, not just at the end. By the time you get to the end of development any major problems should have been picked up and solved. This is vitally important especially when you may have the results of one formula/function being used in another formula/function. If the results generated by the first formula/function are incorrect then the result for the second formula/function will be wrong as well.

Technical testing

Technical testing is checking the functionality of the solution. When developing a spreadsheet solution this will involve testing that the:

- navigation features work
- formulae and functions work and provide the correct answers
- data and instructions on the screen can be read easily (colour contrast, size, positioning)
- outputs such as print-outs or graphs:
  - display the correct data
  - display all the data necessary (nothing is missing).

Testing should be done as each aspect of the spreadsheet is developed to ensure that it works before moving on to the next stage.

Synoptic link

You learnt about spreadsheet errors and how to correct them in Unit R050, Topic area 2, section 2.1.

Key term

Technical testing Checking the functionality of the solution.

Day 1 on the festival

ID Code	Event / Day	Description	Category / Department	Vendor Pos	Cost Price	Mark Up	Retail Price	Tax	Initial Stock	Stock Value	No Items Sold	Stock Level	Income Gross	Profit Net	Notes
F1A	27/07/2023	T Shirts (Adult)	Festival Merch (Clothing)	Festival Stall	£12.00	30.00%	£15.60	21%	200	£2,400.00	98	102	£1,528.80	£1,207.75	Main festival designs
F2A	27/07/2023	Hoodies (Adult)	Festival Merch (Clothing)	Festival Stall	£15.00	30.00%	£19.50	21%	200	£3,000.00	141	59	£2,749.50	£2,172.11	Main festival designs
F1C	27/07/2023	T Shirts (Child)	Festival Merch (Clothing)	Festival Stall	£10.00	30.00%	£13.00	0%	50	£500.00	14	36	£182.00	£182.00	Main festival designs
F2C	27/07/2023	Hoodies (Child)	Festival Merch (Clothing)	Festival Stall	£12.00	30.00%	£15.60	0%	50	£600.00	38	12	£592.80	£502.80	Main festival designs
A1A	27/07/2023	Artist T Shirts (A	Artist (Clothing)	Festival Stall	£12.00	35.00%	£16.20	21%	200	£2,400.00	125	75	£2,025.00	£1,599.75	5% extra mark up to cover festival cost
A2A	27/07/2023	Artist T Hoodies	Artist (Clothing)	Festival Stall	£15.00	35.00%	£20.25	21%	150	£2,250.00	90	60	£1,822.50	£1,439.78	5% extra mark up to cover festival cost
A1C	27/07/2023	Artist T Shirts (Cl	Artist (Clothing)	Festival Stall	£10.00	35.00%	£13.50	0%	200	£2,000.00	135	65	£1,822.50	£1,822.50	5% extra mark up to cover festival cost
A2C	27/07/2023	Artist T Hoodies	Artist (Clothing)	Festival Stall	£12.00	35.00%	£16.20	0%	100	£1,200.00	76	24	£1,231.20	£1,231.20	5% extra mark up to cover festival cost
FH1	27/07/2023	Hat (Style A)	Festival Merch (Clothing)	Festival Stall	£3.00	10.00%	£3.30	21%	200	£600.00	148	52	£488.40	£385.84	
FA1	27/07/2023	Hat (Style B)	Artist (Clothing)	Festival Stall	£3.00	15.00%	£3.45	21%	200	£600.00	137	63	£472.65	£373.39	5% extra mark up to cover festival cost
FO1	27/07/2023	Travel Cup (Festi	Festival Merch (Other)	Festival Stall	£3.00	10.00%	£3.30	21%	150	£450.00	111	39	£366.30	£289.38	
AO1	27/07/2023	Travel Cup (Artis	Artist (Other)	Festival Stall	£3.00	15.00%	£3.45	21%	150	£450.00	133	17	£458.85	£362.49	5% extra mark up to cover festival cost
SO1	27/07/2023	Travel Cup (Spon	Sponsor (Other)	Sponsor Stall	£3.00	10.00%	£3.30	21%	200	£600.00		200		£0.00	
SC1	27/07/2023	T Shirt (Any size)	Sponsor (Clothing)	Sponsor Stall	£5.00	10.00%	£5.50	21%	200	£1,000.00		200		£0.00	
SO2	27/07/2023	Wrist Band	Sponsor (Freebie)	Sponsor Stall	£1.00	-100.00%	£0.00	0%	500	£500.00		500		£0.00	Given away as promotion
P1F	27/07/2023	Wrist Band	Advertiser (Freebie)	Advertiser St	£1.00	-100.00%	£0.00	0%	500	£500.00		500		£0.00	Given away as promotion
P2F	27/07/2023	T Shirt (Any size)	Advertiser (Freebie)	Advertiser St	£5.00	-100.00%	£0.00	21%	500	£2,500.00		500		£0.00	Given away as promotion
Totals:									3750	£16,450.00	1246		£13,740.30	£11,058.98	

Stock Cost	£16,450.00	Only sold at Festival Stalls
Income	£11,658.98	
Profit	-£4,791.02	

Figure 2.53 Worksheet for testing (Google Sheets view)

The testing of the worksheet in Figure 2.53 during development could involve the potential test areas shown in Table 2.12.

All these tests would not be done at once but would be carried out as each column is created. It does look as if there is a lot to do here, but many of these tests are small and would be done as the cells are set up. It would be a quick check that the data appears correctly.

Some of the tests however, such as the ones checking the calculations, would require more time. When testing the calculations, you need to know what the answer would be if the calculation is working properly. To help achieve this one of

Table 2.12 Possible tests

Column in spreadsheet	Content	Why it should be tested
B	Date format	To check that the data appears as a date.
D & E	Validation lists	To check that the data can only be entered from the selected options in a list.
F, H, K, N & O	Price format	To check that the data appears as a price.
G & I	Percentage format	To check that the data appears as a percentage. These percentages are used in calculations, so they need to be correct.
H, K, M, N & O	Calculation check	To check that the calculations work correctly and produce the correct answers.
J, L & M	Data format – whole number only	To check that only whole numbers can be entered, these are items which cannot contain a decimal figure.

the best ways is to use valid data that can be entered and checked easily. For example, using the same worksheet as seen in Figure 2.53 the test data could be as shown in Table 2.13.

Once this has been done then the other types of data (Invalid and Extreme) can be used to test the spreadsheet solution.

Table 2.13 Test data choice and reasoning

Column	Data	Reason for use
F	10	Column H would be 10 + 25% = 12.50
G	25%	
J	100	Column M would be 50 meaning half stock sold
L	50	

If there are any errors or issues, then the changes can be made at this stage.

Usability testing

Usability testing (**user testing**) is carried out by users of the final system. During development this can be carried out by showing sections of the spreadsheet solution as they are developed. Users are then asked to test the section using predefined tests from the test plan to gather their feedback.

Users could be asked to test that the:

- navigation is clear and easy to understand
  - movement forward through the system
  - movement back through the system
  - can get to all the parts needed
- content is readable
  - colours
  - sizes
  - images are clear (if used)
- data entry is clear
  - where to enter data is clearly shown
  - what data needs to be entered
  - messages explaining any data entry errors are helpful
- output production is clear
  - how to produce the necessary outputs
  - how to change the data for different outputs
- can be used by all types of users
  - technical user vs. non-technical user
  - visually impaired users
  - physically impaired users.

This testing is all about making sure that the system is easy and **intuitive** for the end user. What you may think is clear to understand because you have built the spreadsheet may not be clear to other users.

Key terms

Intuitive Actions that can be easily carried out without having to think deeply.

User testing Carried out by a range of users who are likely to use the solution.

The data that is gathered here can be used to make changes to the system at this stage. This data will not be **quantitative** in nature but will probably be **qualitative** statements from users explaining the issues that they have or what they like about the spreadsheet solution.

Testing after development

At the end of the development there should be a final round of testing before it is released to the end user.

Technical testing

At the end of development, the final technical testing is concerned with a final check that everything works as it should. Have any changes been made during the development that had a knock-on effect to other aspects of the solution? There should be no major issues if the system has been tested thoroughly during development.

It is at this stage that the whole system is checked, where you enter the data into the spreadsheet and follow the users' journey, checking that each step works correctly. The testing would involve testing the:

- navigation of the system
- data entry processes
- data output processes
  - is the information correct?
  - is it well presented?
  - is it easy to understand?
  - is anything missing in the output?

Usability testing

This is the final check of the system by the end users. The completed fully functioning system is given to users, who then test it to ensure that it does what they need it to do.

Key terms

Qualitative data Data that is descriptive and cannot be measured.

Quantitative data Data that is measurable and is usually in numerical form.

Activity

Create a workbook with four worksheets named: Cover, Shoes, Shirts and Trousers. Link the pages together using buttons and hyperlinks. (You may have already done this for Topic area 2.)

Show this workbook to someone and ask them to test it to check that the navigation works well.

Note in your exercise book any comments that they make.

Test plan documentation

A spreadsheet solution is not developed in a single day or single sitting at a computer system. The testing of a spreadsheet solution should be systematic and organised. The most effective method of doing this is by using a test plan. A test plan (such as the example shown in Table 2.14) records what tests have taken place, what was tested, the result of the test and any improvements that are needed.

Table 2.14 shows an example of a test plan that was used to check the worksheet shown in Figure 2.52. There was an issue with the validation rules when it was first set up that it allowed 9 hours to be entered. The validation rule was changed and test 1b was rerun as test 2 to check that the validation rule worked correctly.

Test your knowledge

1. What is technical testing?
2. What is usability testing?
3. What are the three types of test data that should be used during testing?
4. Why is it important to test though the whole development process?
5. Why is it important to use a test plan?

Table 2.14 Test plan example

Date	Test number	Test purpose	Type of test data	Test data	Expected result	Actual result	Remedial action needed	Retest number
02/02/2022	1	Check the data validation tool applied to Column J.	Extreme	0 and 8	Data will be accepted by system.	Data accepted	None	
02/02/2022	2							

Assignment practice

Task 3

You need to test the spreadsheet that you created in Assignment practice task 2. Here's a reminder of the scenario:

The headteacher of your school wants a new spreadsheet system to monitor the spending of the different departments in school. The spreadsheet will need an HCI that allows the headteacher to select different departments and see:

- the percentage of their budget that they have spent
- what they have bought in the last month.

The school logo will need to appear on the screen as well as the name and email address of the Head of Department of the department being viewed.

Create a test plan for the new spreadsheet solution that you have created to meet the headteacher's requirements.

You need to ensure that you test both the technical and the usability aspects of the solution.

Topic area 4 Evaluating the spreadsheet solution

Getting started

When a spreadsheet solution has been designed, developed and tested, the final stage of the process is to evaluate its effectiveness.

The evaluation will check that the solution:

- meets the users' needs
- meets the client's needs
- complies with the principles and conventions of HCIs (Human Computer Interfaces).

Find an example of spreadsheet from school, a business or on the internet.

Identify what features have been included to help an end user use the spreadsheet.

Describe how these features help the end user.

Explain how the spreadsheet could be developed further to help the end user.

Synoptic link

Reviewing is covered in Unit R070, Topic area 4.

4.1 Methods used to evaluate the success of the spreadsheet solution

Client requirements

Synoptic link

You learnt about the principles of HCIs in Topic area 1, section 1.2 of this unit.

First, look at the requirements that the client gave you in their brief. Then split your review of these requirements down into functionality and usability, as you did with the testing.

You need to evaluate how your solution meets these requirements from the client. Refer to the teaching content in Topic area 1 and think about how you came up with your solution. Then explain how your system meets these requirements.

For each of the points in your evaluation, you should think about the following:

Statement, **E**vidence, **E**xplanation (you should try to **SEE** it).

- **Statement** What you did to meet the point evaluated (for example, limited choice validation was used to limit user errors).
- **Evidence** Screenshot or description of the technical aspect you used (for example, screenshot of drop-down list).
- **Explanation** How this met the point and the client's requirements (for example, how this drop-down list was used and why it was of benefit).

HCI design principles and conventions

Synoptic link

You learnt about the principles of HCIs in Topic area 1, section 1.2 of this unit.

Your spreadsheet solution should comply with the principles of HCI design. For each of these principles, you should consider how it has been applied to the spreadsheet solution. The principles are:

1. **Accessibility**
2. **Colour**
3. **Layout**
4. **Learnability**
5. **Memorability**
6. **Messages**
7. **Navigation**

Evaluating how well the spreadsheet solution meets these principles is important as this will provide a good indication of whether the solution will be successful or not. If the solution does not comply with these principles, then the chances of users not finding the system easy to use are high. In turn this could lead to low adoption of the system, leading to the possibility that the client will not accept the completed solution.

Having carried out user testing, the chances of the client not accepting the solution should be minimal. Evaluating the application of the HCI principles at this stage is about learning lessons for future developments and how the solution could be improved for the client.

Activity

Day 1 on the festival

ID Code	Event / Day	Description	Category / Department	Vendor Pos	Cost Price	Mark Up	Retail Price	Tax	Initial Stock	Stock Value	No Items Sold	Stock Level	Income Gross	Profit Net	Notes
F1A	27/07/2023	T Shirts (Adult)	Festival Merch (Clothing)	Festival Stall	£12.00	30.00%	£15.60	21%	200	£2,400.00	98	102	£1,528.80	£1,207.75	Main festival designs
F2A	27/07/2023	Hoodies (Adult)	Festival Merch (Clothing)	Festival Stall	£15.00	30.00%	£19.50	21%	200	£3,000.00	141	59	£2,749.50	£2,172.11	Main festival designs
F1C	27/07/2023	T Shirts (Child)	Festival Merch (Clothing)	Festival Stall	£10.00	30.00%	£13.00	0%	50	£500.00	14	36	£182.00	£182.00	Main festival designs
F2C	27/07/2023	Hoodies (Child)	Festival Merch (Clothing)	Festival Stall	£12.00	30.00%	£15.60	0%	50	£600.00	38	12	£592.80	£592.80	Main festival designs
A1A	27/07/2023	Artist T Shirts (Adult)	Artist (Clothing)	Festival Stall	£12.00	35.00%	£16.20	21%	200	£2,400.00	125	75	£2,025.00	£1,599.75	5% extra mark up to cover festival cost
A2A	27/07/2023	Artist T Hoodies (Adult)	Artist (Clothing)	Festival Stall	£15.00	35.00%	£20.25	21%	150	£2,250.00	90	60	£1,822.50	£1,439.78	5% extra mark up to cover festival cost
A1C	27/07/2023	Artist T Shirts (Child)	Artist (Clothing)	Festival Stall	£10.00	35.00%	£13.50	0%	200	£2,000.00	135	65	£1,822.50	£1,822.50	5% extra mark up to cover festival cost
A2C	27/07/2023	Artist T Hoodies (Child)	Artist (Clothing)	Festival Stall	£12.00	35.00%	£16.20	21%	100	£1,200.00	76	24	£1,231.20	£972.65	5% extra mark up to cover festival cost
FH1	27/07/2023	Hat (Style A)	Festival Merch (Clothing)	Festival Stall	£3.00	10.00%	£3.30	21%	200	£600.00	148	52	£488.40	£385.84	
FA1	27/07/2023	Hat (Style B)	Artist (Clothing)	Festival Stall	£3.00	15.00%	£3.45	21%	200	£600.00	137	63	£472.65	£373.39	5% extra mark up to cover festival cost
FO1	27/07/2023	Travel Cup (Festival)	Festival Merch (Other)	Festival Stall	£3.00	10.00%	£3.30	21%	150	£450.00	111	39	£366.30	£289.38	
SO1	27/07/2023	Travel Cup (Sponsor)	Sponsor (Other)	Sponsor Stall	£3.00	10.00%	£3.30	21%	200	£600.00		200		£0.00	
SC1	27/07/2023	T Shirt (Any size)	Sponsor (Clothing)	Sponsor Stall	£5.00	10.00%	£5.50	21%	200	£1,000.00		200		£0.00	
SO2	27/07/2023	Wrist Band	Sponsor (Freebie)	Sponsor Stall	£1.00	-100.00%	£0.00	0%	500	£500.00		500		£0.00	Given away as promotion
Totals:									3750	£16,450.00	1246		£13,740.50	£11,658.98	

Stock Cost	£16,450.00	Only sold at Festival Stalls
Income	£11,658.98	
Profit	-£4,791.02	

No sold	1246
Min sold	14
Max sold	148
Average sold	104

Evaluate how the spreadsheet above meets the client’s requirement to reduce data entry errors.

Activity

Evaluate how the principles and conventions of HCIs have been applied to **three** of the following.

- Domestic appliance
- Smart TV
- E-reader
- Satellite navigation system
- Gaming console
- Smartphone home screen

Consider whether the principles and conventions have made the HCI effective or not.

Test your knowledge

1. Which **two** aspects should you consider when evaluating how well a spreadsheet solution meets the client's needs?
2. What is house style?
3. What is accessibility?
4. What is memorability?
5. Why may a client not accept the final spreadsheet solution?

Assignment practice

Task 4

You now need to evaluate the spreadsheet you created in Assignment practice task 3. Here's a reminder of the scenario:

The headteacher of your school wants a new spreadsheet system to monitor the spending of the different departments in school. The spreadsheet will need an HCI that allows the headteacher to select different departments and see:

- the percentage of their budget that they have spent
- what they have bought in the last month.

The school logo will need to appear on the screen as well as the name and email address of the Head of Department of the department being viewed.

Evaluate how the spreadsheet solution that you created has met the headteacher's requirements.

Explain how the principles and conventions of HCI design have been applied to the spreadsheet solution.

Case study

Andrea has decided to get an allotment to grow her own food. It will cost her £20 a month to rent the allotment land.

Andrea wants to grow a range of vegetables and fruit on the allotment so that she can grow most of her own food all year.

Andrea would like a spreadsheet developed that will help her budget for her allotment. The spreadsheet needs to include:

- land rent
- seed prices (at least six different vegetables)
- garden tools that she needs to buy
- fertilisers for the soil
- what she has planted in which month
- when the vegetables should be ready for harvest (month).

Following the process that you learnt in Topic areas 1-4, develop a spreadsheet solution for Andrea to use to manage her allotment.

Unit R070

Using augmented reality to present information

About this unit

In this unit, you will learn what augmented reality (AR) is, what it is used for, and how it is used. You will also learn about the different devices that can be used to view an AR resource. You will learn how to plan and design an AR resource, as well as develop and test the prototype version. It is always important to reflect on work that you have carried out, so you will learn how to reflect on the processes that you followed and consider what you have learnt from your studies and the practical activities you have carried out.

Topic areas

In this chapter you will learn about:

1 Augmented reality (TA1)
2 Designing an AR model prototype (TA2)
3 Creating an AR model prototype (TA3)
4 Testing and reviewing (TA4)

How will I be assessed?

You will be set an assignment which will provide you with a scenario to create an AR model prototype. You will then need to use the skills that you have learnt to plan, design, create, test and review an AR model prototype solution to meet the requirements set out in the assignment.

The assignment will cover the following performance objectives:

PO2 – Apply knowledge and understanding

PO3 – Review knowledge, understanding and performance for the processes followed

PO4 – Demonstrate and apply skills and processes relevant to the subject area

Topic area 1 Augmented reality

Getting started

In small groups, prepare a leaflet to explain what you think AR is and how it is different from **virtual reality (VR)**. Use examples to help your explanations.

Each group will share their leaflet with the main group and agree a short statement defining the term 'augmented reality'.

1.1 Purposes and uses of AR

AR is a collection of technologies that are used to combine computer-generated information with the user's natural senses. AR has become a real revolution due to advances in mobile personal computing such as smartphones and tablets.

What AR is and its purposes

AR is a way of viewing the real-world environment with an overlay of computer-generated inputs, such as audio, video, graphics, photos and text. The two environments (the real-world and the augmented content environment) are totally separate and do not communicate with each other. This means that the computer-generated content does not recognise physical objects in the real-world environment. AR is a combination of the real world seen by the user and a computer-generated virtual world that **augments** the entire scene while also providing additional information. The virtual scene is designed so that it enhances the user's sensory perceptions of the virtual world they are seeing/interacting with. The purpose of AR is that the user cannot tell the difference between the real world and the virtual augmentation of it.

Key terms

Augment To make something larger by adding to it.

Virtual reality (VR) A computer-generated simulated environment. A person can interact within the simulated environment using special VR glasses, screens and even gloves fitted with sensors. The use of VR glasses stops the user from having any view of the real-world environment.

There are hybrid versions of AR known as **mixed reality (MR)** and **extended reality (ER)**, but for this unit you are only going to focus on AR.

The sectors where AR can be used

There are a number of sectors and industries that use AR, putting the technology to good use. Industries are continually implementing AR for the benefit and improvement of human performance as well as to support customers and encourage growth. Let's take a look at some of them.

Architecture

Architects and designers include not only people who design buildings, but also those who design gardens and other types of outdoor spaces (landscapers). One of the most important benefits to an architect of using AR is that it enables them to give their clients a sense of scale (size and proportion) that they would not have from looking at a computer screen or design drawings. Architects can show their planned projects in a 3D format using AR technology. The client can use a smartphone or similar device to walk around the objects and get a sense of the space and size of rooms, buildings, gardens, parks, and so on. Previously, a client could not have a tour of a building such as a house until it was physically built.

AR is also a useful resource for home improvements and renovations. It is possible to look at the potential changes that can be made and decide whether they are as expected or as required. This is more cost effective for the clients as they do not have to pay for the work to be done, only to discover that it is not what they wanted or does not suit the original purpose.

Key terms

Extended reality (ER) This is the overall term for all forms of real and virtual environments and includes AR, MR and VR.

Mixed reality (MR) MR enables contents to interact with objects in the physical world. This means that a computer-generated object can be partially obscured by objects in the physical world. For example, you could have a computer-generated person, animal or robot, partially hidden behind a tree in a forest.

Education

AR helps classroom education to be interactive. Teachers can show virtual examples of subjects, for example looking at a Saxon village in a History lesson or exploring organisms in a Biology lesson.

It is often easier to remember something that is visual than something that is text based. Using AR in education can help motivate students because it is more exciting and interesting.

AR is often used in professional training. Industries such as aviation, aerospace, healthcare and the military all use AR. It reduces the costs of equipment and event transportation to carry out activities. AR allows training to remain interactive but based in a classroom.

Entertainment

When people think of AR and entertainment, they often think of gaming. While AR was originally designed for games and interactive gamers, it is now used within other areas of the entertainment industry.

Gaming

Within the gaming sector, AR has defined what is known as immersive gaming. When Pokémon GO was released in 2016, for example, it captured the attention of millions of players around the world. People would walk around the streets trying to catch Pokémon, often gathering in places where there was a virtual 'Pokémon Gym'. This is because it focused on users physically interacting with the game.

Figure 3.1 This gamer can see a mythical creature superimposed in the real world

Travel and tourism

The use of AR in travel and tourism is referred to as a **travel portal**. This enables people to 'travel' the world using the screens on their smartphones or tablets. Travel industry marketing departments use AR to promote locations, products and movies so that users can explore them. Travellers can now view hotels and hotel rooms, walk around cities and even see what the seat is like on the plane they are going to fly on. AR is one of the best tools used by travel and tourism marketeers.

Art and museum galleries

AR is used to add additional information and explanations to exhibitions. Visitors can access information using their smartphones or tablets when viewing an artefact or piece of art. Some museums use AR to display digital views of the artists next to their work, who then provide a narrative. AR gives a third dimension to displays and brings objects and scenes to life.

Theatre

The use of AR has been successful in theatres. It has enabled theatregoers to have a more interesting experience. AR **avatars** can be projected on the stage alongside the actors, combining fictional worlds with the real world. Many theatres use a combination of AR and VR to provide a more **immersive** experience for their audience.

Key terms

Avatar A digital representation of a person or the person's character. It can take a 2D form as an icon used in internet forums or a 3D form in games and virtual worlds.

Immersive In relation to digital technology, this is the creation of a 3D image that appears to surround the user.

Travel portal Provides a virtual travel experience through a smartphone's AR application to help users choose the destination, hotel and holiday experience.

Music

Music fans can use AR to access information about artists, lyrics and composers, for example, or watch music videos. They simply use an app to scan the cover of the CD, or the online album cover on a streaming platform. Music artists have started to incorporate AR into their concerts. Imagine a band on the stage: members of the audience can point their smartphones towards the stage and the lead singer appears in a much larger form and looks like they are floating above the crowd.

Another use is where the artist or band is on stage and you are at home watching the concert on your television or computer. By pointing your smartphone at the screen, you have a sense of actually being at the concert.

Television

There are a number of television dramas and series that use AR – viewers point their smartphones or tablets at the screen to access additional information and feel as if they are a part of the scene. They have a totally immersive experience. The television programme *Strictly Come Dancing* uses AR to incorporate additional 'scenery' to enhance the experience of the story that the dancers are depicting through their performance.

Retail

AR applications can be used to provide 'try-before-you-buy' experiences. This includes being able to see what a piece of furniture or other products look like in a room. IKEA was one of the first retailers to implement this concept. Fashion retailers, such as Gucci and Louis Vuitton, have implemented AR so people can use a photograph of themselves to 'try on' clothing from the comfort of their own home. Dulux paint has provided an app called the Dulux Visualiser, where the customer takes photographs of the walls in the room they want to decorate and then selects different colour schemes to see what their walls will look like once painted. Even some jewellery retailers have introduced AR tools enabling customers to 'try on' different earring styles.

Lifestyle

People who enjoy carrying around and using the latest gadgets have been using AR without even realising it. An example is Snapchat. It has used AR to revolutionise the culture of selfies by detecting faces and overlaying them with a range of filters. AR enables the continuous tracking of faces. This means that it does not make any difference what strange expression a person makes – they will not distort the filter. Some of the filters available in Snapchat require the user to pull funny faces to trigger some of the special effects that are available.

Some industries, such as beauty and fashion, use AR and facial recognition to provide an immersive experience for their customers. Snapchat enables people to change their appearance using virtual makeup, for example using a different shade of eyeshadow or lipstick. Beauty brands offer the use of AR on their websites. You can upload a photo of your face and try different makeup styles and colours before buying.

All of these uses of AR can have an impact on your lifestyle if you choose to engage with them. You can take virtual tours of towns, cities, national parks, beaches, the countryside and even outer space without physically travelling. Marketeers are using AR more and more to bring products and locations to customers in their homes. The immersive experience received by the customer provides them with more information and a 'feel' for what the products or locations are like. This can give the customer more confidence in what they are paying for.

Research

Research how AR is used to train the following services:

- mountain rescue
- police
- fire
- ambulance
- coastguard or Royal National Lifeboat Institute (RNLI).

Make notes from your research and consider:

- the type of training
- how AR is used for the training
- the benefits and limitations of delivering training in this way.

Activity

Work in small groups. Each group selects a different service from the research activity. For the service you have selected, prepare a presentation to include:

- what AR is
- the type of training where AR is used
- how AR is used to deliver the training (and where appropriate, how it is used to test the participants in the training)
- the benefits and limitations of delivering the training in this way.

Consider using images and, where possible, video links within the presentation to demonstrate how the training is used.

Prepare an infographic which includes examples of the training, how AR is used and the benefits and limitations.

Your group will deliver the presentation to the rest of the class, answer any questions and provide the class with a copy of the infographic.

Uses of AR

Training

AR can enhance the learning and understanding of the workforce and can increase the engagement and safety awareness of the participants. In addition, it can reduce training costs.

Engagement

Many people learn by 'doing'. AR provides the opportunity for this by providing a 'hands-on' experience in a structured and interactive way. Employees can practise work activities in real-time and at their own pace, without any pressure from outside influences such as customers and managers.

Training costs

The initial cost of the equipment required to use AR can be high. But the equipment is reusable, and many people can use their own smartphones. The use of AR headsets and apps can even replace the need for people to attend expensive seminars, external training sessions or classes.

Safety

Some workplace activities are dangerous and therefore the training required to learn how to complete these activities safely can also be dangerous, for example firemen entering burning buildings where there is not only fire but poisonous gases. AR enables employees to practise these activities in a safe environment without the risk of injury or involving themselves in real dangerous situations.

Cognitive barriers

Job training can be challenging. The use of AR provides training to show how something is supposed to work in an interactive way rather than a theoretical way which, in turn, helps people to manage things when they go wrong because they have the knowledge about how something works.

Other benefits of using AR in training include the following.

- AR can motivate people to learn about the work activity and the organisation they work for. This is because it is a more exciting and imaginative experience.
- Training is available on demand.
- It helps the participants to retain information, knowledge and skills.

Many sectors already use AR for training, such as retail and healthcare.

In retail, AR is used to simulate interactions with customers.

In healthcare, hospitals such as St Mary's Hospital in London have doctors and surgeons who use AR during reconstructive surgery. Before the use of AR, surgeons would use handheld scanners to locate major blood vessels near the injury. With the use of AR they can now find these major blood vessels directly and accurately by displaying them on a screen as a three-dimensional image.

Virtual tours

What is a virtual tour? Imagine walking into a shop or a building such as a hotel, or a town or city for the first time. You have a look around and walk up to objects to take a closer look. You walk around and go along the different streets of a town or city, or different rooms within a building. Now you can do this by using the screen of your smartphone or your computer screen. This is called a virtual tour. There are many virtual tours available, such as The Harry Potter Experience in London and the Louvre Museum in Paris.

Visualisation of designs, interiors and concepts

AR technology is popular with architects and designers. It enables them to transfer their projects, ideas (concepts) and drawings from a 2D static representation into a 3D dynamic model.

AR enables designers to take the design from the screen and place it in the real world as an overlay in full-scale size. People can walk around the project and understand its size within the context of the space surrounding it and its general environment.

Basically, AR brings products to life, whether it is a piece of equipment or furniture, plants for a garden or a new building being built on land. It allows us to view the product within its context. In addition, AR provides the opportunity for a more collaborative design process regardless of where the designers are situated in the world.

Marketing

Markets are driven by the needs and desires of customers (consumers). AR is an emerging trend within marketing and sales and enables brands (McDonald's, Virgin and BT are all examples of brands) to provide their customers with unique experiences. These experiences are conveniently available to the customer through the use of their smartphones.

AR allows the customers to 'try before you buy'. Earlier in this section under the heading 'Retail' there were a number of examples of how the 'try-before-you-buy' concept had been implemented. Facebook's first AR-related advertisement enabled potential customers to try on sunglasses using the camera on their smartphone.

Starbucks has provided an AR experience enabling potential customers to tour one of its coffee shops. Potential customers can scan objects within the shop and access a virtual tour with additional information.

Within the automotive industry, Hyundai was the first manufacturer to create an AR manual for drivers. Customers could scan the manual using a smart device and it would provide them with information to do with certain parts of the cars, including instructions on how to carry out some basic maintenance.

The branding materials used by businesses, such as business cards and brochures, can be enhanced with AR. Users can access information about the business or representative of the business by scanning the printed materials with a smart device. An example could be a product within a brochure and by using the app on a smart device, the user can access a video highlighting some of the important features of the product and how it works.

More and more businesses are using AR to create a more exciting experience for their customers. In Zurich, Uber has created AR experiences to amuse its passengers by adding virtual adventures at Zurich station.

This link shows what it has created using AR:

https://youtu.be/bCcvEVyAXQ0

These exciting experiences have generated more than one million YouTube views. The use of AR for marketing purposes is endless.

Research

Research how AR is used to promote virtual tours and how it can be used for marketing purposes. It could be a virtual tour of a place, a hotel, an exhibition, a new house or a building design.

Find photos and videos that show how AR has been used within the virtual tours you have selected as part of your research.

Activity

The headteacher of your school wants to implement a marketing campaign for the school. You have been asked to come up with some marketing ideas and want to use AR but your headteacher does not understand what this is.

Create a presentation that explains how AR could be used to market the school. Include images and videos to make your presentation interesting.

Test your knowledge

1. Explain the difference between AR and MR.
2. Identify **two** ways that AR has been used within the entertainment industry.
3. Describe the term 'immersive'.
4. Explain how AR is used within the travel and tourism sector.
5. Discuss how AR can have an impact on people's lifestyles.

1.2 Types of AR and user interaction

There are several types of AR, and you are now going to look at the different types with examples of how they are used.

Types of AR

Object recognition/marker-based

This type of AR uses **markers** to **trigger** an augmented experience. The markers can be made

Key terms

Markers Visual prompts that trigger the display of virtual information.

Trigger The trigger activates the function of the AR experience.

with distinct patterns such as **QR codes**, logos or the packaging of products. These markers act as **anchors** for the technology to use. When a marker in the physical world is recognised by an AR application, the digital content is placed on top of it. It is commonly used in marketing and retail. Think of business cards that can talk to you or holiday brochures that can move.

Figure 3.2 The barcode/QR code is scanned by a shopper to purchase the product

Figure 3.3 A warehouse manager scanning packaging to identify picking and delivery time of products

How it works

Marker-based AR uses a specifically designed marker placed in the real-world space for the camera of the device or **computer vision** to lock on to. As stated above, this specifically designed marker could be a QR code, a logo or product packaging. Once the AR software has locked on to the marker, it will display the digital information associated with it.

The chocolate manufacturer Kinder includes a leaflet with a QR code on it with the toy in its Kinder Surprise egg. When the QR code is scanned by the AR app on a smartphone, it shows an AR version of the toy.

Research

Search on the internet for examples where QR codes, logos and product packaging are used as triggers for an AR experience.

Here are some links to YouTube clips to get you started.

- Using a QR code: **https://youtu.be/9w6_QBNuNuA**
- Using a logo: **https://youtu.be/cidBVt0ZkJE**
- Using product packaging: **https://youtu.be/YnJ0m-uzJbl**

For each of the types of triggers (QR code, logo and product packaging), consider how it could be used in different sectors. How could you provide an AR experience to a customer who wants to buy a washing machine by using the washing machine packaging as a trigger?

Remember, when carrying out your research think about the search criteria that you use (keywords). Try to be as specific as possible by using examples of:

- the use of QR codes as triggers for AR
- the use of logos as triggers for AR
- the use of product packaging as triggers for AR.

Markerless/location-based

Markerless AR is more versatile than marker-based AR. This means that it is more adaptable to

Key terms

Anchor Objects that AR software can recognise.

Computer vision How a computer understands the environment. It 'sees' via a digital image or video.

QR code A two-dimensional barcode that can be read using a digital device. It stores information as a series of pixels in a square-shaped grid.

Figure 3.4 This card game uses an AR app to bring the characters to life

many different functions and activities. It enables the user to decide where to put the virtual object. It relies on the device's hardware, including the camera, **Global Positioning System (GPS)**, **digital compass** and **accelerometer** to gather the information needed so that the AR software can work as required. Markerless AR is very popular in gaming, for example Pokémon GO.

The following types of AR also come under the heading of markerless AR because they do not require a physical marker to trigger the digital content.

- **Location-based AR:** This is where the digital content (AR content) is tied to a specific location. This is often used for navigation. For example, you are walking down a street in a location you are unfamiliar with. You use the camera on your smartphone to view the street and a virtual street sign will be displayed, giving you the name of the street. This is location-based AR.

Key terms

Accelerometer In a mobile phone, the accelerometer detects the orientation of the phone.

Digital compass A sensor that uses the Earth's magnetic fields to find direction. A digital compass will always find north.

Global Positioning System (GPS) A global navigation satellite system that provides the location of an object.

It will allow you to reach your destination with directions for where to go that are displayed on the streets in front of you. Another example of location-based AR is the game Pokémon GO.

Figure 3.5 This smartphone app uses AR to give the visitor information about nearby businesses and services

- **Superimposed:** This is where an object that is in the physical world is recognised by the superimposition AR. It is then enhanced in some way to provide an alternative view. The enhancement can relate to just a portion of the object being enhanced or the whole object.

Figure 3.6 The marker is the bathroom within the image, the digital content is the sink that is overlaid on top; this allows the customer to see what a particular sink will look like in their bathroom

Research

Research 'IKEA Place'. You might want to look on YouTube for videos on how it works, for example:

www.youtube.com/watch?v=UudV1VdFtuQ

Explain to another member of the class how IKEA Place uses AR and how it helps IKEA's customers.

Discuss with your classmate how the same AR experience could be used within your school.

User interaction/layers

AR is where the real world has layers of digital information projected onto it. A number of different examples were given in the previous section, such as the image of the location-based AR where the digital information relating to the street names and interesting places to visit is projected (overlaid) onto the real-world street view. So, imagine that you are standing in the centre of London and you use an AR app on your smartphone to navigate. Using the camera on your smartphone the app will recognise the location and overlay the digital content.

User interaction

Whenever you are going to design an AR app, you need to consider how the user will interact with objects. How the user interacts will depend upon the devices being used.

AR headset

This uses gaze and hand tracking for interaction. The AR headset will use gaze-based navigation to track where the user is looking. It will then target items in the environment. Once an item has been targeted, the user can interact with that item using hand gestures.

Figure 3.7 shows an artist wearing an AR headset. The artist is working on abstract 3D jellyfish sculptures, using hand gestures to create multimedia concept art with animation effects.

Figure 3.7 An artist wearing an AR headset working on an abstract 3D jellyfish sculpture

When you design an AR experience for someone wearing a headset, it is important that the user's hands remain within the viewing area of the headset. In addition, your design must be able to work with the specific hand gestures accepted by the headset. Users should also be notified when their hand gestures are getting near the visual boundaries of the headset. The AR app will not function as intended if the headset cannot see the hand gestures because they are out of view. The most important thing is that the interactions are kept as simple as possible.

User interaction for mobile devices

Many of the design principles for user interaction apply to both headsets and mobile devices. But there is a big difference between the interactive functionality of AR headsets and mobile AR experiences. The interactions for mobile devices use different rules.

It is still important that user interaction remains simple and includes feedback to the user when placing, or interacting with, an object. On mobile devices, most user interaction happens in a 3D space (real-world space) using gestures by touching the screen instead of using hand gestures (like the artist in Figure 3.7).

Most mobile device users are already used to using gestures, for example single-finger taps, drags, two-finger pinching and rotating. Users understand these interactions through using the two-dimensional world on the screen instead of the three-dimensional real world.

Voice interaction

Some AR devices support voice interaction, such as some AR headsets. Voice interaction can be a convenient way to control the application. It is important to think about the end user and how you can incorporate voice interaction and still ensure the app is simple to use. Consider the following.

- Keep commands simple as people have different dialects and accents.
- Voice interactions may be triggered by sound effects close by or by other people talking; it is important that any command can be stopped, undone, reversed.
- Do not use similar-sounding interactions. If the interactions sound too similar, the wrong command may be triggered. An example is 'make reference' and 'make preference'. These two commands sound too similar and, therefore, could be confused by the app and trigger the wrong action.

- Do not use voice commands that are pre-set system commands, such as 'home screen'. If 'home screen' is a system command for the AR device and you create a new command using the term 'home screen', you will overwrite the original command and the system may stop functioning.
- Provide feedback to the user. The voice interactions should provide feedback to the end user in the same way as any other interaction method. The device must provide confirmation that the voice command has been heard and understood. Consider how Alexa and Google Home function through the use of voice commands. The feedback could be an audio response or written text on the screen of the device.

Activity

Investigate the voice commands used by Amazon's Alexa or Google Home. Create a table identifying the commands used by the device you have selected and state what each command does.

In a group, consider what commands you could use for a new device similar to Alexa and Google Home but that are not the same commands (using the same words in the same way).

Static or interactive

Static

If the digital content in an AR app is text, visual cues or 3D models (whose appearance does not alter during interaction with the user), then this is known as static content. For example, consider using an AR app in an art gallery to view a painting that is on display. When the painting is identified within the app, text appears that tells you about the painting, who the artist is, when it was painted, and so on. This is an example of static content. Static visualisations do not show any form of continuous movement.

Interactive

This is where the digital content such as animation or video changes its appearance during interaction with the user. These objects change continuously with time and represent a continuous flow of movement. For example, consider using an AR app to view a globe. Through user interaction, the globe can be rotated, and the user can view the different countries shown on the globe.

The type of digital content used will depend upon the purpose of the AR app.

Test your knowledge

6 Explain the term 'superimposed/superimposition'.
7 Describe the difference between marker-based and markerless.
8 Identify **three** different methods of user interaction.
9 Give **one** example of a static AR experience.
10 Give **one** example of an interactive AR experience.

1.3 Devices used with AR

Types of devices AR can be used on

There are a number of different devices that can be used for AR.

Table 3.1 AR devices

Device	Mobile device	Smart device	Computer/PC
Smartphones	X	X	X
Tablets/phablets	X	X	X
AR headsets	X	X	X
AR glasses	X	X	X
Kiosk systems/AR installations		X	X
Desktop computers			X
Laptops	X		X

Mobile devices

A mobile device is any electronic device that is portable (it can be easily carried from one place to another). These include smartphones, tablets (and **phablets**), and laptop computers. If you want to design an AR app that people can use anytime, anywhere, then designing the app for mobile devices is the best solution. Tablets/phablets have more computing power and a larger display than smartphones and this may be another factor to consider when designing an AR app.

Smart devices

Smart devices are interactive electronic gadgets that are able to connect to, interact with, and share with the user and other smart devices. There are many smart devices such as refrigerators, televisions, watches, and so on. But when referring to AR, smart devices include:

- the mobile devices identified above
- AR glasses (these are not the same as smart glasses)
- AR headsets
- AR kiosks
- AR installations.

AR headsets and AR glasses are also mobile as they can be transported from one place to another.

AR glasses

AR glasses use a front-facing camera. They add 3D images, animations and videos to the user's real-world environment by overlaying computer-generated/digital information. They can retrieve information from computers, smartphones and other devices as they can support Wi-Fi, Bluetooth and GPS. Here are some examples of how AR glasses can be used.

Key term

Phablet A combination of a phone and a tablet (**PH**one-t**ABLET**).

When used with AR software designed for decorating the home, the software will recognise things such as the window frames or where two walls join. Using this information, the software can generate images, for example curtains, furniture, lights, and so on, and situate them in the view of the user by projecting the items onto the lens of the AR glasses.

If the AR glasses also have an integration microphone, they can communicate with Alexa or Siri to carry out voice-controlled searches. The results will appear on the lenses of the AR glasses.

Message alerts can be discreetly displayed on the lens. The user can then note and dismiss them without having to use the smartphone.

Using integrated GPS, virtual arrows will appear in the user's view and help them navigate where they are going.

Figure 3.8 AR smart glasses used by a customer to buy a product in a store

Smart contact lenses are already in production and cameras can be controlled through blinking the eye. They can be used to monitor a person's health data including the identification of glaucoma symptoms and blood sugar levels.

AR headsets

AR headsets allow viewers to see images that are superimposed on the real-world environment of the user. They work in a similar way to AR glasses but because they cover the eyes completely, they are more immersive.

Figure 3.9 An engineer wearing an AR headset when designing a prototype of an electric motor

AR kiosks/installations

AR kiosks and installations are often used by museums, art galleries and retailers. But the opportunities for their uses are vast. Users do not have to carry smartphones or any other device with them to access the AR experience. The graphic quality is usually of a higher standard because there is greater computer power.

Figure 3.10 An AR kiosk

Figure 3.11 An AR installation

Have a look at these YouTube clips for some examples:

- a photobooth kiosk using AR: **https://youtu.be/rfafnNsXlEA**
- a photokiosk linked to Hong Kong's Museum of History: **https://youtu.be/8k1Tz0Zrspg**
- an installation in Singapore called Story of the Forest: **https://youtu.be/0Mv92Dpcgfl**
- A website showing examples of AR kiosks and how they are used in museums: **www.magicmirror.me/Industry/Augmented-Reality-Kiosk-for-Museums**

Research

Work in a group of three or four and research examples of the use of AR kiosks and AR installations. Remember to use sensible keywords to help your research when using the internet.

To get you started, look at this example of a young boy having fun using an AR kiosk in Disney, Florida:

https://youtu.be/8UxWkZtUKal

In your group, prepare a presentation to deliver to the rest of the class. The presentation should include video/photographic content showing examples of how AR kiosks and installations are used and where they can be used.

Finish your presentation by sharing some ideas with your class on how an AR kiosk/AR installation could be used in your school.

Laptop/PC

Desktop AR is a technology that enables laptops and PCs to create an illusion of 3D objects that float in front of the screen. This is achieved by rendering red–blue 3D images according to the user's viewing position.

Users can download and use desktop AR apps using their laptop/PC webcam and red and blue (anaglyph) glasses. An AR desktop is virtually free because it only requires a laptop/PC and a webcam. Anaglyph glasses are readily available to buy online and cost very little. The user experience can be improved by using 3D monitors.

There is a difference between the user experiences when using mobile AR and desktop AR. For mobile AR, the user's experience is not enhanced directly. It indirectly enhances the videos that the users see in their mobile device. The quality of the user's experience is not as good as it is with desktop AR. Desktop AR directly augments the user's perception of the real world. It displays images that are corrected for each user's eye. This creates a more immersive experience.

There is a collection of desktop AR apps available. The following link can be used to access apps that you can download and use on your laptop/PC without any charge:

www.holo-sdk.com/sample-apps

Figure 3.12 shows you an example of developers using a sophisticated desktop AR app.

Figure 3.12 Developers using a sophisticated desktop AR app

Test your knowledge

11 Identify **two** mobile devices that can be used for AR.
12 Identify **two** types of businesses that could use AR kiosks.
13 Describe the term 'desktop AR'.
14 Describe how AR glasses work.
15 The quality of mobile AR images is better than desktop AR images. True or false?

Topic area 2 Designing an AR model prototype

Getting started

In small groups, look on the internet for an example of an AR app that has been created. Look at how the app works, what it is required to do and who you think the app is aimed at (the audience).

In your group, make a list of all of the things that you would need to think about if you were creating this same AR app. The list should be detailed and include everything that you would need to think about, for example what sources you would use, where you would get them from, what software you would use, and so on.

Prepare a presentation to deliver the results of your research to the rest of the class.

2.1 Planning and design considerations

The more you interact with AR experiences, the more you will be become aware of which are good experiences and which are not. When you get started on your journey of designing and planning an AR app, there are some simple tips and tricks that you can use to improve the user's experience.

Purpose and user requirements

Do your research

You need to ask yourself *why* the user experience would be better if you used AR.

It is important to understand how your users will benefit from your AR app. As you have read in the previous topic areas, there are many reasons for using AR.

It is important to carry out as much research as you can, especially about your target market.

For example, if you are creating an AR app for education or for the travel industry, ask:

- who is your target audience?
- what are you trying to tell them?

When carrying out research you will see plenty of design ideas. So you need to understand what is and what isn't possible with the software that you have and the devices that will be used by the end users.

You need to have a balance between the functionality of the design and the technical capabilities of the target audience. The most important thing is to keep your target audience (the user) as the focal point of your design.

Consider constraints and opportunities

AR is new and exciting, so it can be tempting to include everything that it can do and provide the user with endless features. This is not a good idea – your design will be more effective if you keep it simple.

Too many features can make it overly complex if there is no requirement or real benefit to the user. Remember: the user can do only so much at any one time.

Keep it simple and keep your user focused on the AR experience. A major constraint of AR is the **viewfinder**. A person can only see and interact with what is in their view at any moment in time. The user is in control of the movement and therefore they are controlling the viewfinder. For users new to AR, this can be quite challenging at first.

Most AR users use their smartphone, so use your own smartphone to see what sort of view the end user will see. Consider:

- how much real-world space can be seen?
- what size image can be displayed?
- how much information can be displayed?
- and so on.

Remember you cannot control where the user is looking, so this is a challenge when designing an AR app. Think about how your user will use their device. Will they hold the smartphone or tablet with both hands?

You must carefully plan any interaction for the user. Ask yourself: can the user take one hand off the device to touch the screen?

Key term

Viewfinder Part of the camera that a person looks through, and part of the camera within the device being used by the user.

In many cases, the answer is 'yes', but it can also be a challenge for many people. This is especially relevant if the app is to be used on larger devices.

Consider the use of navigation buttons or quick options that will ensure the user can remain focused on their AR experience and navigate at the same time.

Help the user on their journey

The AR app that you design may be the first AR experience that a person is having. So it is important that, before starting, they are provided with clear instructions that introduce them to the basics, for example they might need a flat surface with plenty of light. If you do not tell them, they will not know. If the user is going to be using a smartphone, then consider using similar interaction that they will use, for example pinching fingers together to reduce an image size, and so on.

Simple instructions with images can help a novice to get the most out of an AR experience. But remember, there will be users who are familiar with using AR who need to be able to 'skip' instructions.

Think about the user's environment

Will the user be using the app indoors or outdoors? It is also important for the user to know whether the experience is intended for a large space, such as a room, or a small space, such as a table top.

You may be designing an AR app where the user is playing a sport such as football or netball. Football and netball pitches are large spaces so it may be a good idea to include a virtual pitch so that the user can concentrate on using the app to play the game as opposed to finding a suitably sized space within their environment.

Think about what the user can interact with

It must be clear to the user what elements they can and cannot interact with. A visual indicator can be used to help the user.

Visual indicators could be outlines of something, for example the outline of a swimming pool or circles placed under chairs. Depending on what the interactivity is, it may be helpful to show what object is selected and indicate this by highlighting it. This is especially helpful if there are multiple objects that can be seen by the user.

It is also important that users can access other interactions quickly, for example to move things around. Ask yourself: how would they do this? Would they drag the object, or touch the image and use a menu of options? What happens to the object when it is moved? Usually, an object that is moved gets smaller so that the user can confirm that the object has moved.

Will the user be able to use standard rotation, for example to rotate a chair? Will they be able to scale the object? If so, how? Will it be a pinch action similar to when you resize the screen, or an object on the screen of a smartphone?

You have no control over the user's environment. Their environment may be too dark, or they may find themselves outside the boundaries of the app and not know how to get back. Some apps use an 'off-screen' indicator with an error message that helps a user to get back within the boundaries.

Make it believable

The environment you create must be realistic (believable). The virtual objects you use need to look real so that they do not look out of place in the user's environment. Light and space are important considerations. The height of objects should be maintained if they are being moved around in space.

For example: If a user was using an AR app to learn about planets and the solar system, they could select a planet and be provided with information about it and asked to place it in its appropriate position in the solar system. If the planet has to be moved further back into the solar system, it will reduce in size (because it is further away from the user), so it must be able to adapt to the view and become the size required.

Lighting is very important when trying to create realism. If the lighting does not reflect the typical lighting within the environment, then the experience will not be believable. Using highlights, shadows and reflections all help to make things look more realistic.

Using detail and texture is also important for the virtual objects. Texture brings objects to life. Flat coloured surfaces are not perfect and, therefore, need to look natural.

You need to consider what should – and should not – be in the AR world. Where do things such as game-scoring information belong? It depends on the app, but controls and messages should not be in the direct view (viewpoint) of the user unless absolutely necessary.

It is also important to consider the consistency of the design. The Human Computer Interface (HCI)/user interaction must be as consistent as possible. Common HCI design elements should be used consistently, such as icons, components and messages. These should all be predictable to the user throughout the use of the app. Think of using colours – such as green for start and red for stop – as part of the commands and instructions when designing the HCI.

Synoptic link

You learnt about HCIs in Unit R050, Topic area 2 and Unit R060, Topic area 1.

Think about safety, safety, safety

This is the most important consideration. Immersive experiences are great fun, but there is also the possibility that the users can forget what is actually happening in their environment. It is, therefore, very important to design AR experiences with safety in mind.

Key term

Visual indicator The app displays an indicator on the screen, for example the outline of a square with grid lines. This is used to show where an object can be placed.

Do not ask your users to, for example, walk backwards or do anything else that may put them at risk of falling over or put them in danger. Include 'reminders' as the users may be focused on walking around holding their smartphone, using their AR headsets or AR glasses, and so on.

Consider including resting points within the app through in-app notifications. If a user is going to pause, make it easy to store progress so that they can 'pick up' where they left off. It is also important that users are not required to do anything that is physically demanding or that makes them feel uncomfortable.

Target audience

As with any design idea, you need to understand who your target audience is. Are they busy people who just want to access the information quickly? Are they people who want to use something quick and flashy to capture their short attention span? It is, therefore, important to determine the demographics of your target audience. This will help you to narrow down the type of AR technology that is appropriate for your project.

It is also important to consider something known as the 'customer journey'. Is your target audience researching options, such as looking for new furniture for their home, trying on clothes via online shopping, or considering where to go on holiday? If this is the case, then you should focus on making sure the target audience is aware of what is being offered.

Are the users ready to purchase a product, such as a new television, car or house? If so, you should focus on providing information relating to the features and benefits of the product and of buying from a particular supplier. The customer journey is an important focus for digital marketing, but it is just as important when designing an AR app for a specific purpose.

Using a table – such as Table 3.2 – can help you clearly see who your target audience is and their reason for using the AR app.

Table 3.2 Table indicating purpose of an AR app and the information required

Why AR app is used	Example	Information needed for the user journey
Researching items to buy	New furniture in the house	• Features of the furniture: • Size • Style • Colour • Price • Benefits of product • How it looks in the room
Learning new information	The planets of our solar system	• Names • Locations on map • Details of planets: • Size • Atmosphere

Synoptic link

You learnt about demographics in Unit R050, Topic area 5, section 5.5.

Content

When planning the content for your AR design, there are four key principles that you must consider:

- How will you represent the physical setting?
- How will you anchor the content?
- How will you format the content?
- How will you source the content?

The physical setting

It is important to understand what the physical environment is like so that you can make relevant content for it. You need to consider:

- the use of image markers, such as QR codes embedded on objects, to place the content against

- the use of computer vision to detect flat surfaces or walls for a **surface plane**.

Anchoring the content

With AR, the user can see the real world through the display of the device. The device and the software have to be able to recognise something that is in the real world and create the AR experience around it. In other words, it needs to know where to place the augmented content. This is called an anchor. The anchor then triggers the experience.

An example of the use of anchors are those used in social media that allow people to add rabbit ears or glasses, or change their hairstyle and mouth shape. The anchor used is the general shape of the face. When the user looks into the camera, the anchor identifies the person's face and then they can augment ears, glasses, hairstyles, mouth shapes, and so on, onto their own face.

Figure 3.13 Image of a young girl who has augmented her features using TikTok

Content format

Content can be displayed in many different formats, such as text, images, data, sound and videos.

Sourcing content

The sources used for the content can come from a variety of places, but it is always important that copyright and licensing laws are complied with.

Sources can be paper-based or digital. They can be images, videos or audio, and they can already exist or be created for the project. You could ask people to provide audio clips (for example, to provide some information about a subject) or video content (for example, to demonstrate how to use a particular tool).

Synoptic link

You learnt about the Copyright, Designs and Patents Act in Unit R050, Topic area 4, section 4.4.

Assets

You previously learnt that AR consists of the overlaying of digital content with the user's view of the real world. This digital content is referred to as virtual assets. These can consist of audio, video, graphics, photographs and text. Whatever virtual asset(s) you use, they should be the best quality you can get.

Audio

If using audio within an AR app, it is important to consider what the purpose of the audio is.

If you want to create an audio clip of someone explaining something, then you must ensure that the recording is clear and that the person can be easily understood. For example, if you wanted to record someone explaining about a location on a walking tour of a village or town, you want the recording to be clear so that the user can understand what is being said and can hear it clearly, above any background noise. It

Key term

Surface plane The boundaries of a surface, such as a table top, desk or wall, that a virtual object can be placed on.

will be of no use to the user if they cannot hear the recording properly or understand what the person is trying to tell them.

Audio recordings could include sound effects. These must be good quality, and you should consider their volume. If the sound effect is of an explosion, for example, you do not want to damage the user's ear drums by having the sound effect too loud. Users do not always consider turning the volume of the device up and down.

Charts and graphs

Graphs and charts help explain and analyse data. It is important that the graphs and charts are appropriate for the data being presented, clearly and correctly labelled, and of good quality, for example the colour and weight of lines in a graph need to be considered to ensure they are visible when overlaid on the real-world environment.

Hyperlinks/weblinks

If you are going to include a hyperlink or a weblink into your AR experience then you need to consider the following:

- Can you guarantee that the links will be available for the lifetime of your AR product?

  It is disappointing to the end user if a link doesn't work – this can damage the reputation of your AR product.
- How will the user interact with the links? Will it be through touching the screen, or providing a specific voice command?

Photographs/images

Photographs and images used in AR should have a high level of detail and contrast, including any unique patterns. If the level of detail and contrast is poor, the AR experience can still take place, but there will be a reduction in the quality of the experience.

Select a unique photograph from your own collection or create a design yourself. If you use photo library photos, someone else may have also used the same photograph.

Imagine two people in the same room in close proximity using AR apps that have been created using the same software by two different people, using the same photographs (but for different purposes). The AR experience created by one person and the AR experience created by the other person will be distorted. The software will recognise the image, but may not be able to select the correct information/object for the person using the app. In other words, the two different applications will try to work as one app if they are close to each other.

Do not use logos as marker images. A logo can appear in multiple materials for different contexts. It can be confusing to the computer vision and prevent the correct content becoming available when the target image is scanned. If you want to include a logo, include it in the instructions.

Avoid using the same images or symbols within your design. All elements should be unique. In order for the computer vision to recognise the marker image, it must recognise approximately 70 per cent of its feature points. If the same images/symbols are used for different reasons within the design, the computer vision will be unable to decide what content you want for each image/symbol.

Images should not be blurred. Computer vision cannot interpret blurry images. So do not use images/photographs with blurry backgrounds whenever possible. Look for photographs and images that have high resolution and different textures. Remember, there are no feature points when something is blurred!

It is important to remember that, when your AR marker is scanned with a mobile device, it must take up at least 50 per cent of the camera screen as well as keeping any white space to a minimum.

Refer to Topic area 1.2 for explanation of the term 'computer vision'.

Text

With AR, the user's view can change every time they move. So it is important that text remains legible regardless of the colour of the background, the texture or the depth. It is good practice to select fonts that have open letter shapes and sufficient letter spacing.

Poorly designed and implemented text can distract the user from the immersive AR experience. Text that is designed and placed well can add to the AR experience. Helvetica is a popular text font to use for AR.

Video

Video content may or may not include sound. This very much depends on the purpose of the video. The images must be clear and of good quality. It is important that the required specification for the video is supported by the AR development software that you are using.

There may be a minimum requirement with respect to the number of pixels permitted/recommended. If the video is to contain audio, then this must also be sufficiently loud to hear and clear with respect to the speech. 360° cameras have become popular for the creation of more immersive video content for AR.

Research

Pepsi used AR to advertise Pepsi Max in bus shelters across London:

https://youtu.be/GB_qT6rAPyY

Watch the video and look for other examples of similar ideas to the 'bus shelter augmented reality' created by Pepsi.

Show the examples you have found to your classmates and discuss the following with them:

- How have they used sound and vision (in your examples as well as Pepsi's)?
- Do you think it is an effective use of AR?
- Could a similar AR experience be created for your school?

Triggers

What do we mean by the term 'triggers'? To display the AR experience, you use the AR app on the device to scan a trigger/marker image. This image then triggers the device to show the augmented digital content.

The trigger causes the device/software to function and show the augmented digital content associated with the trigger image.

There are three types of AR trigger:

- Object recognition/marker-based
- Markerless/location-based
- Superimposed (sometimes called superimposition)

Synoptic link

You learnt about the three types of AR trigger in Topic area 1, section 1.2 of this unit.

Consider these important questions you should ask yourself before a user can interact with your digital world:

- What content do you want to display on the user's live camera view?
- Where exactly do you want the content to be placed within the user's view?

Your answers will depend upon which AR application you are using. Each AR application can require different types of user interaction.

- If you want to display AR content in a specific position in the view of the user's real world, you would use object recognition/marker-based triggers.
- If you want to display AR content and it does not matter what the user's real-world view is, you would use a markerless trigger.
- If you want to display AR content that provides information that is linked to the location that a person is viewing in their real world, you would use a location-based (GPS) trigger.

  For example, a person is walking through the streets of London and, as they look through their viewfinder, information appears through the AR app, providing the street names for the area in which they are walking, or an image appears showing where the nearest underground station is.
- If you want to fully or partially overlay an AR image over the user's real-world view (or even the user themselves), then you would use a superimposed trigger.

Layers/user interaction

Synoptic link

You learnt about layers/user interaction in Topic area 1, section 1.2 of this unit.

Action flow

You want the AR experience of the user to appear smoothly and flow from one area to the next. It is, therefore, important to consider the following:

- How will the user interact with the AR app to move from one 'area' to another? Will there be multiple layers?

  For example, you select the door of a house, it takes you into the hallway, you then have a choice of doors to open and view the rooms. So, by selecting a particular room you can enter, look around, exit the room back into the hall and go into the next room, and so on.
- How will the action flow? Flow charts are a good design tool when designing the flow of the AR experience.

Static

Will the digital content alter during any user interaction? If the answer is no, then this will be a static layer.

For example, you only want some information to appear on the screen when the user clicks on a trigger. Consider an image of a Formula 1 car. By clicking on the image, text will appear informing the user who the manufacturer is, who its drivers are, and so on.

Interactive

Will the digital content alter during user interaction? If the answer is yes, then this will be an interactive layer.

For example, you want the user to rotate an image of a room so that they can see the various views of the room. The user will interact with the image and rotate the image as if they were turning round to look at different parts of the room. This is interactive.

Test your knowledge

1. Explain why it is important to carry out research when planning and designing an AR app.
2. What is the purpose of a visual indicator?
3. Describe the key points to remember when using photographs and images for an AR app design.
4. Explain the difference between a marker-based and a markerless trigger.
5. Explain the term 'static' with reference to layers and user interaction.

Assignment practice

Task 1

You have been asked to create an AR app for students at Key Stage 3 to use in a Geography lesson about the Antarctic and the impact of global warming. The AR app can be for use with a smart device and/or a PC.

Prepare a document or presentation that explains your planning and design considerations for the AR app.

2.2 Design tools

The first stage of any development process is to design the solution. The design stage and use of design tools helps you to check that the solution you plan will:

- meet the requirements of the person you are designing the solution for (the client) and the end user
- be fit-for-purpose and provide the information required, as well as providing the end user with an exciting AR experience
- enable the end user to use the AR app as intended regardless of their skill level when using the technology.

Synoptic link

Design tools were covered in Unit R050, Topic area 1, section 1.1.

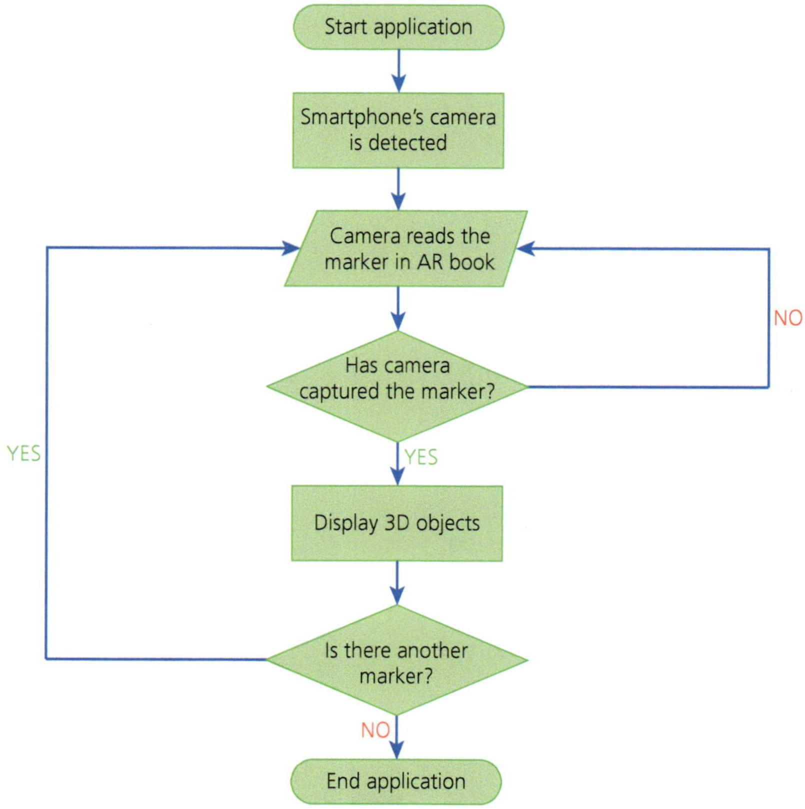

Figure 3.14 A typical flow chart for an AR app

Flow charts

A flow charts is a useful design tool when designing the action flow of your AR app. You will include the steps and decisions that are required for the AR app to access the AR digital content and the user interaction for how they will move through the AR app.

Mind maps

Using a mind map is a useful way to note your creative ideas for an AR app. The central node will be the purpose (and type) of AR experience you are designing. You can then use the nodes and sub-nodes to document your different ideas. It is a useful way to share your initial ideas with the person who has asked you to create the AR app.

Mood boards

A mood board is a physical or digital collection of images, text and other design considerations which are placed in a format that represents the style of the final design.

Figure 3.15 A designer's physical mood board with ideas for colours, fonts and shapes

Purpose

Mood boards can be used to:

- organise ideas about a project, such as the design for an AR app
- ensure that the style and aesthetics remain consistent during the design process

- refine the style of the design prior to the actual development of the product
- provide information about the look and feel of the final design.

Uses

Mood boards are used:

- as a starting point for any creative design and are particularly useful when designing an AR app
- to collect sample materials and ideas relevant to the overall purpose of the AR app.

A mood board is not used to provide a view of what the product will look like – that is what the prototype is for. The mood board is a view of the ideas.

Contents

The contents of physical mood boards include:

- images (photographs, logos, posters, advertisements and so on)
- text, triggers, fonts and styles
- types of surfaces, objects, lighting and size
- colours, for example the colour scheme to be used within the AR app.

As well as the contents above, a digital mood board may include sound and video clips. (A physical mood board would include the source reference and an explanation of the content for these elements.)

Storyboards

A storyboard is a sequence of images placed together to represent a series of steps. Storyboards can be used to show how the interaction in an AR app would take place and how it would appear. This allows the user to clearly see what will happen using images instead of trying to understand it by reading words only.

The storyboard allows you to find out the user's point of view (POV) from scene to scene and to provide accurate detail on the surroundings, the space and the user interaction. Storyboards must:

- visually tell the story
- detail the idea, the models, characters, settings, surroundings, sequence of events and interaction
- reflect the design ideas for the AR app and the potential point of view of the user.

For each scene within the storyboard you must state the areas of interest to include, such as:

- the field of view, for example what are the surroundings that the user will see including horizons, floors, ceilings, ground and sky, as well as the objects that may be in these surroundings
- an estimation of the user's POV, for example where will the user be positioned when in their surroundings – will they be looking down a street in a town or city, or will they be standing on top of a mountain?
- the start and end points for each scene
- what user interaction is taking place and what the user is doing during this scene:
  - Will they be required to interact with their surroundings, for example to walk in certain directions?
  - Will they be required to perform any interactions, for example on screen, give a voice command or hand gestures?
  - Will they be viewing an image, listening to an audio clip, or watching a video?

The storyboard is also where you state what a user can and cannot do during each scene.

Storyboards should also include documented information relating to any special effects, voiceovers and notes.

Visualisation diagrams

A visualisation diagram enables you to visualise your AR app without actually creating it. It can be hand drawn or digitally created using visualisation software. You can share your visualisation diagrams with others to exchange ideas and to receive feedback.

A visualisation must include:

- sketches/drawings of the AR app
- photographs/images/audio/video to be used
- text including font style, size and colour
- the overall colour scheme to be used within the AR app.

It is also important to include annotations that explain the choices you have made within your design.

Wireframes

Wireframes are created during the AR app design stage to document what the AR app will do (unlike the visualisation diagram that shows what it may look like).

It is important to read the section about wireframes in Unit R050, Topic area 1, section 1.1 Design tools, especially the reference to high- and low-fidelity wireframes.

Synoptic link

Refer to Unit R050, Topic area 1, section 1.1, Design tools.

Figure 3.16 Wireframe diagrams used for an AR app design

Test your knowledge

6 Explain the purpose of using a flow chart when designing an AR app.
7 Describe the components of a mind map.
8 You want to include samples of the actual video and audio in your AR app. Would you create a hand-drawn mood board or a digital mood board?
9 Describe each component for each scene that should be included in a storyboard.
10 Identify **two** things that should be included in a visualisation diagram.

Assignment practice

Task 2

Using the planning and design considerations that you created while working on Assignment practice task 1, design the content and action flow for your AR app.

You are required to use:

- a mind map
- a flow chart
- a mood board
- a storyboard
- a visualisation diagram
- a computer-generated wireframe (high-fidelity wireframe).

Topic area 3 Creating an AR model prototype

Getting started

Create an infographic to explain to people what a prototype is, why it is used and who uses it. You have some information in the section above, but may need to carry out research to gather further information.

3.1 AR model prototype

One of the important requirements during any design process is the designing and development of prototypes. In this topic area, you will learn about different prototypes and the things you need to consider and include when creating an AR prototype.

The prototype provides the client and the end users with an idea of how the AR app will look and work before creating the final product. It allows you to focus on important elements of the AR app, for example interactivity, triggers, views, and so on. Creating a functional prototype will provide you and the end user with a clear indication of what the final AR app will look like and how it will function.

Types of prototype

Feasibility prototype

- Used for trying out new technological or software-related ideas.
- Helps to understand any technical risk relating to performance.
- Used to test a specific design element or feature of a product and not the product as a whole.

Example: A new robotic design has been developed to be used for the extraction of oil from an oil field. A feasibility prototype would be created to look at how the robotic device would work to extract oil safely. It would include how it extracts the oil from the oil well and what risks (especially to health and safety) there could be.

Low-fidelity user prototypes

- Do not look real and are basically an interactive wireframe.
- Used to simulate processes to identify any user issues as early as possible.
- Do not include user interaction.

Example: This is where the processes using the robotic design for oil extracted from the well are tested.

High-fidelity user prototypes

- Look real and simulate how the design will work.
- Used to present the design ideas to clients and end users.
- Used to see what the client/end user does not like about the design as well as what they do like (gather feedback).
- Allow real user interactions.
- Look as close as possible to the final product.

Example: An AR app is designed for a teacher to use in a Science lesson. It is important that the prototype reflects the final product as closely as possible so that it can be tested by the end users. Therefore the HCI, action flow, triggers, and so on, must be available for the user to use.

For this unit, you will be required to create a high-fidelity user prototype.

Live-data prototypes

- Have access to live data.
- Should not impact on any processes running outside of the design.

Example: A person has created a spreadsheet to calculate the rate of production for extracting oil from an oil well.

The live-data prototype will be used to run alongside the original system so that results can be compared and amendments made to the design if required, prior to the final spreadsheet being developed and implemented into the current system.

Characteristics

When designing AR products, you may use one or more of the above prototypes during the design stage in your design documentation. But for the purpose of this unit and the set assignment, you will be required to create a high-fidelity prototype only.

Not full product

It is important to remember that the prototype is not the final product. It will simply contain sufficient interaction and use of triggers, and so on, for the user to see how it will work, what it will look like and what the intended AR experience will be.

Confirms functionality

The prototype must be able to confirm that the HCI, triggers and layers, and so on, work as intended.

Confirms aesthetics

The prototype must show how the product will look and feel to the user. The user's first impression of any product is the visual (look) of the product. Therefore it is important that the prototype provides a good visual of how it will look. This could include:

- the colours to be used
- the quality of the audio/video
- the quality, such as sharpness of the images, photographs and/or video content
- the style, such as how things are laid out in the viewfinder for the user
- the scale of text/images/photographs, and so on.

Has access to real data

If the purpose of the AR app is to access and use real data, then the prototype must show that this can happen, if appropriate how it happens, and the possible results from the access of the data. All of this will depend upon the overall purpose of the AR app.

3.2 Triggers

Trigger characteristics

A trigger image is one of the basic building blocks when creating an AR app. When the image is detected as the user views it through the viewfinder, an overlay appears (the augmented content).

For example, if you wanted to use a trigger image that would launch a video of you and your friends having a party, you would use a photo of yourself and your friends as the trigger image. The video of you and your friends at the party would then be overlaid as the digital content. Each time you point your smartphone at the photograph, the video will play.

So, what makes a good trigger image? A good trigger image should have plenty of detail on it. If using a photograph, try to use one that has been taken head-on (in other words, taken pointing directly at you and your friends).

Do not use an image that has anything reflective. The reflection will not allow sufficient detail of the image to be seen. Images of water, mirrors and white paper, white or very light clothes all reflect light – these will also reduce the quality of the image and there will not be enough detail. Brown paper, for example, is not reflective and does not reflect light. Also avoid anything that moves or is not flat. So a trigger image could be a flat photograph of a person with their family or friends. You would not be able to create a trigger out of a moving image such as a video clip.

Trigger images must be unique.

Different trigger images should be used to trigger the different AR content. The image size is also important to ensure that you have the recognisable view for image recognition and tracking by the AR app. Small images (that are so small it is difficult to see what the image is of), do not contain enough graphical information to show the feature points. The feature points must be unique, sufficient and equally balanced so that they can be easily detected and tracked by the AR app.

Trigger images must not contain blurred images, too much text or too much blank space.

Blurred images do not show sufficient detail which means it will be difficult for the AR app to recognise them.

Figure 3.17 This image is too blurred to be used as a trigger

Too much text causes unreliability when AR content is displayed on top of it. If you have a page of mostly text, then it is advisable to select an area of the page that contains an image and to use the image as the trigger marker.

Lots of blank space can confuse image recognition technology. It needs a clear image/icon to cause the trigger to work. This can affect the marker's readability and reliability/stability.

Figure 3.18 This photograph of yellow plums has too much blank space

Object recognition/marker-based

Synoptic link

You learnt about object recognition/marker-based in Topic area 1, section 1.2 of this unit.

In section 1.2, you learnt to use markers to trigger an augmented experience. The markers can be made with distinct patterns such as QR codes, logos or the packaging of products. These markers act as anchors for the technology to use. When a marker in the physical world is recognised by an AR application, the digital content is placed on the top of it. This is commonly used for marketing and retail.

This link shows you an example of the use of object recognition:

https://youtu.be/FEqBW3cKF2k

Location-based/markerless

Synoptic link

You learnt about location-based/markerless in Topic area 1, section 1.2 of this unit.

In section 1.2, you learnt that a more flexible option is the user of markerless. You can decide where to put the virtual object. For location-based, the AR digital content is linked to specific location.

This link shows you an example of the use of markerless:

https://youtu.be/kS6u_-1EVtc

Superimposed

Synoptic link

You learnt about superimposed (sometimes referred to as superimposition) in Topic area 1, section 1.2 of this unit.

You learnt in section 1.2 that superimposition is where an object that is in the physical world is recognised by the superimposition AR. It is then enhanced in some way to provide an alternative view.

This link shows you the use of superimposition:

https://youtu.be/wVZ2oFm4B3w

Remember that the type of trigger you use depends upon the context for using the trigger, for example to overlay street names on a street, to provide information on an object, and so on.

3.3 Layers/user interaction

Single and multiple layers

A single layer is where you create one trigger and overlay an AR asset over the top of it. The asset could be information, an image, audio, video, photograph, chart or graph, and so on. When the user activates the trigger, the asset that is overlaid is shown or played.

Figure 3.19 Someone using AR technology to simulate the installation of new equipment

With multiple layers, you use one or more triggers to overlay multiple assets. For example, you could create a marker of a karaoke machine. You could then overlay the recording of a song, and at the same time display the words of the song or a photo of the artist. The photo and the audio recording are multiple layers linked to the marker.

Another option is to still create the marker of the karaoke machine, but this time when the marker is triggered a photo of the pop artist appears. Then if the artist's image is selected, an audio recording of the song plays. This is an example of multiple steps/layers of interaction.

The important thing is not to overcomplicate the layers. They should be kept simple, especially if the user is required to interact with the AR app to trigger further augmented content to appear. Where you have multiple layers, it is advisable to merge them together (linked into layers) as with the first example for the karaoke machine.

Layers should always be provided with appropriate names that give a clear indication of what they include, or what they are for, as well as how you have organised them.

Layers have to be able to use the triggers, so every layer has to be set up.

Figure 3.20 This is an AR app used by an engineer when monitoring equipment. It contains a number of layers

Activity

Review this video:

https://youtu.be/oFSEe6iaNUQ

It shows how to develop an AR layered image into an AR experience.

The person in the video is using Adobe Aero, but you can create a similar AR experience using a wide variety of AR software. There are many good, free products available for smartphones.

Have a go at creating a multi-layered AR experience to promote **one** of the following:

- a holiday
- a music festival
- a sporting event.

Access to layers

Synoptic link

You learnt about static and interactive interaction with layers, and the many forms that this could take in Topic area 1, section 1.2 of this unit.

When creating a mobile app, you can have single and multiple layers that may have static or interactive accessibility.

Static

Static accessibility is where the object being viewed, for example text, does not alter even during interaction with the user.

Interactive

Interactive accessibility is where the user physically controls the layers of the app using a variety of pre-programmed forms of control. These can include swipe, click/select and voice.

Swipe

Think about how you use apps on a smartphone. You can swipe by dragging your finger across the screen and change screens.

Click/select

Think of how you use a smartphone or a tablet. You can click on an icon or menu and this will select the action that you want to perform. The same applies to using an AR app.

Voice

A lot of apps now allow you to control them by giving voice commands. Siri allows you to control an iPhone, Google Assistant can be used to control an Android. A similar idea can be used to control an AR app.

3.4 Information output

Synoptic link

You learnt about the different types of information output that could be used in Topic area 2, section 2.1 of this unit.

In section 2.1, you learnt about the different types of information output that you can have for your AR app design. Do not just use a specific output unless it is going to be effective and enhance the AR experience for the user.

Audio

This can be music, a song, someone speaking or just sound effects.

Charts and graphs

These are usually used to help explain numerical information by providing a pictorial representation of the data. Imagine using an AR app showing a map of the world. You could use a trigger for each country, where a graph or chart would appear showing statistics about the population or about the wildlife species within the country,

Hyperlinks and weblinks

An engineer who is trouble-shooting a problem may use an AR app that provides them with hyperlinks and/or weblinks to access information on the problem and potential solutions.

Photographs and images

You have learnt a lot about photographs and images and how they can be used with AR. You could point at an object which represents the planet Earth and it could trigger a photograph or image of the solar system and show you where Earth is placed within the solar system.

Text

You could point at an object using an AR app and text could be the information output telling you about the object. For example, you could have a photo of a human skeleton or an actual skeleton model. By using the AR app to point at different areas of the skeleton, text could appear that provides the user with information about the bone structure, the name of the bones, and so on.

Video

Video is a combination of moving images and audio. So, video can be used to provide a more visual display of information. An example could be to use an AR app to look at an image of a car. The image would then trigger a video of the car being driven, or a video showing the inside of the car and how the controls work.

Depending on the context, you may want to create single or multiple layers using different types of information output. Always remember to make sure that any asset you use is of the best quality possible. Think about how you would layer the assets, the types of triggers you would use and any user interaction.

Test your knowledge

1 Describe the term 'feasibility prototype'.
2 Explain the difference between a high-fidelity and low-fidelity prototype.
3 A prototype is a full working product. True or false?
4 Identify **two** characteristics of triggers.
5 Describe the term 'multiple layers'.

Assignment practice

Task 3

Review your plans and design for the AR app for the Key Stage 3 Geography lesson you created for Assignment practice tasks 1 and 2. Following your designs and using the assets that you identified during the planning stages, create an AR model prototype.

Topic area 4 Testing and reviewing

Getting started

Research an example of an AR app on the internet and identify:

- what tests would have been carried out on the AR app?
- who would have carried out the tests?
- how would each test be carried out?
- what would be the expected result for each test?

Create a report stating the purpose of the AR app you considered and include the tests and points you identified. Justify the choices you made.

4.1 Testing

Synoptic link

You learnt about testing in Unit R050, Topic area 3, section 3.5.

How to carry out testing of an AR model prototype

Producing and testing a prototype allows you to bring your design to life. It will highlight its functionality and how it looks. But testing will also identify any problems that you can address before the complete product is created. It is very difficult to test your design ideas without a prototype. Although creating the prototype can be time-consuming, it can save a lot of time compared to building a complete product so that you can test whether it will work as intended.

Here are some important reasons why testing must be carried out:

1 It is much easier to understand something that you can physically see and use, than just being told about it. Testing (for example, end-user testing) allows people to see, touch, feel and test the prototype, and share their experiences.
2 Usability tests are very practical and provide you with a lot of information. User testing should be carried out by people who you would expect to use your AR app. Their role is to provide you with feedback on your design and their personal physical experiences of using it.

It is always advisable to provide users with tests and instructions that you want them to carry out for you. You are then able to analyse the results from all the tests and make decisions on what you need to do before creating the final product. You may need to rectify some errors or reconsider the HCI to make it more accessible and user-friendly.

3 Do not be afraid of failure. It is important that your prototype can be tested in such a way that any failure with the design can be changed so that the final product can work properly.
4 Having a working prototype that shows that the final product will actually work is a good way of attracting investors. They will be interested in investing in a design/product that has been thoroughly tested using a prototype. It gives investors confidence in the product.
5 Test your prototype against the product design brief you created. Ask yourself whether it meets the design brief and works as intended. Make sure you do not get carried away and ignore your design priorities.
6 The testing period is a critical and important stage for the development of any product. The use of a prototype can reduce costs and time wasted from trying to botch or fix problems once the complete product has been developed.

Technical testing

This is the testing of the AR app prototype (and eventually the final product) to see if there are any errors, bugs, defects or anything else that an end user may come across when they use the AR app.

Reports are produced during technical testing that will identify any issues with the AR app or any potential improvements that could be made.

The technical tester will identify the types of tests to be carried out and develop a test plan to reflect the tests and the results.

User testing

This is sometimes referred to as usability testing. This is when users from your target audience try out the AR app prototype (and eventually the final product). It allows you to see how your target audience interacts with your AR app.

You should test your prototype with several different users where they try the different features and the action flow of your prototype. You must set the tests you want your users to carry out and record the results. You then analyse the results, which will help you consider potential improvements that you could make.

Using a test plan

Synoptic link

You learnt about the requirements for a test plan in Unit R050, Topic area 3, section 3.5.

When preparing your test plan, it is important that you think carefully about the following.

Test number

Always include your test number; this helps you to track your tests/retests and encourages you to carry out the tests in a logical order.

What is being tested?

What are you trying to test? Do not group tests together. For example, do not say 'testing triggers' but instead be specific by saying 'testing the trigger for...'. How are you going to test it?

Expected result

What is the expected result and the ideal result you want from the test?

Actual result

What was the actual result from the test? Do not simply say 'X trigger did not work'. Did anything else happen? Did it do nothing at all, or did something else happen instead?

Remedial action

How did you resolve the problem? Explain what you did. This is also known as remedial action.

Have you retested (carried out the test again), to make sure that you now get the results you expected?

Always enter any retesting onto your test plan using the next available test number.

Testing should be carried out iteratively. This means that you should be testing as you work through creating the prototype.

4.2 Reviewing the process of creating the AR model prototype

Ways to review

It is always important to review the processes you are following when developing any product. This is not just about whether your product meets the defined purpose, but also about considering the processes you followed. Ask yourself what worked, what didn't work, and what lessons you learnt.

Think about your learner journey throughout this unit.

- **Topic area 1**: You learnt about the purposes and uses of AR. You also learnt about the different types of AR, user interaction and the devices that you could use for an AR experience.
- **Topic area 2**: This is where you started being creative. You learnt how to plan an AR app and the things you needed to consider. You also learnt about the different design tools you could use.
- **Topic area 3**: You learnt about the different types of prototypes and then created a high-fidelity prototype using triggers and layers/user interaction, as well as the different types of information output you could use.

> **Assignment practice** ✔
>
> **Task 4**
>
> For Assignment practice task 3, you created the AR model prototype following your design plans for the AR app for the Geography class. For Assignment practice task 4, you will prepare the two types of test plans. One will be a technical test plan and the other a user test plan.
>
> - Prepare two test plans, one for technical testing and one for user testing.
> - Carry out the technical testing and record the results. Rectify any faults and if necessary make changes to your design documentation and the prototype.
> - Once you have completed the technical testing, give a copy of your user test plan to at least four people in your class and ask them to carry out the tests and record the results.
> - Remember to observe your users testing your AR app. You want to get an idea of how they are using it.
> - Analyse the results of all of the tests and any other feedback your users give you.
> - Document your analysis from the technical and user testing and identify any areas where you need to rectify problems, adjust your design, and so on. Make adjustments to the prototype model as well.

- **Topic area 4**: You learnt about testing – what you need to think about and do when testing your AR app prototype.

In your review, you will therefore need to reflect on Topic areas 2, 3 and 4. It is important that you refer to the assignment brief and the unit specification as well as any notes you have made.

Planning and design considerations

Think about how you went through the process when planning your design and the things that you needed to consider. Look at the teaching content for Topic area 2, section 2.1 to remind yourself about what you did and how you did it. Do not forget to consider any lessons you have learnt while working through the planning and design process.

Design tools

This is where you think about all the design tools that you used. Look at the teaching content for Topic area 2, section 2.2 to remind yourself of the range of different design tools you learnt about. Also look at the design tools you used and any notes you may have made. Think about how you used the design tools throughout the design process and how they helped you when developing the prototype. Do not forget to consider any lessons you have learnt while selecting and using the design tools.

Creating the prototype

This stage will need a lot of careful thought as it is probably the stage that took you the longest. Think about how you worked through the process of creating the prototype and the things that went smoothly as well as those that did not go so well. Think again about how you planned and designed the prototype and the design tools you used and whether you could have done things differently. Do not forget to consider any lessons you have learnt while creating the prototype.

Testing the prototype

You will have learnt that testing is an important task when creating the prototype. There are the two forms of testing: technical and user. Consider the tests that you selected for both types of testing and how this helped you through the process of creating the prototype. Think about whether you carried out sufficient testing and how well you analysed the results of the tests. Do not forget to consider any lessons you have learnt while testing the prototype.

Activity

Research an example of an AR app that has been created to enhance the user's experience using AR. It can be an example that you found during the activities, an example you have been provided with, or a new example.

Make sure that you understand the purpose of the AR app and the intended user AR experience. Carry out a review of the example you have found and consider whether it is fit for purpose. To be fit for purpose it must provide a user with an AR experience that is easy to use as well as exciting and interesting. It must also meet the intended purpose for its use. While carrying out the review, think about your own experiences with creating the AR model prototype and lessons you may have learnt.

Test your knowledge

1 Identify **four** components of a test plan.
2 Describe the term 'user testing'.
3 Explain what technical testing is for.
4 When carrying out a review, state **three** questions you should ask yourself about the testing of the AR model prototype.
5 Explain **two** reasons why testing should be carried out on an AR model prototype.

Assignment practice

Task 5

Carry out a review of the AR model prototype that you created for the Geography class in Assignment practice task 3. Follow the guidance provided in section 4.2 above. Write a report for the review of the processes you followed while planning, designing, creating and testing your AR model prototype.

Case study: Assignment

The Science teacher in your school has asked you to create an AR app for the Year 4, Key Stage 2 class on the topic of sound. The students have to look at the creation of sound through vibration and changes in pitch and volume.

Following the processes that you have learnt in Topic areas 2, 3 and 4, develop an AR model prototype that the Science teacher could use with the students in the class.

Glossary

Accelerometer In a mobile phone, the accelerometer detects the orientation of the phone.

Access rights Control over who has access to a digital system, folder, files, data and/or information.

Alphanumeric A combination of letters and numbers.

Anchor Objects that AR software can recognise.

Augment To make something larger by adding to it.

Automatic Number Plate Recognition (ANPR) A system used by the police; it checks the number plate of every vehicle that the police car sees.

Avatar A digital representation of a person or the person's character. It can take a 2D form as an icon used in internet forums or a 3D form used in games and virtual worlds.

Backlight A built-in light source that is needed to produce a readable display.

BODMAS An acronym to remember the order in which calculations are carried out (Brackets, Orders, Division, Multiplication, Addition, Subtraction).

Civil Aviation Authority (CAA) The organisation that regulates civil aviation in the United Kingdom.

Closed question A question where there is only a set number of answers to be chosen. For example, the question 'Can you ride a bicycle?' can be answered either 'Yes' or 'No'.

Column A series of cells running vertically/up and down in a worksheet.

Computer vision How a computer understands the environment. It 'sees' via a digital image or video.

Concurrent processes Processes that can be carried out at the same time.

CSV file A plain text file where the fields are separated by commas and the records are separated by carriage returns/enter key.

Cyber-security The practice of defending digital devices, including computers, servers, mobile devices, electronic systems, networks and data, from malicious attacks.

Data Raw facts and figures before they have been processed.

Data at rest Data stored on a digital device or storage media.

Data controller The person who needs to apply for permission to collect and store data. The data controller is often the person in charge of the business, but sometimes a different person who works in the business may have this responsibility. This person decides what data needs to be collected and what it will be used for and how.

Data in transit Data being sent to two or more authorised users.

Data integrity Making sure that the data has nothing missing (is complete), that it is error free and up to date. This will mean that the data is reliable for use in its specific context.

Data packets Small units of data which are sent and received when accessing the internet or any other type of network.

Data subject The person the data is being held about.

Delimiter These are the separators between the values in text files. These can be commas, spaces or semi-colons.

Digital compass A sensor that uses the Earth's magnetic fields to find direction. A digital compass will always find north.

Display screen equipment (DSE) Devices or equipment with a display screen, such as laptops, touch screens, smartphones and other similar devices.

Distribution channels The methods (channels) that can be used to share data and information by individuals, organisations or businesses.

Driver and Vehicle Licensing Agency (DVLA) The government organisation that holds more than 49 million driver records and more than 40 million vehicle records.

Encryption code (or encryption key) A set of characters, a phrase or numbers that are used when encrypting or decrypting data or a file.

Encryption software Software that is used to encrypt a file or data.

Extended reality (ER) This is the overall term for all forms of real and virtual environments and includes AR, MR and VR.

Extreme data Data that is on the boundary between valid and invalid data for a spreadsheet solution.

Field An individual data item within a record. Each field has a unique name and contains a single data type.

Formula A calculation created by the user that uses cell references and operators.

Function A tool or calculation that is pre-built into the spreadsheet application.

Global Positioning System (GPS) A global navigation satellite system that provides the location of an object.

High-fidelity wireframe A wireframe that shows actual content, fonts, colours, image dimensions and branding.

House style A set of rules set by an organisation covering how all its documents are formatted. This can cover: colours, font sizes and style, logo style, text alignment.

Human Computer Interface (HCI) An HCI allows communication between the user and a digital system.

Immersive In relation to digital technology, this is the creation of a 3D image that appears to surround the user.

Information Commissioner The person who enforces the Data Protection Act. This is the person who organisations need to apply to in order to gain permission to collect and store personal data.

Information Commissioner's Office (ICO) The organisation that oversees the Freedom of Information Act; it reports to the UK parliament.

Intellectual property (IP) Creative work which can be treated as an asset or physical property. IP covers four main areas – copyright, trademarks, design rights and patents.

Internet service provider (ISP) A company that provides access to the internet to both personal and business customers.

Interviewee The person answering the questions.

Interviewer The person asking the questions.

Intuitive Actions that can be easily carried out without having to think deeply.

Invalid data Data that is unacceptable for the spreadsheet solution.

Light emitting diode (LED) A small device that emits light when an electric current is passed through it; lots of LEDs are used together to make self-illuminating displays.

Liquid crystal display (LCD) A type of display that uses a liquid crystal film sealed between glass plates.

Low-fidelity wireframe A wireframe that uses basic shapes and image placeholders with limited specific details.

Markers Visual prompts that trigger the display of virtual information.

Mixed reality (MR) MR enables contents to interact with objects in the physical world. This means that a computer-generated object can be partially obscured by objects in the physical world. For example, you could have a computer-generated person, animal or robot, partially hidden behind a tree in a forest.

Open question Allows the person completing the questionnaire to give a detailed answer in their own words.

Opt-in When a person has to take a specific positive step, for example ticking a box, sending an email or clicking a button or icon, to say they consent to receiving marketing.

Opt-out When a person must take a positive step to refuse or unsubscribe from marketing.

Organic light emitting diode (OLED) display A type of display that produces its own light; it is flexible and can include a touch response layer.

Permissions A set of attributes that determine what a user can do with files and folders, for example read, write, edit or delete.

Personal data Any information relating to an identified or identifiable living individual.

Phablet A combination of a phone and a tablet (PHone-tABLET).

Public authorities These include government departments, the National Health Service (NHS), state schools and the police force.

QR code A two-dimensional barcode that can be read using a digital device. It stores information as a series of pixels in a square-shaped grid.

Qualitative data Data that is descriptive and cannot be measured.

Quantitative data Data that is measurable and is usually in numerical form.

Radio-frequency identification (RFID) Access badges or tags that use radio frequency to transfer data from the tags to a digital system; for example, to allow access to a room.

Range A group of cells containing data used in a formula or function. First and last cells in the range are separated using a colon ':' (B22:B32)

Rank order Requires the person completing a survey or questionnaire to compare a list of the same type of items. The items are then ranked, for example from 1 to 10 where 1 is most important and 10 is least important.

Rating Requires the person completing a survey or questionnaire to compare different items. The items are then ranked, for example from 1 to 10, where 1 is most important and 10 is least important.

Real-time backup When a backup is made automatically each time the data changes.

Real-time data (RTD) Data that is delivered immediately after it has been collected.

Record A collection of data about a single item, such as a single student or customer. Each record must be unique.

Reliability Data and information from a reliable source can be trusted to be correct or true.

Row A series of cells running horizontally/across in a worksheet.

Sector An area on a storage device that stores data.

Smart city An urban area that uses the IoE and digital devices to collect data to allow well-informed decisions to be made and to improve the quality of life of the people who live and work there.

Spreadsheet A software application for organising, analysing and storing data in tables.

Surface plane The boundaries of a surface, such as a table top, desk or wall, that a virtual object can be placed on.

Table Contains data about 'things', such as students, customers or orders. Each table has a unique name and contains data held in records.

Technical testing Checking the functionality of the solution.

Telematic Vehicle onboard communications and applications that communicate with one another via GPS receivers and other devices.

Text file A plain text file used for importing into a spreadsheet. A text file uses tabs or spaces as delimiters for the fields. It uses carriage returns/ enter key to separate the records.

Travel portal Provides a virtual travel experience through a smartphone's AR application to help users choose the destination, hotel and holiday experience.

Trigger The trigger activates the function of the AR experience.

User adoption The number of users who start to use a system because it suits their needs.

User testing Carried out by a range of users who are likely to use the solution.

Valid data Data that is acceptable, sensible and reasonable for the spreadsheet solution.

Validity The quality of being correct or true; valid data and information is also, generally, reliable.

Value A specific piece of data contained in a cell.

Vehicle-to-everything (V2X) The wireless transmission of data between vehicles, traffic infrastructure, networks and devices.

Vehicle-to-vehicle (V2V) The wireless transmission of data from vehicle to vehicle to increase safety while driving.

Viewfinder Part of the camera that a person looks through, and part of the camera within the device being used by the user.

Virtual reality (VR) A computer-generated simulated environment. A person can interact within the simulated environment using special VR glasses, screens and even gloves fitted with sensors. The use of the VR glasses stops the user having any view of the real-world environment.

Visual Basic for Applications (VBA) code A programming language that can be used within spreadsheet software programs.

Visual indicator The app displays an indicator on the screen; for example, the outline of a square with grid lines. This is used to show where an object can be placed.

Voice over Internet Protocol (VoIP) A system that enables voice calls to be made over the internet.

White space Empty space used to separate elements on a screen or document.

WIMP (Windows, Icons, Menus, Pointer) A style of graphical user interface that uses windows, icons, menus and pointers.

Workbook A collection of one or more worksheets into a single file.

Worksheet A single table of cells within a spreadsheet application.

WYSIWYG (What You See Is What You Get) What is shown on screen is exactly how it will look when printed.

Index

Index